I0491596

The Gods Must Be Crazy!

DRAGON vs. EAGLE

The Trillion-Dollar Autonomous Demolition Derby

SAJI MADAPAT

ALSO IN THE GODS MUST BE CRAZY! SERIES

The Gods Must Be Crazy II:
A Rooseveltian Renaissance for Trump 2.0
Available at amazon.com/dp/B0FFX51PL3

This book is a strategic forecast written from the perspective of February 2026. Events cited after 02-20-2026 are scenario projections based on the current trajectory.

This book provides analytical frameworks and educational discussion of investment strategies. It does not constitute personalized investment advice. The author holds positions in several securities discussed. Consult a qualified financial advisor before making investment decisions.

ABOUT THE AUTHOR

Saji Madapat is a contrarian strategist who has spent three decades navigating the corridors where capital, geopolitics, and technology collide—from Fortune 10 boardrooms to 40 countries across 6 continents—as a BIG4 financial transformation architect and a Clinton Global Initiative Fellow.

His authority on the US-China autonomous vehicle divide draws on this rare intersection: enterprise architecture for global corporations (Ernst & Young), strategic leadership across emerging and developed markets, graduate-level immersion in China through the Clinton Global Initiative's GIFT program (Hong Kong and Cambodia), and published expertise spanning artificial intelligence, enterprise performance management, and geopolitical risk—with over fifty papers presented globally and contributions to all five major PMI standards.

He is also a *Kala Sreshta* laureate—recipient of the Most Accomplished Artist award—and a practitioner of Theyyam, the ancient ritual art form of northern Kerala in which performers become living deities. The epistemological tradition of *ullil kaanal* (inner vision) that underlies Theyyam is the diagnostic lens through which this book reads the autonomous vehicle industry's grandest illusion.

Kala Sreshta (Most Accomplished Artist) Award
Prof. MN Karasseri to Saji & Subhash Chandran(Chief Editor Mathrubhumi))
-Sculpture by Kanayi Kunhiraman

In the backwaters of Kerala, two currents flow through the same channel. The brackish tide pushes inland from the Arabian Sea, and the freshwater descends from the Western Ghats. They coexist in the same body of water, each governed by its own logic, meeting without mixing. The boatmen do not choose between currents. They read both.

— From the oral traditions of the Kuttanad boatmen

The market can remain irrational longer than you can remain solvent.

— A. Gary Shilling

He who controls the granaries controls the kingdom; he who controls the trade routes controls the granaries.

— Kautilya, Arthashastra, c. 300 BCE

CONTENTS

Contents

Michael E. McGrath

Author of *Autonomous Vehicles: Opportunities, Strategies, and Disruptions*

The author of this book and I first connected because we share a deep conviction that autonomous vehicles are not just another technology cycle, but a civilizational transition in how mobility, data, and capital interact. My own work in Autonomous Vehicles: Opportunities, Strategies, and Disruptions has focused primarily on the United States and the regulatory and commercial deployments unfolding across American cities. Saji Madapat has come at the same phenomenon from the other side of the world, mapping China's rapidly evolving AV ecosystem, its regulatory architecture, and the global ramifications of both. What emerged in our conversations was a simple realization: we were looking at the same river from opposite banks.

One of the central arguments of this book is that there is a vast and growing gap between how Western markets *value* autonomous vehicle businesses and what is actually happening on the ground in China. On the one hand, US-listed or US-anchored AV narratives command extraordinary valuations despite relatively small fleets, expensive hardware, and still-experimental robotaxi operations. As I have previously written in my Seeking Alpha articles, I believe that some of this is what I call the "Tesla Distortion": overvaluing its robotaxi opportunity at almost $1 trillion, even though it has yet to prove viability.

The book's Māyā Meter in the prologue does something especially well: it converts a vague sense of valuation excess into a concrete side-by-side comparison of implied per-vehicle valuations across US and Chinese AV operators. Once you see that table, the scale of the disconnect—and the roughly 3,000-to-1 gap it implies—becomes very difficult to dismiss.

On the other side, Chinese players like Baidu Apollo Go, Pony.ai, WeRide, BYD, XPeng, Huawei ADS, and others are already operating large, fully driverless fleets, achieving city-level breakeven economics, and shipping autonomy-capable vehicles at price points that look almost impossible from an American perspective. The market, as this book shows in detail, has chosen to watch one current and almost ignore the other. It is hard to read this book and come away believing that US companies are competing against a single Chinese firm. They are competing against a system.

I agree with the author that this valuation gap is not entirely explained by technology, safety performance, or even business fundamentals. It is, in significant part, a "valuation illusion"—what he calls Māyā—driven by narrative gravity around US names (especially Tesla), a systematic "China discount" in global portfolios, and a tendency to treat Western AV stories as the default template for the future. At the same time, I believe an important part of that gap also reflects something more mundane but very real: the difference in the underlying ride-hailing markets that autonomy is competing with. In China, ride-hailing and taxi fares are structurally much lower than in the US. Most estimates show that the equivalent fares in China are approximately half of those in the US. Baidu's ability to reach breakeven in Wuhan, where base fares are roughly 30 percent below those in China's Tier-1 cities and far below those in US major metros, demonstrates an AV system robust enough to survive at the bottom of the global fare spectrum. In the US, by contrast, robotaxis are being tested against much higher prevailing ride-hailing prices, which both support higher revenue per mile today and subtly encourage investors to extrapolate higher long-term margin potential for American operators.

That difference in pricing doesn't invalidate the book's thesis; in many ways, it strengthens it. If Chinese operators can make the numbers work at Wuhan or Guangzhou price levels, the same cost structures and technologies deployed into higher-fare markets—Dubai, London, parts of Europe, and the Gulf—should, in principle, produce very attractive competitive economics. The author makes this point clearly when he notes that Apollo Go's breakeven at Wuhan price points implies even better economics in markets where fares are three to five times higher. As someone who has spent a lot of time looking at US ride-hailing dynamics, I see that as a crucial nuance: the American market's higher prices buy its AV companies more room for error in the short run, but they do not guarantee a durable structural advantage once low-cost platforms arrive with materially lower vehicle, sensor, and compute costs.

One of the book's most thought-provoking arguments is the author's "Industrializer thesis." It suggests that a decisive factor in autonomous driving may not be the most elegant algorithm or the most famous Silicon Valley brand, but the ability to mass-produce autonomy. BYD illustrates the point vividly: advanced autonomous features are deployed as standard equipment at roughly $385 per vehicle across millions of consumer cars. At that price, autonomy stops being a laboratory experiment or a luxury add-on and becomes a mass-produced data engine, generating enormous volumes of real-world driving data every day. This is not the heroic story of a single technological breakthrough. It is the quieter—and potentially more consequential—logic of manufacturing scale, cost compression, and continuous iteration. Whether or not one ultimately agrees with the author's conclusions, the Industrializer argument forces a central question about the future of autonomous mobility: will the winners be the hunters chasing the perfect system, or the industrializers who make "good-enough" autonomy ubiquitous first?

The book highlights a clear difference between China's "smart road, smart car" approach and America's default of "dumb road, smart car," arguing that China is developing vehicle-road-cloud integration—roads equipped with perception units, C-V2X radios, edge computing, and digital twins—so the infrastructure itself shares the cognitive load with AVs. In contrast, the US largely keeps 1950s-style highways unchanged, requiring each AV to carry a more costly, fully self-reliant sensor and compute "temple" on its roof. From my perspective, such deeply integrated smart-infrastructure development will likely never be politically or institutionally feasible in the US: our fragmented, multi-tier system—federal agencies competing over spectrum, fifty state DOTs, thousands of cities and counties, each with veto power but no single authority or budget to coordinate a $100 billion nationwide V2X rollout—means American AVs will have to assume the road remains mostly silent and uninformed. The profound implication is that US AV technology platforms must be more capable, more redundant, and more costly per vehicle, increasing capital needs and slowing deployment, while Chinese systems can rely on cheaper vehicles and smarter corridors to achieve autonomy at significantly lower costs per mile. This architectural difference will influence not just who leads in AV technology but also where each ecosystem can profitably compete as autonomy expands globally.

Where I find myself strongly aligned with this book is in its sober assessment of the risks to the US market if it continues to think of autonomy as a primarily American race. The US has remarkable strengths: world-class research labs, iconic AV brands, and a deep capital market willing to fund very long-term bets. But it also has structural vulnerabilities that this book does not flinch from: fragmented regulation across fifty states, an absence of true "mass-market industrializers" that can ship autonomy-ready vehicles for under $30,000, and a political environment that can, at times, be more comfortable with symbolic hearings than with building coherent national standards. The result, as the author convincingly argues, is a "gilded river" of brilliant technology and fragile economics, moving more slowly than many Americans realize.

For investors and strategists who, like me, started by primarily studying US and allied-market AV players, that realization is uncomfortable, but it also opens up one of the most interesting contrarian opportunities of the next decade. If you accept even a portion of the evidence assembled here, that Chinese AV and ADAS platforms are further along in cost, scale, and unit economics than their current valuations imply, then it follows that at least some of these companies are undervalued relative to their Western peers. That does not mean there is no risk. Regulatory, geopolitical, and governance risks are real and non-trivial. But it does mean the upside/downside profile for a carefully constructed portfolio that includes Chinese AV names may look very different from that of a US-only allocation that is already paying for American narratives.

It is important to acknowledge a major protective barrier that the author describes: for at least the next several years, Chinese AV companies are effectively locked out of the US market. The Bureau of Industry and Security's Connected Vehicle Rule prohibits Chinese-developed autonomous-driving software in US vehicles starting with model year 2027, and Chinese connected-vehicle hardware starting in 2030, effectively closing the door to Baidu Apollo Go, Pony.ai, WeRide, BYD, Huawei ADS, and their peers on American roads. That legal 'iron curtain through the dashboard' does more than signal national-security concerns; it also buys the US ecosystem time. Time for American AV operators, chipmakers, and automakers to drive down costs and mature their own offerings without facing a full-scale price war against much cheaper Chinese AVs. This insulation may or may not be permanent, and it comes with opportunity costs abroad, but it does create a protected window in which US players can work to become cost-competitive and commercially robust before the global AV market becomes a true head-to-head contest.

Ultimately, what I appreciate most about this book is that it is not asking the reader to pick a side in a simplistic "dragon versus eagle" contest. It is asking you to learn to read both rivers. As someone whose early work in this space was heavily US-centric, I found that both humbling and energizing. The AV race will not be decided solely in Phoenix or San Francisco, nor solely in Beijing or Shenzhen. It will play out across Wuhan and Dubai, Guangzhou and Abu Dhabi, Wolfsburg and Singapore—and it may well produce two increasingly distinct AV ecosystems built on different cost structures, regulatory architectures, and infrastructure philosophies.

My challenge to you, as you begin this book, is to approach it with genuine open-mindedness. Set aside, for a moment, the stocks you already own, the headlines you have already absorbed, and the narratives you are most comfortable with. Let the data speak. Let the case studies from Wuhan and Guangzhou sit alongside what you know from Phoenix and Austin. Ask yourself not "Which country do I prefer?" but "Which systems, in which markets, at which price points, are actually working?" If you do that, I believe you will come away better equipped to understand the competitive dynamics of this emerging industry, and better prepared to navigate both the risks and the opportunities that autonomous vehicles will create on a truly global scale.

Michael E. McGrath
Author of Autonomous Vehicles: Opportunities, Strategies, and Disruptions

INTRODUCTION

Technological revolutions rarely unfold where the market is looking.

Niels Pluijmen

Founder and Lead Analyst, Business Ignition Research

In autonomous driving, technology may determine what is possible, but regulation and market structure determine what becomes profitable. Investors tend to follow spectacle. Product launches, keynote presentations, and viral robotaxi videos create the impression that autonomous driving is moving toward a single, obvious outcome. From a distance, the industry appears to be a global race where the fastest developer eventually wins.

That narrative is convenient. It is also misleading.

Autonomous driving is not one race but a set of systems evolving under very different regulatory structures, industrial ecosystems, and economic conditions. The contrast becomes particularly clear when comparing the two largest arenas shaping the industry today, the United States and China.

In the United States, companies such as Waymo operate in an environment that resembles a traditional market expansion model. Once regulators approve operations in a city, scaling is largely determined by operational execution and the capital a company is willing to deploy. Waymo's fleet illustrates this dynamic clearly. As the first large-scale operator in several cities, it has established a meaningful first mover advantage and expanded capacity to meet demand at premium pricing.

China operates under a different logic. Companies such as Baidu's Apollo Go, WeRide, and Pony deploy within regulatory systems that tightly govern where fleets operate and how quickly they expand. Growth follows staged approvals, district-level permits, and controlled fleet caps rather than open scaling driven primarily by capital deployment.

The result is a different competitive environment. In the United States, scale largely follows capital and operational execution. In China, scale follows regulatory sequencing and controlled market access. Both systems produce capable operators, but they shape those operators in very different ways.

As an analyst who has spent the past year building bottom-up operational models across autonomous mobility platforms, I have become increasingly skeptical of narratives that treat autonomy as a single global race. The closer one looks at the mechanics of the industry, the clearer it becomes that deployment pathways diverge sharply between markets.

Those differences shape economics, strategy, and ultimately valuation. Autonomous technology itself extends well beyond ride-hailing. It is increasingly appearing in consumer vehicles through advanced driver assistance systems and through software licensing into OEM platforms. Robotaxi fleets may represent the largest long-term opportunity, but ADAS deployments and software diffusion often provide the earliest path to scale.

Robotaxi fleets remain the first large-scale environment where the economics of autonomy become visible. Fleet deployment, ride utilization, and cost structures provide the earliest signals of whether these systems can evolve into sustainable businesses rather than technological demonstrations.

One of the most persistent analytical errors in the debate is the assumption that deployment follows a purely market-driven model. In reality, regulatory design plays a central role in shaping how autonomy reaches public roads. In many markets deployment follows regulatory sequencing rather than manufacturing speed. A company may produce hundreds of vehicles, yet the pace of real deployment is determined by permits, district approvals, and operational constraints.

Vehicles do not become economic assets when they are produced, but when they are permitted to operate and connected to rider demand that generates sustained utilization. A robotaxi operating continuously along a high-demand corridor, such as an airport-to-business district route, produces fundamentally different economics from a vehicle that spends long periods idle between rides.

Operational variables compound. Whether a vehicle is allowed to operate, how many units regulators permit to deploy, which city and corridors they serve, and whether they run on a dominant demand platform can dramatically alter the economics. In practice, these differences often determine whether one fleet earns several times more per vehicle than another.

Taken together, these forces, regulation, demand aggregation, fleet operations, software capability, and industrial supply chains, form the architecture of the autonomous vehicle industry.

This is where the author's concept of the Māyā Meter enters the discussion.

By comparing the implied valuation of autonomous fleets across companies, the book exposes the gap between market perception and operational evidence. In several cases companies operating substantial fleets appear dramatically undervalued relative to competitors commanding far larger market capitalizations.

The metric is deliberately provocative. It compresses a complex ecosystem into a single ratio and forces readers to confront the possibility that narrative has outpaced observation.

The argument becomes most compelling in the operational data beneath those comparisons.
Inside the autonomous mobility ecosystem, progress is measured less by announcements than by economic thresholds. Remote assistance ratios determine whether fleets can scale without recreating labor costs in another form. Sensor prices determine whether vehicles remain expensive prototypes or become deployable infrastructure. Utilization determines whether robotaxi fleets become sustainable businesses.

These indicators rarely dominate headlines. Yet they quietly shape the future of the industry. Markets often mistake visible progress for economic progress. In autonomous mobility, the two are not always the same. Good analysis begins by questioning the assumptions everyone else takes for granted.

This book does exactly that.

It challenges the narrative simplicity that has shaped much of the public discussion around autonomous driving. Along the way it introduces conceptual lenses, including the author's Hunter vs Farmer framework, to explain how different industrial systems approach technological deployment. Behind every robotaxi demonstration and valuation narrative lies a more complicated system.

Regulation determines where vehicles can operate.
Economics determine whether fleets can scale.
Demand networks determine whether vehicles generate rides or sit idle.

Understanding how these forces interact may prove more important than identifying the next technological breakthrough.

The pages ahead push that argument much further. Once the surface narratives fall away, the structure of the autonomous mobility industry looks very different. It is also where the deeper contrast between competing technological systems becomes impossible to ignore.

Niels Pluijmen
Founder and Lead Analyst
Business Ignition Research

PROLOGUE

Two Rivers, One Mountain

The pyre's fire reveals more than ashes to Kerala's boatman–he reads the currents beneath the surface. So it is in automotive finance: outsiders fixate on plain diesel sales, ignoring the undercurrents reshaping an entire industry. This is not the eulogy of the last car but the birth of the first embodied robot. In three movements–descents, ascents, counts–we will navigate those currents.

I

The Two Currents

Stand on the narrow boat at Kumarakom, where the Vembanad Lake opens into a labyrinth of waterways older than recorded history, and you will witness something that confounds every instinct of Western hydraulics. Two rivers occupy the same channel. The brackish tide, heavy with the salt of the Arabian Sea, pushes inland with the patient insistence of an empire. Simultaneously—not sequentially, not alternately, but *simultaneously*—the freshwater current descends from the Western Ghats, carrying the accumulated rainfall of a monsoon that falls with a totality the temperate world has never known. They do not mix. They do not fight. They coexist in the same body of water, each governed by its own density, its own temperature, its own internal logic, separated by a halocline so subtle that only the boatmen can read it.

The boatmen of the Kuttanad, who have navigated these paradoxical waters for centuries, do not ask which current is *real*. Both are real. They do not ask which is *stronger*. Strength depends on the season, the lunar cycle, and the monsoon's mood. They ask only one question, the question that separates the drowned from the living: *Which current carries my boat where it needs to go?*

This is the autonomous vehicle industry in 2026. Two civilizations are building the same technology through entirely different logics—one gilded and theatrical, the other turbid and relentless—and they flow through the same global channel without acknowledging each other's existence. The Western financial markets watch one current. The Chinese industrial machine rides the other. Moreover, the investors, the policymakers, the executives who will determine how this trillion-dollar transformation unfolds? Most of them are standing on the bank, watching only one river, and wondering why their models keep drowning.

A word on the lens through which this book sees. The Gods Own Country (Kerala, India)—the narrow strip of land between the Western Ghats and the Arabian Sea—is my homeland. Theyyam, the ancient

ritual art form in which a performer, through elaborate transformation, becomes a living deity, is my practice. The concept of *ullil kaanal* (the inner vision, the seeing-beyond-seeing) is the epistemological tradition in which I was raised. When I describe Wall Street as a temple economy, I am not reaching for color. I am making a structural observation about how belief systems generate, sustain, and occasionally destroy economic value. When I speak of *Māyā*, I am naming a specific cognitive distortion—the elevation of partial truth to the status of the whole—that no term in the English-language financial lexicon captures with equivalent precision. The metaphors in this book are not decoration. They are the diagnostic instruments.

This book is a boatman's manual. It teaches you to read both currents.

● ● ●

II

The Arithmetic of Disbelief

There is a word in Malayalam—*Māyā*—that means illusion, but not the kind that merely deceives. It is the grand illusion, the cosmic misdirection, the architecture of perception built upon a premise so elegant that questioning it feels like sacrilege. In the Advaita Vedanta tradition, *Māyā* is not a lie. It is something more dangerous: a partial truth elevated to the status of the whole. The global autonomous vehicle industry, as it stands in early 2026, is a masterclass in *Māyā*.

Consider the arithmetic that defines this psychosis.

Tesla commands a market capitalization of approximately $1.5 trillion. Wall Street analysts routinely attribute $450 billion to $700 billion of that figure to robotaxi potential—a business that, as of this writing, operates ~42 vehicles in Austin and ~158 in the Bay Area(Musk's Q4 2025 earnings call claimed "well over 500"), each still requiring human safety monitors for most rides, with the National Highway Traffic Safety Administration investigating 58 incidents across 2.9 million Full Self-Driving vehicles, including 14 crashes and 23 injuries. It is, to borrow a phrase from the temple festivals of Kerala, a deity's procession valued at the price of a kingdom but unable to walk without attendants.

Now turn the page to the parallel universe.

Pony.ai—a company most Western investors have never heard of—operates over 1,000 fully driverless robotaxis across four of China's tier-one cities, has achieved city-wide unit-economics breakeven in Guangzhou, maintains operations in eight countries across four continents, and is scaling toward 3,000 vehicles by year's end. Its entire market capitalization? Approximately $5.6 billion. WeRide fields 1,600 vehicles across eleven countries, posts 32.9 percent gross margins, and runs fully driverless rides on Uber in Abu Dhabi. Its market cap: $2.5 billion. Baidu's Apollo Go has completed over 17 million rides with 1,000-plus driverless vehicles at a per-vehicle cost of $28,000. Moreover, BYD—the world's largest electric vehicle manufacturer—has equipped 2.3 million consumer vehicles with autonomous driving capabilities at $385 per unit, generating 160 million kilometers of training data *every single day*, a data monsoon so vast that the metaphor is not literary indulgence but mathematical understatement.

The Māyā Meter: The Valuation Gap in One Table

Note: Per-vehicle metrics are illustrative strategy mirrors, not precision instruments. Market capitalizations encompass multiple business lines. A "Steelman" column acknowledges the legitimate factors that sustain each valuation. But the directional signal is unmistakable—and the magnitude of the gap is what demands explanation.

Company	Market Cap	AV Vehicles	Per-Vehicle Valuation	Steelman
Tesla (robotaxi attribution)	$450B–$700B (analyst attribution)	~250 supervised (Austin)	~$2B per vehicle (Morgan Stanley)	Global EV manufacturing, energy storage, Musk narrative gravity, 1.1M FSD subscribers
Waymo (Alphabet)	$126B (Feb 2026 round)	2,500–3,000 driverless	~$50M per vehicle	World-class safety record (Swiss Re: 88% fewer claims), 20M+ rides, 6th-gen cost reduction
Pony.ai	~$5.6B	1,000+ fully driverless	~$5.6M per vehicle	Guangzhou unit-economics breakeven, 8 countries, Toyota JV, MSCI China inclusion
WeRide	~$2.5B	1,600 across 11 countries	~$1.6M per vehicle	32.9% gross margins, Uber Abu Dhabi partnership, L4 permits in 8 countries
Baidu Apollo Go	~$5–8B (estimated)	1,000+ driverless	~$5–8M per vehicle	17M+ cumulative rides, unit-level profitability in Wuhan, $28K per-vehicle cost
BYD God's Eye	~$112–137B (whole company)	2.3M ADAS-equipped	~$385 per vehicle (ADAS cost)	World's largest EV manufacturer, 160M km/day training data, zero additional consumer cost

Valuation ratios: Waymo vs. WeRide: 14:1. Tesla (Morgan Stanley attribution) vs. WeRide: 244:1. Tesla (ARK attribution, independent tracker) vs. WeRide: >10,000:1.

A reasonable sceptic—and this book respects reasonable sceptics, because unreasonable ones write their own books—would object. The 3,000-to-1 gap is not *entirely* irrational. Tesla's valuation encompasses a global EV manufacturing operation, an energy storage business, and the gravitational pull of Elon Musk's narrative machine on retail capital flows. Chinese ADRs trade under the perpetual shadow of delisting risk, opacity around VIE structures, and the geopolitical discount that attaches to any asset denominated in a yuan-adjacent trust. The Holding Foreign Companies Accountable Act is not a phantom. Waymo's safety record—Swiss Re's finding of 88 percent fewer property damage claims than human drivers—is genuinely world-class. These are real factors.

However, here is what they do not explain. They do not explain a per-vehicle implied valuation gap of 3,000-to-1. They do not explain why the market prices Tesla's *promise* of a robotaxi future at $2 billion per supervised test vehicle while pricing WeRide's *operating, profitable, multi-continent* driverless fleet at $1.6 million per vehicle. A 30 percent geopolitical discount is rational. A 99.97 percent discount is *Māyā*. Moreover, the distance between 30 percent and 99.97 percent is the distance between market pricing risk and a market pricing narrative—and, as the temple priests of both civilizations know, narrative is the most expensive architecture ever built.

Here is the question this book will address over fifteen chapters, three acts, and two civilizations: **Is the 3,000-to-1 gap a geopolitical discount, a market inefficiency, or a fundamental misreading of industrial reality?** Moreover, for the investor reading this with capital to allocate, **is the gap closing—and if so, what is the trade?**

The answer, as the boatmen of Kuttanad would tell you, depends on which current you are reading. Moreover, most of the world is reading only one.

• • •

III

The Hunter and the Farmer

In *The Gods Must Be Crazy II: A Rooseveltian Renaissance for Trump 2.0*, I introduced a framework for understanding how different civilizations approach economic transformation. I called it the Hunter and the Farmer. The metaphor was drawn from the anthropology of pre-agricultural societies, but its application to modern capital markets is, if anything, more precise than the original.

The Hunter stalks the singular prey—the perfect algorithm, the transcendent technology, the kill so magnificent that a single success justifies a decade of patience and a hundred billion dollars of capital. The Hunter's economy is organized around the moonshot. Its heroes are visionaries. Its temples are venture capital firms. Its sacred texts are pitch decks. Its liturgical calendar runs from earnings call to earnings call, each one a high mass in which the faithful gather to hear the oracles of consensus EPS estimates, and the high priests of Wall Street perform the ritual sacrifice of long-term R&D on the altar of short-term shareholder returns. The Hunter does not eat regularly, but when the kill comes, the feast is legendary.

The Farmer does not hunt. The Farmer prepares the field. The Farmer plants seeds across a million acres and trusts the monsoon to do the rest. The Farmer's economy is organized around *yield per hectare*, not yield per unicorn. Its heroes are not visionaries but *executors*—the methodical, the incremental, the almost agricultural logic of making something ten percent cheaper this quarter, then ten percent cheaper again next quarter, until the cost curve has collapsed so far that the product becomes as ubiquitous as running water. The Farmer's temple is the factory floor. Its sacred text is the bill of materials. Its liturgical calendar runs from Five-Year Plan to Five-Year Plan.

In the autonomous vehicle industry, the Hunter is America. The Farmer is China.

The Hunter's trophy: Waymo closed a $16 billion funding round in February 2026 at a $126 billion valuation—the largest autonomous vehicle financing in history, a coronation ceremony for patient capital and vertical integration. Its sensor suite costs approximately $175,000 per vehicle. Its fleet of 2,500 to 3,000 vehicles delivers 450,000 paid driverless rides per week across six American metros. It is, by any measure, the most advanced autonomous driving platform on Earth. It is also, by any measure, a service that cannot yet scale to the mass market at its current cost structure. The Hunter has killed the prey. The Hunter cannot yet feed the village.

The Farmer's harvest: BYD's "God's Eye" autonomous driving system ships as standard equipment on the $9,550 Seagull—the world's best-selling electric vehicle—at a per-unit ADAS cost of $385. Not $385,000. Not $38,500. Three hundred and eighty-five dollars. LiDAR sensors from Hesai and RoboSense, which cost $150,000 a decade ago, now sell for approximately $150 from Chinese manufacturers. Pony.ai's Gen-7 robotaxi has achieved a 70% reduction in autonomous-driving kit costs compared to the previous generation. The Farmer has not killed the singular prey. The Farmer has planted a million fields, and the monsoon has arrived.

Beneath the cultural metaphor lies a mechanical explanation. Both civilizations have built self-reinforcing flywheels, but they spin on different axes. **The American Flywheel** is a patience machine: capital intensity buys safety proof; safety proof earns regulatory permission; permission unlocks city expansion; expansion generates data; data reduces cost; lower cost attracts more capital. It is elegant, rational, and agonizingly slow. Each node requires years; each city requires separate regulatory negotiations; and the entire system rests on the assumption that the technology must be *perfect* before it can be *ubiquitous*.

The Chinese Flywheel is a monsoon machine: mass-market ADAS diffusion generates billions of kilometers of training data, ferocious OEM competition drives steep cost deflation, government guardrails create structured L3/L4 stepping stones, and each step generates revenue that funds the next iteration. It does not require perfection. It requires *volume*. It does not wait for the algorithm to achieve transcendence. It lets the algorithm learn from a hundred million cars on a million roads in a thousand cities, improving incrementally, failing publicly, correcting quickly, and arriving at competence through sheer statistical inevitability. The Chinese flywheel does not ask for permission. It arrives with a totality that rearranges everything it touches.

The Western financial imagination, trained for generations to worship at the altar of the moonshot, cannot process the Farmer's logic. It sees BYD's $385 ADAS system as a cheap imitation. It examines Pony.ai's $5.6 billion market capitalization and identifies a geopolitical risk. It looks at WeRide's

32.9 percent gross margins and sees nothing, because it has never heard of WeRide. The Hunter's temple does not have a pew for the Farmer. Thus, the Farmer keeps planting, the monsoon keeps falling, and the 3,000-to-1 gap keeps widening—not because the market is efficient, but because *Māyā* is the most elegant architecture ever built.

• • •

IV

The Voyage Ahead

Both flywheels work. Both will produce commercially viable autonomous vehicles. However, they will produce *different kinds* of commercially viable autonomous vehicles at different price points for different markets under different regulatory regimes. Moreover, the resulting bifurcation—two parallel, increasingly incompatible autonomous driving ecosystems, separated by the Bureau of Industry and Security's Connected Vehicle Rule like an Iron Curtain drawn through the dashboard—is not a temporary condition. It is the industry's permanent architecture. This book maps that architecture.

Act I: The Gilded River (Chapters 1–5) takes you inside America's autonomous temple—where the technology is breathtaking, the capital is staggering, and the regulatory labyrinth may strangle the revolution before it reaches the mass market. This is the story of brilliance trapped in amber.

Act II: The Turbid River (Chapters 6–10) crosses into the current that Western analysts cannot see and Western media will not cover—where $28,000 robotaxis achieve unit economics, where the road itself has learned to think, and where the monsoon is already reshaping every market it touches. This is the book's primary original contribution, and it will change how you think about China.

Act III: Where the Rivers Meet (Chapters 11–15) brings the two currents together into a single diagnosis and a single question: given everything both rivers reveal, where is the trade? It begins at the burning ghat, where the 150-year ICE empire meets the embodied-intelligence platform that is cremating it — not one disruption but five, feeding each other through an Interdependency Web whose compound force no single-sector analysis can capture. This is where analysis becomes architecture—where the Burning Ghat's Dinosaur Meter, Interdependency Web Score, and Quarter-Kelly Sizing give you the instruments to price the wreckage and size the trade—and where the Māyā Meter, the Six Temples, and the Three Monsoons tell you which current to ride and how much cargo to load. Act III requires both preceding acts. Read the rivers before you attempt the sea.

A final note for the contrarian investor, the reader who picked up this book because the title promised an "autonomous demolition derby": you are the reader for whom this book was written. The gods are not crazy. They are simply Chinese and American, racing on the same highway, priced in different currencies, and valued by different temples. Your job is not to choose a god. Your job is to read both rivers, navigate both currents, and arrive at the ocean with your cargo intact.

The tiller is in your hands.

• • •

Evidence Anchors

World Economic Forum, Autonomous Vehicle Roadmap (April 2025). • McKinsey & Company, Autonomous Vehicle Expert Survey (January 2026) • Bureau of Industry & Security, Connected Vehicles Final Rule (January 16, 2025) • Pony.ai Q3 2025 Earnings Release (November 25, 2025); Toyota JV Production Update (February 2026) • Morningstar / Wolfe Research Tesla Robotaxi Valuation Analysis (January–February 2026)

ACT I

THE GILDED RIVER

The American Autonomous Vehicle Landscape

The Schism

From Cruise Control to Cognitive Machines

In the great temple festivals of northern Kerala, two processions often approach the same gate from opposite directions. Each carries its own deity, its own drummers, its own logic of the sacred. The crowds do not ask which procession is correct. They ask which one reaches the sanctum first.

— From the Pooram traditions of Thrissur

1.1 The SAE Taxonomy as Strategic Framework

Every great schism begins with a taxonomy. Martin Luther had his ninety-five theses. The autonomous vehicle industry has six levels, numbered zero through five, bestowed upon it by SAE International with the solemn bureaucratic precision of an organization that also standardized bolt thread pitches. Moreover, like most taxonomies designed by engineers and adopted by marketers, the SAE levels have been simultaneously indispensable for understanding and catastrophic for honesty.

The taxonomy is simple enough on paper. **Level 0** is your grandfather's Buick: no automation, full human responsibility. **Level 1** adds a single guardian angel—cruise control or lane-keeping, but never both simultaneously. **Level 2** is where the modern story truly begins: the vehicle handles steering *and* acceleration simultaneously, but the human must supervise at all times. This is Tesla's Full Self-Driving (Supervised), General Motors' Super Cruise with its 620,000 subscribers, and Ford's BlueCruise. At this level, the machine *assists*. It does not *drive*. The distinction is not semantic. It is the difference between a co-pilot and a captain—and in the event of a crash, the legal liability, the insurance claim, and the eulogy all fall squarely on the human behind the wheel.

Level 3 is the Bermuda Triangle of autonomous driving. At this level, the machine assumes full control under specific conditions but demands that the human stand ready to retake control within seconds when those conditions evaporate. As of early 2026, exactly one commercial vehicle on Earth offers genuine Level 3 capability: the Mercedes-Benz Drive Pilot, available on the EQS and S-Class sedans, legal in California, Nevada, and Germany, and limited to speeds below 40 miles per hour in congested highway traffic. Mercedes has already stepped back from deploying L3 in the 2026 S-Class for the American market, quietly substituting an "L2++" system instead—a retreat so elegant it would make a French diplomat blush. In China, Changan's Deepal SL03 received the nation's first L3 conditional driving permits in December 2025, though restricted to 50 km/h in Chongqing. The handoff problem—the terrifying cognitive gap between a distracted human and an overwhelmed machine—remains unsolved. Asking a person who has been checking email for twenty minutes to become a competent driver immediately is not a safety strategy. It is a liability architecture dressed in marketing copy. The only people who love Level 3 are personal-injury attorneys and the actuaries who price their premiums, which, if you think about it, is the same thing said twice.

Here is the insight that most industry commentary misses: the autonomous vehicle industry did not progress linearly up this ladder. The breakthrough came from *skipping* Level 3 entirely and leaping to **Level 4**—full automation within geographically defined domains—where the vehicle requires no human backup. Waymo's robotaxis in Phoenix, San Francisco, and Los Angeles are Level 4. Aurora's driverless trucks on Interstate 45 between Dallas and Houston are Level 4. Baidu's Apollo Go robotaxis across Chinese cities are Level 4. The commercially operational autonomous vehicles in the world are not semi-autonomous cars nervously begging their owners to grab the wheel. They are fully autonomous machines operating in carefully circumscribed environments where they have been proven to work.

For the investor, the strategic reframing is essential. Forget the staircase. Think in business model categories: **L2 is a feature** (sold inside personal vehicles, monetized through subscriptions and insurance discounts—Tesla's 1.1 million FSD subscribers generating a recurring revenue stream that analysts love even when the feature itself is still supervised, at a hardware cost of roughly $2,000–$3,000 per vehicle). **L3 is a regulatory quagmire** (liability ambiguity makes underwriters weep and lawyers salivate). **L4 is a commercial platform** (fleet robotaxis and autonomous trucks generating per-mile or per-ride revenue—the only level producing actual transportation revenue from actual passengers who paid actual money; Waymo alone delivered 15 million rides in 2025, more than tripled, with an annualized revenue run rate exceeding $350 million). Moreover, **Level 5**—full automation everywhere, in every condition, from a Montana blizzard to a Mumbai monsoon to a Kozhikode morning with cows, autorickshaws, and a wedding procession sharing one lane—remains the industry's asymptotic aspiration. No vehicle on Earth has achieved it. Every earnings call that implies otherwise is, to use a technical financial term, *aspirational*.

1.2 Camera-Only vs. Sensor Fusion: The Philosophical Schism

If the SAE levels are the industry's creed, the sensor debate is its denominational split. Moreover, like all great theological schisms, it is fought with the ferocity of people who agree on ninety percent of everything but are prepared to burn each other at the stake over the remaining ten.

On one side stands the Church of Sensor Fusion, whose high temple is Waymo's campus in Mountain View—the creed: a vehicle must perceive the world through *multiple, redundant, complementary* sensing modalities. Waymo's fifth-generation system deployed LiDAR, cameras, radar, and high-definition maps in a layered architecture where each sensor compensates for the others' blind spots. LiDAR measures distance with centimeter precision but cannot read a stop sign. Cameras read stop signs but struggle in direct sunlight and total darkness. Radar penetrates rain and fog but produces blurry spatial data. HD maps provide the contextual metadata—signal timing, right-on-red rules, parking lot geometry, construction zone routing—that no onboard sensor can infer in real time. The philosophy is institutional, conservative, and deeply unfashionable: *trust no single source of truth*. It is, in the language of Kerala's Theyyam rituals, the *ullil kaanal*—the inner seeing that requires multiple mirrors to reveal what any one mirror conceals. The Theyyam performer wears a mask with many faces, not because the deity is confused about its identity, but because, in the Kerala epistemological tradition, truth is always *compound*. Sensor fusion is the engineering expression of that ancient insight.

On the other side stands the Church of Pure Vision, whose prophet-in-chief is Elon Musk. The creed: if a human brain can drive a car using only two eyes, then a sufficiently powerful neural network can drive a car using only eight cameras. Tesla's Full Self-Driving system uses no LiDAR, no radar (both were removed from production vehicles in 2021–22 in a move that was either visionary or reckless, depending on which of your retirement accounts holds TSLA), and no pre-mapped routes. The philosophy is radical, elegant, and intoxicating: the car must learn to see the world as a human does, and the data exhaust from more than a million customer vehicles will train it faster than any fleet of purpose-built sensor platforms.

The theological beauty of the cameras-only argument is that it is simultaneously the cheapest solution *and* the most ambitious. Tesla's FSD hardware—the HW4 onboard computer and eight cameras—costs approximately $2,000–$3,000 per vehicle, roughly one-sixtieth of Waymo's fifth-generation sensor stack, which costs $175,000 per Jaguar I-PACE. If cameras-only work, Tesla wins everything: every vehicle is a potential robotaxi, every mile driven is free training data, and the marginal cost of scaling approaches zero. It is the *sola scriptura* of autonomous driving—the belief that scripture alone, without the accumulated tradition of institutional redundancy, is sufficient for salvation.

Moreover, the faithful are not fools. The argument for pure vision has genuine structural appeal: it scales with manufacturing, it avoids the supply-chain dependency of LiDAR (a market where China's Hesai commands ~65 percent global share for L4 applications), and it bets on the one curve that has never disappointed in computing history—the exponential improvement of neural networks given sufficient data. If you believe that silicon will eventually match biology, cameras-only is the rational long-term wager. The Reformation, after all, produced some very good theology before it gave rise to centuries of war.

The verdict, as of early 2026, has been rendered not by theologians but by commercial results. Moreover, the results are, to put it as diplomatically as a Kerala communist in a temple town, *directionally unambiguous.*

Waymo delivers approximately 400,000 paid, fully driverless rides every week across six American cities, with no human safety driver on board. It has driven over 200 million fully autonomous miles on a fleet of roughly 2,500–3,000 vehicles. Its safety record, per Swiss Re's actuarial analysis of 25.3 million miles published December 2024, shows 88 percent fewer property damage claims and 92 percent fewer bodily injury claims than human drivers—a result that held even when benchmarked against newer ADAS-equipped vehicles. Waymo's total lifetime funding now exceeds $27.1 billion across five rounds, and its February 2026 raise valued the company at $126 billion—the largest single autonomous vehicle financing in history.

Tesla operates roughly 500 vehicles—combined across Austin and the San Francisco Bay Area — according to its Q4 2025 earnings call, with safety monitors present in most rides. Independent trackers found as few as 30 to 60 vehicles actively operating in Austin at any given time, a number that suggests either a very generous definition of "operating" or a very ambitious definition of "five hundred." Tesla began tentative unsupervised testing in Austin in late January 2026. NHTSA's Preliminary Evaluation PE 25012, opened in October 2025, is investigating more than 80 reported incidents involving 2.9 million FSD-equipped vehicles, documenting at least 14 crashes and up to 23 injuries. Tesla's crash rate in supervised Austin operations runs approximately many times higher than the human average—a figure that, had it appeared in any other company's safety filing, would have triggered congressional hearings, activist short-sellers, and at least one Netflix documentary. However, narrative immunity, as we shall see in Chapter 2, is the most expensive insurance policy in the history of American capital markets, and Tesla's premium is fully paid.

The comparison, placed here where both companies first stand side by side, is stark. Waymo delivers approximately 450,000 paid, fully driverless rides per week. Tesla's supervised Austin fleet delivers, by the most generous independent estimates, fewer than 1,000. On a *rides-delivered basis*, Waymo's sensor fusion approach outperforms Tesla's cameras-only approach by a factor of roughly *eight hundred to one*. On a *safety-adjusted basis*, the gap is wider still. FSD as transubstantiation—the belief that a camera, through the miracle of sufficient data and sufficient faith, can *become* a driver— remains an article of devotion. Like all articles of faith, it commands a premium from believers that no amount of actuarial data can displace. We will examine the elaborate financial architecture of that faith, and the temple economy that sustains it, in Chapter 2.

1.3 The Agentic AI Frontier: Beyond Camera vs. LiDAR

However, here the narrative takes a turn neither denomination fully anticipated. While the Western theological debate rages between cameras and LiDAR—a dispute increasingly resembling a 16th-century argument about the precise number of angels on the head of a pin—the 2026 frontier has already moved *beyond* both positions. The new paradigm is **Agentic AI**: autonomous driving systems that do not merely *perceive* the world but *reason* about it; that do not merely react to obstacles but understand context, interpret intention, and generate plans, as a seasoned driver processes a chaotic intersection—not pixel by pixel, but holistically.

Vision-Language-Action (VLAs) models represent the fusion of large language models with visual perception and motor control. Where a traditional AV system processes sensor data through hand-engineered rules or narrow neural networks, a VLA model can "read" a complex traffic scenario the way a human reads a sentence: parsing context, inferring intention, and generating action. A construction worker waving traffic through a one-lane detour while simultaneously holding a sign that says STOP. A school bus with its lights flashing on a road where a police officer's hand signal has temporarily overridden the posted speed limit. A wedding procession occupies the left lane at 3 miles per hour on a two-lane highway in rural India, while oncoming traffic plays chicken in the opposite direction. These are not edge cases for VLA models. They are the *raison d'être*.

Moreover, here is the data point that should send a small electric current through the spine of any investor still operating under the comfortable assumption that Chinese AV companies are merely cheap imitators playing catch-up to Silicon Valley's genius. In December 2025, **XPeng Motors**—a Chinese EV and autonomous driving company most Western analysts classify as a mere "Industrialiser"—had its paper *FastDriveVLA: Efficient End-to-End Driving via Plug-and-Play Reconstruction-based Token Pruning* accepted at **AAAI 2026**, the premier international artificial intelligence conference, which accepted only 17.6 percent of 23,680 submissions. The paper, a joint effort with Peking University, introduces **ReconPruner**, an adversarial foreground-background reconstruction strategy that mimics human driving attention patterns. The result: a **7.5-times reduction** in computational overhead—from 3,249 visual tokens to 812—while maintaining planning accuracy on the nuScenes benchmark. The team also constructed nuScenes-FG, a 241,000-image segmentation dataset—the kind of painstaking, unglamorous infrastructure-building that venture capitalists never tweet about but that makes the difference between a demo and a deployable system.

This is not incremental optimization. This is a company, according to most Western analysts, classified as a *farmer*, a manufacturer, a hardware company, an industrialiser—operating at the absolute bleeding edge of algorithmic AI research. The Farmer showed up at the most selective AI conference on Earth and outperformed the laboratories that the Hunter funds with billions in R&D. XPeng's President Brian Gu has called this dynamic the **"DeepSeek Moment"** for autonomous driving: the point at which Chinese firms achieve comparable or superior performance at radically lower cost, not through brute-force spending but through architectural innovation that Western incumbents did not anticipate and, more troublingly, may not yet fully understand.

If DeepSeek demonstrated that a Chinese AI lab could match GPT-4's performance at a fraction of the training cost—a revelation that briefly wiped nearly a trillion dollars from American tech market capitalization—then FastDriveVLA demonstrates that a Chinese automaker can make Vision-Language-Action models efficient enough to run on production electric vehicles that cost $25,000, not $175,000. The implications for the sensor debate are profound: if the reasoning layer becomes sufficiently powerful, the sensor hardware becomes less decisive. The schism between cameras and LiDAR is beginning to look less like a fundamental theological divide and more like an argument over which type of eyeglasses to wear. At the same time, the real cognitive revolution happens in the brain.

File this thought carefully: a Chinese company that simultaneously manufactures vehicles at scale, develops its own full-stack AV software, *and* publishes frontier AI research at top-tier academic conferences. The American ecosystem has no structural equivalent. No American company inhabits that combination of roles. In the next chapter, we will introduce a framework—what I call the Four Temples—that explains why this matters, why the American competitive landscape has empty stalls where China has occupants, and what it means for the returns that accrue in the decade ahead. The empty stall is not a curiosity. It is the thesis. By Chapter 11, it has become the central argument of this book.

1.4 The HD Map Advantage: Why Geography Is Not a Bug

There is a persistent critique of Waymo's approach—advanced most loudly by Tesla partisans and most quietly by Waymo's own engineers who wish they could do without the expense—that geofencing is a limitation. That confining an autonomous vehicle to pre-mapped territories is an admission of inadequacy, a concession that the technology cannot handle the real world in its full, uncharted, potholed complexity. That Waymo's cars are, to put it indelicately, very expensive pets that can only find their way home if someone has pre-drawn the route in crayon.

This critique misunderstands the nature of the advantage. Geofencing is not a concession. It is a *strategy*. Moreover, as we will see in Act II, it is the strategy China is deploying at the level of civilization.

High-definition maps are not just GPS routes with higher resolution. They are dense metadata layers encoding information that no onboard sensor can reliably infer in real time: the precise timing of every traffic signal, including unposted yellow-light durations that vary by municipality; the local convention on right-on-red (permitted in Arizona, prohibited at specific intersections in San

Francisco, a matter of existential philosophical debate in New York City); the geometry of parking lot entries that deviate from standard lane markings; the routing implications of recurring construction zones that have been "temporary" since 2019; the school-zone speed reductions that activate on weekdays but not weekends and not on teacher workdays, which no one including the teachers can reliably predict. This is institutional knowledge—the accumulated memory of a city's traffic nervous system—baked into a digital substrate that the vehicle consults, as a seasoned cab driver consults decades of muscle memory.

Waymo's sixth-generation Driver system, deployed operationally in February 2026 on the new Zeekr RT ("Ojai") platform, demonstrates what the geofenced approach enables at an industrial scale. The total sensor count decreases by 42 percent—from 29 cameras to 13 and from 5 LiDARs to 4—while targeting hardware costs below $20,000 per unit, an 80-plus percent reduction relative to the fifth-generation I-PACE configuration. The total vehicle cost falls from approximately $175,000 to roughly $75,000. As the maps mature and the software improves, the hardware requirements *shrink* rather than *expand*. This is the opposite of what the cameras-only apostles predicted. Moreover, it is worth pausing on the Chinese comparison point that will become Act II's central exhibit: ADAS-grade LiDAR from Hesai and RoboSense—sensors that cost $150,000 a decade ago—now sell for $200 to $500 per unit from Chinese manufacturers who command ~65 percent of the global L4 LiDAR market, with Hesai alone delivering 2 million cumulative units in 2025 and expanding to 4 million annual capacity in 2026. The cost curve is not converging. It is a rout.

The deeper analogy—one that establishes the central architectural argument of this book—is civilizational. The American approach makes the car smart enough to navigate dumb infrastructure. Waymo's vehicle must carry the full cognitive burden: sensing, interpreting, reasoning, acting. Every watt of computation, every photon of LiDAR, every polygon of HD-map data exists because the road itself offers *nothing*. American infrastructure is passive, indifferent, fundamentally unchanged since Eisenhower's Federal-Aid Highway Act of 1956—a magnificent fossil in which the most technologically advanced element remains the reflective paint stripe, itself a 1930s innovation. The American road does not communicate. It does not perceive. It simply *is*, and whatever intelligence is needed to navigate it must be carried entirely on the vehicle's roof, at the vehicle's expense, within the vehicle's power budget. It is, if you step back far enough, a $175,000 confession that America has not built a new piece of transportation infrastructure worth mentioning since the Eisenhower era—and has instead elected to bolt the intelligence onto each car, one sensor cathedral at a time.

The Chinese approach, as Act II will demonstrate in forensic detail, inverts this logic entirely. China is developing smart infrastructure that can share the cognitive load with vehicles. Vehicle-to-everything communication. Roadside perception units mounted on lampposts and gantries. Smart highway corridors with embedded sensors that can detect a stopped vehicle around a blind curve before any onboard sensor could. The vehicle does not need to carry a $175,000 temple on its roof because the road itself *is* a temple—equipped with eyes, ears, and a nervous system of its own.

These are not two versions of the same strategy. They are two civilizations, two epistemologies, two answers to the same fundamental question: *who should think?* The American answer is: the vehicle. The Chinese answer is: the system. One scales upward in per-unit sophistication. The other scales outward in per-system coverage. Moreover, the investment implications of that civilizational divergence—what it means for your portfolio, your industry, your country's competitive position— are the subject of every chapter that follows.

The schism between cameras and LiDAR, between faith and redundancy, between the elegant bet and the institutional hedge, is the founding fracture of the American autonomous vehicle landscape. However, two processions are still approaching the same gate. One carries a $175,000 sensor cathedral on its roof and the safety record to justify every dollar. The other carries a $385 autonomy kit inside the world's best-selling electric vehicle and a data monsoon that generates 160 million kilometers of training data every day. The crowds, as the Pooram traditions of Thrissur teach, do not ask which procession is correct. They ask which one reaches the sanctum first.

In the next chapter, we examine who stands on each side of the American crack: the undisputed king who just raised $16 billion, the challengers building purpose-built vehicles and platform empires, the heretic-prophet whose market capitalization exceeds most nations' GDP but whose autonomous fleet can still be counted on one's fingers and toes—and whose "narrative immunity" may be the most expensive insurance policy in the history of capital markets—and the graveyard of those who thought the temple could be built on faith alone. The question is not whether the gods will be pleased. The question is whether the offering is real.

Evidence Anchors

Tesla 10-K (FY, 2025); NHTSA PE 25012 Preliminary Evaluation (Oct 2025, expanded Dec 2025) • Waymo 2025 Year in Review; $16B funding announcement (Feb 2, 2026); Waymo Safety Impact Data Hub • Swiss Re–Waymo Actuarial Safety Study (Dec 2024, 25.3M miles; published in Heliyon) • XPeng FastDriveVLA (AAAI 2026, accepted Dec 28, 2025); VLA Models for Driving survey (arXiv, Dec 2025) • SAE J3016 Standard; Mercedes-Benz Drive Pilot certification; Waymo Open Dataset documentation

---

CHAPTER 2

The Kingdom, The Challengers, and The Heretic

America's AV Hierarchy in the Age of Scale Capital

After the flood recedes, you see who is still standing.

— Kuttanad proverb (*vellam ozhinja shesham, kaanaam enthu nilkkunnu*)

In the Kerala backwaters, the boatmen have a phrase for what happens after the monsoon scours the channels: *vellam ozhinja shesham, kaanaam enthu nilkkunnu*—after the flood recedes, you see who is still standing. The American autonomous-vehicle industry has just endured its own monsoon. Between 2022 and 2025, more than $30 billion in cumulative capital was destroyed across a dozen failed ventures. Cruise burned through $10 billion and imploded after dragging a pedestrian beneath its chassis in San Francisco. Apple spent a decade and assigned 5,000 engineers to Project Titan before cancelling it in a 12-minute meeting that allowed no questions. TuSimple, once valued at $8.5 billion, collapsed amid fraud allegations and a bizarre geopolitical defection to Asia. Embark, Motional, Argo AI—the roll call of the dead reads like the casualty list of a Napoleonic campaign, except the soldiers were software engineers and the battlefield was a parking lot in Chandler, Arizona.

What remains after the flood is a landscape so consolidated it would make a trust-busting Teddy Roosevelt weep: one undisputed king, two credible challengers, one distribution kingmaker who owns no vehicles, and one heretic-prophet whose market capitalization exceeds most nations' GDP but whose actual driverless fleet, upon forensic inspection, fits comfortably inside a mid-size parking garage. This is the hierarchy of the American autonomous-vehicle market in February 2026. It is a hierarchy defined not by technological superiority alone—the theological schism of Chapter 1 saw to that—but by the most unglamorous virtue in Silicon Valley: *patient capital deployed with operational discipline.*

The survivors share a structural trait that the dead lacked. They understood, before their funding ran out, that building an autonomous vehicle is an engineering problem, but *running an autonomous transportation service* is an operational one—and operations are harder. A Theyyam performer does not merely learn the choreography; he must sustain the trance for hours, manage the fire, read the crowd, and emerge unburned. The technology is the choreography. The operations are the fire.

2.1 Waymo: The Undisputed King

On February 2, 2026, Waymo closed a $16 billion funding round at a post-money valuation of $126 billion—the largest single raise in autonomous-vehicle history. Lead investors included Dragoneer, DST Global, and Sequoia Capital, joined by Andreessen Horowitz, Mubadala, Silver Lake, Tiger Global, T. Rowe Price, Fidelity, Kleiner Perkins, and Temasek. Alphabet, the majority owner, contributed an estimated $13 billion of the round, a figure so staggering it suggests either supreme confidence or a pathological inability to let go—or, more likely, both. Total lifetime funding now exceeds $27.1 billion across five rounds. That is not a venture investment; it is the GDP of a small European nation funneled into self-driving vehicles in Phoenix.

The operational metrics that justified that valuation are, for once, not aspirational. Waymo delivered 15 million rides in 2025, quadrupling year-over-year volume and surpassing 20 million lifetime rides. Weekly paid driverless rides settled to approximately 400,000 by February 2026 across six US metros: Phoenix, San Francisco, Los Angeles, Austin, Atlanta, and Miami. Annualized revenue exceeds $350 million. Co-CEO Tekedra Mawakana has publicly set a target of one million weekly rides by year's end. The safety record—detailed in Chapter 1—remains the industry's gold standard.

The expansion roadmap is the most aggressive in AV history. Waymo is laying groundwork for ride-hailing operations in more than twenty additional cities in 2026, including Dallas, Denver, Detroit, Houston, Las Vegas, Nashville, Orlando, San Antonio, San Diego, and Washington, D.C. Internationally, London testing began in December 2025 with fleet partner Moove, and Tokyo testing launched in April 2025 through a partnership with Nihon Kotsu and the GO taxi application. If even half these cities reach commercial launch, Waymo will have more operational geography than any taxi company in world history.

The 6th-generation Driver—deployed on the Zeekr RT platform, detailed in Chapter 1 —brings total vehicle cost from approximately $175,000 to roughly $75,000, transforming Waymo's economics from boutique to scalable. This is not merely a cost reduction; it is the difference between an exhibition of fine art and a printing press.

For the Gordon Gekko in the room: Waymo's $126 billion valuation implies approximately $50,000 per vehicle on its current fleet—absurd on a static basis but rational on a forward basis if the fleet scales to 50,000–100,000 vehicles by 2030, each generating $70,000–$100,000 in annual revenue. At that scale, the implied price-to-revenue multiple of 5–8x on 2030 estimates is expensive but defensible for a natural monopoly in the making. The key question for Act III is not whether Waymo can scale. It is whether any Chinese company *needs* to replicate its model—or whether an entirely different architecture, built on $200 LiDAR and $7,800 vehicles, renders the question moot.

2.2 The Credible Challengers

Zoox: The Temple Builder

If Waymo is the established cathedral, Zoox is the architect who decided to design an entirely new one from the foundation up—and then convinced Amazon to pay for it. Zoox's purpose-built, bidirectional robotaxi has no steering wheel, no pedals, and no front or back—it drives equally well in both directions, a design philosophy that is either brilliantly efficient or magnificently hubristic, depending on how patient your capital happens to be.

The operational milestones are tangible. NHTSA granted Zoox its first demonstration exemption on August 6, 2025—the first ever issued for an American-built autonomous vehicle. A commercial exemption petition followed on September 24, 2025, and remains pending. Without it, Zoox cannot charge fares, which means its current operations in Las Vegas and San Francisco are free public rides: a generous if expensive form of market education. The Hayward, California, manufacturing facility—220,000 square feet and opened in June 2025—is designed to have a production capacity of 10,000 robotaxis per year at full scale—current fleet: approximately 50 vehicles. The gap between capacity and deployment tells you everything about where Zoox sits on the maturity curve.

Amazon's backing provides the balance-sheet patience that Cruise lacked, but patience is not a strategy. The binary is stark: either the bespoke manufacturing line becomes an unassailable moat that no competitor will casually replicate, or Zoox becomes the most expensive proof-of-concept in Amazon's long history of expensive proofs-of-concept, which is saying something. It is either a $75,000 TCO moat or a $10 billion monument to vehicular indecision. There is no middle outcome.

Uber: The Demand-Side Moat

Uber's autonomous-vehicle strategy is a masterclass in what management consultants call "asset-light platform arbitrage" and what everyone else calls "letting someone else do the hard part." Having sold its own AV division to Aurora in 2020 after a fatal crash in Tempe, Arizona, Uber pivoted to a pure platform play: aggregating autonomous supply from multiple AV providers without owning a single driverless vehicle. It is the Airbnb of robotaxis—all the demand, none of the real estate.

The partnership roster is staggering in its breadth. Waymo vehicles are bookable through the Uber app in Phoenix, Austin, and Atlanta. Avride launched robotaxi rides in Dallas in December 2025. Nuro and Lucid received $300 million each from Uber, with purchase agreements for more than 20,000 Lucid Gravity SUVs over six years. An NVIDIA partnership envisions 5,000 Stellantis Level 4 vehicles. In January 2026, Uber launched AV Labs to collect driving data across more than 600 cities for its robotaxi partners—a demand-side data flywheel that no AV company can replicate on its own. CEO Dara Khosrowshahi expects robotaxi services in ten or more countries by late 2026.

The strategic logic is the ultimate hedge: if autonomous vehicles work, Uber owns the marketplace and earns a platform fee. If Avride undercuts Waymo on price, Uber earns a platform fee. If both fail and human drivers persist, Uber already has them. It is the only bet in the American AV landscape that wins regardless of which god answers the prayer. The risk, of course, is that Waymo decides it no longer needs Uber's demand aggregation—that once you own the restaurant, you stop paying the food-delivery app. However, for now, the marriage of convenience holds, because Waymo needs riders in Austin and Atlanta more than it needs to save on platform fees.

A quieter but strategically significant development: the Lyft–Waymo integration and the expansion of Flexdrive's fleet management signal that the platform wars will eventually include multiple demand aggregators competing for AV supply. For investors, this means the platform layer may commoditize faster than the AV stack itself—a counterintuitive outcome in an industry obsessed with algorithmic differentiation.

2.3 Tesla: The Heretic-Prophet

And then there is Tesla.

This book introduces a concept called **narrative immunity**: the phenomenon in which a company's stock price becomes decoupled from its operational performance and instead becomes attached to a story so compelling, so emotionally resonant, so deeply woven into the identity of its shareholder base, that no quantity of empirical evidence can displace it. Narrative immunity is not unique to Tesla—it has precedents in the dot-com bubble, in the housing derivatives market of 2007, and in the cryptocurrency manias of 2017 and 2021—but Tesla's version is distinctive in its duration, scale, and the sophistication of the institutional investors who participate in it. Understanding narrative immunity is essential to understanding why the Māyā Meter from the Prologue shows a 3,000-to-1 valuation gap between Tesla's robotaxi promise and WeRide's operating reality. It is the financial architecture of *Māyā* made manifest.

In the Theyyam tradition of northern Kerala, the *kolam*—the performer who channels the deity— enters a state where the boundary between the human and the divine dissolves. The crowd does not ask whether the *kolam is* the god; they experience the performance as if he were, and that is sufficient. Elon Musk occupies a similar ontological space in the American capital markets. His believers do not require evidence that Full Self-Driving works. They require the *performance* of inevitability—the earnings-call incantation, the cryptic tweet, the timeline that slides perpetually forward like a mirage in the Sonoran Desert—and that performance has sustained a market capitalization of $1.2–$1.6 trillion, of which analysts attribute $450–$700 billion to robotaxi potential alone.

The operational reality occupies a different universe. Tesla's Q4 2025 earnings call claimed "more than 500 vehicles between Austin and the Bay Area," with approximately 700,000 paid miles total. Independent trackers found a rather more modest picture: as few as 30 to 60 vehicles identifiable by VIN in Austin, with 3 to 10 actively operating at any given time. The crash rate and NHTSA investigation documented in Chapter 1 tell the rest of the story: a company whose entire thesis rests on superhuman driving capability is arguing, in regulatory filings, that most of its crashes were someone else's fault.

The *ullil kaanal*—the inner seeing of the Theyyam—demands that we look past the performance to the structure beneath. Moreover, the structure reveals that Wall Street operates as a temple economy. The quarterly earnings call is the ritual. The consensus EPS estimate is the liturgy. The analyst upgrade is the benediction. Moreover, the long-term R&D investment required to build a functioning autonomous transportation network is the sacrifice demanded by the deity but deferred by the priests, because the congregation does not want to hear about deferred gratification when the oracle is promising transcendence by next quarter.

Consider the structural absurdity. Waymo has delivered 20 million fully autonomous rides, published peer-reviewed safety data, and operates across six cities—valuation: $126 billion. Tesla has delivered approximately 700,000 supervised rides in two cities, with a fleet whose actual operational count appears to be measured in the dozens, and it is under active federal safety investigation. The portion of Tesla's market capitalization attributed to its robotaxi potential: $450–$700 billion—three to five times Waymo's entire valuation —for a service that has not yet completed a single unsupervised commercial ride. If this were a pharmaceutical company, the FDA would have concerns. If this were a real estate transaction, the appraiser would lose his license. However, this is the American capital market, where narrative immunity converts future tense into present value with the zeal of an evangelist and the precision of a fortune cookie.

The steelman deserves its day. Tesla began testing unsupervised robotaxi rides in Austin in late January 2026—a genuine milestone. Cybercab production is targeted for April 2026. Expansion plans include Nevada and Phoenix. ARK Invest's Cathie Wood projects robotaxi at 60 percent of Tesla's expected value; Wolfe Research models $250 billion in robotaxi revenue by 2035. If Tesla's camera-only architecture works at scale without geofencing or HD maps—if *sola scriptura* proves sufficient—then the entire sensor-fusion orthodoxy collapses, and Tesla's valuation will look prescient rather than delusional. That remains a possibility.

However, the *ullil kaanal* also sees the compensation architecture beneath the product announcement. On February 14, 2026—Valentine's Day, which is either a coincidence or the most expensive romantic gesture in automotive history—Tesla pivoted FSD to a subscription-only model. This is not a pricing decision. It is a compensation trigger. Musk's 2025 CEO Performance Award, one of the largest executive compensation packages in corporate history, includes milestones tied to

10 million active FSD subscriptions. The subscription model converts every Tesla owner into a potential contributor to a metric that directly unlocks billions in personal compensation for the CEO. The reader who files that structural observation alongside the narrative immunity concept will find both waiting in Chapters 11 and 12, where they converge with the Māyā Meter to devastating analytical effect.

The investor who asks "when will Tesla's robotaxi be profitable?" is asking the wrong question. The right question is: "What does it mean for capital allocation in the world's deepest equity market when a $700 billion valuation wedge rests on a technology that has crashed once every 31,000 miles?" The answer is that it means precisely what it has always meant in American finance: the story is the product, the stock is the delivery mechanism, and reality is a long-term catalyst that arrives, eventually, to devastating effect. The *kolam* cannot stay in the trance forever. Eventually, the fire demands a reckoning. The reader from Kerala will recognize the pattern. In every temple festival, the fireworks are spectacular. The cleanup comes the next morning.

2.4 The Four Temples: A Diagnostic Framework

The reader has now surveyed the American landscape: its king, its challengers, its platform, its heretic. However, surveying the terrain is not the same as mapping it. To understand why this landscape feels simultaneously advanced and structurally incomplete—and to prepare the diagnostic lens we will need for Act II's Chinese ecosystem—we need a taxonomy that captures not just *who* competes, but the roles a healthy, autonomous-vehicle ecosystem requires.

In Kerala temple architecture, a great temple complex is never a single structure. It is an ensemble—the *kshetram*—composed of multiple temples, each serving a different deity, each performing a different function in the spiritual economy, all contained within a single sacred compound. The *chuttambalam* protects the sanctum. The *koothambalam* hosts the rituals. The *kulam* purifies. The *gopuram* announces. No single temple is the complex. Together, they form a civilization.

This book introduces the **Four Temples Framework**: a taxonomy for mapping the autonomous-vehicle ecosystem across civilizations. The four archetypes are:

> **1. The National Champion:** the state-anointed or market-anointed standard-bearer, backed by sovereign or megacap capital and regulatory privilege. In China: Baidu Apollo Go. In America: Waymo—not by government designation but by sheer capital accumulation and market dominance.

> **2. The Pure-Play Scaler:** the company whose entire existence is organized around operating autonomous vehicles at a commercial scale. In China: Pony.ai, WeRide. In

America: Waymo again—which is the first structural asymmetry. America's National Champion *is* its Pure-Play Operator. There is no second.

3. The Industrialiser: the manufacturing colossus that pushes autonomy into the mass market through volume, cost compression, and ADAS-to-L4 stepping stones. In China: BYD, XPeng, NIO. In America, *the stall is empty*. No American automaker is building a $9,550 autonomous vehicle. No American manufacturer is generating 160 million kilometers of daily training data from consumer fleets. This is the most consequential vacancy in the entire competitive landscape.

4. The Stack Integrator: the company that builds the autonomous driving software stack and licenses it to OEMs, embedding its technology across the ecosystem like a nervous system through a body. In China: Huawei, Momenta, DeepRoute.ai. In America: *another empty stall*. No American company occupies this role at comparable scale.

Each temple serves a different god. Together they form a civilization—or, in the case of America, they reveal the gaps where a civilization should be. Map the US companies onto this taxonomy, and the geometry is stark:

Waymo = occupies both the National Champion and Pure-Play Scaler stalls. One company filling two roles is a concentration, not a strength.

Tesla = Aspirational Industrialiser. Manufactures vehicles at a massive scale and aspires to embed autonomy, but its AV operations remain supervised, geographically constrained, and statistically unsafe relative to both human drivers and Waymo. It is an industrialiser by manufacturing volume but not yet by autonomous capability.

Uber = Platform. No stack integration. No manufacturing. No vehicles. Pure demand aggregation—immensely valuable but structurally dependent on someone else's technology.

The Empty Cells. No American equivalent to BYD—a company manufacturing millions of vehicles per year with advanced autonomous features as standard equipment at price points accessible to hundreds of millions of consumers. No American equivalent to the Huawei–Momenta–OEM tripartite model. The American temple has one occupied altar and two that echo with emptiness. Chapter 5 will diagnose why. Act II will reveal what fills those stalls on the other side of the Pacific. Moreover, by Chapter 11, those empty cells will have become the argument's center of gravity.

2.5 The Graveyard: They Built Cars, Not Companies

Every Kerala village has its *Kaavu*—the sacred grove where the spirits of the dead reside. The American AV industry has its own. The names inscribed there are instructive not for what they attempted but for what they failed to understand.

Cruise: The $10 Billion Pyre

General Motors invested more than $10 billion in Cruise over the program's life, spending approximately $600 million per quarter at peak burn. The collapse was triggered by the October 2, 2023, incident in San Francisco, in which a Cruise vehicle struck a pedestrian who had been thrown into its path by a hit-and-run driver, then dragged her twenty feet while attempting a pullover maneuver. The incident was horrifying; Cruise's response was worse. The company initially showed regulators an edited video that omitted the dragging sequence—a deception that transformed a tragic accident into an existential credibility crisis. California revoked permits. NHTSA opened an investigation. Half the workforce was laid off.

GM exited the robotaxi market on December 10, 2024, and pivoted to integrating Cruise's technology into Super Cruise—its hands-free highway ADAS system—which by late 2025 had 620,000 subscribers generating $234 million in revenue. The lesson is not subtle: $10 billion in robotaxi investment was converted into a subscription feature for personal cars—a retreat so thorough it suggests the original strategy was less a plan than an expensive experiment conducted in public.

Apple: The Twelve-Minute Funeral

Project Titan was cancelled on February 27, 2024, after approximately ten years and an estimated $10–15 billion in cumulative spending. At its peak, five thousand Apple employees worked on the project. COO Jeff Williams and VP Kevin Lynch delivered the news in a twelve-minute all-hands meeting that permitted no questions—a format so brutally efficient it could only have been designed by a company that prizes user experience above all else, except when the users are its own employees. Apple spent a decade and fifteen billion dollars learning what every taxi driver already knows: the hard part is not the car. It encompasses cleaning, permitting, fleet management, regulatory negotiations across 50 jurisdictions, and the 3 a.m. phone call when a vehicle clips a fire hydrant in a school zone.

The Common Failure Mode

Add Motional ($5 billion, wound down 2024), Embark ($5.2 billion peak valuation, dissolved 2023 with fewer than fifty trucks), TuSimple ($8.5 billion peak, delisted amid fraud allegations), and Argo AI ($3.6 billion, shut down October 2022 with Ford taking a $2.7 billion write-down in a single quarter)—and the pattern becomes unmistakable. **Every failure shares a common structural deficiency: they treated autonomous driving as a technology problem and, too late, discovered it was an operations problem.** Building a car that can drive itself is enormously difficult. Building a system that dispatches, monitors, maintains, cleans, charges, insures, permits, and continuously improves thousands of such cars across dozens of cities—that is a different order of difficulty entirely. It is the difference between composing a symphony and running an orchestra across forty venues simultaneously, in cities with different noise ordinances. Silicon Valley, for all its genius, had confused writing the score with filling the seats—and discovered that the audience was not yet seated, the concert halls were not yet built, and the municipal permits for the concert halls had not yet cleared committee.

The technology is the choreography. The operations are the fire. Moreover, the fire claimed billions.

2.6 The Hierarchy Hardens

The American AV landscape of February 2026 is thus a study in Darwinian selection. The fittest survived not because they were the smartest or the most innovative—Argo's technology was widely respected; Cruise's engineering was formidable—but because they possessed the institutional patience to endure a decade of capital incineration and the operational humility to expand one city at a time. Waymo had Alphabet's balance sheet. Zoox has Amazon's. Aurora has $1.5 billion in liquidity and a freight-first strategy that generates revenue before robotaxis. Uber had the cunning to exit the technology race entirely and position itself as the marketplace. Each survivor found a different way to solve the same problem: how to stay alive long enough for the technology to mature and the market to materialize.

This is what separates the American model from the Chinese one—and what makes the comparison in Act II so structurally illuminating. America's AV hierarchy was forged through venture-capital attrition: dozens of companies entered, billions were destroyed, and a handful emerged with monopoly-scale ambitions and the institutional backing to pursue them. China's ecosystem, as we shall see, was cultivated through a fundamentally different mechanism: state-directed industrial policy that nurtures multiple players simultaneously, distributes risk across the system, and treats failure as a data input rather than a death sentence. The Hunter stalks the singular prey—the perfect algorithm, the winner-take-most platform. The Farmer prepares the field, plants many seeds, and trusts the monsoon to water them all.

Tesla alone defies the pattern. Its survival is not a function of operational excellence but of narrative immunity—a market-cap shield forged in the fires of cult-like shareholder devotion and analyst projections built on assumptions that would make a medieval astrologer blush. Whether that shield holds or shatters will depend on what happens in Austin and San Francisco over the next twelve months. The Theyyam performer cannot remain in trance indefinitely. Eventually, the fire demands a reckoning.

However, before we examine the regulatory labyrinth that constrains this hierarchy, we must first leave the passenger cabin and climb into the truck cab. While robotaxis capture headlines and the venture capital imagination, the first billion dollars of autonomous-vehicle revenue may not come from moving people at all. It may come from moving freight—along the interstate highways of Texas, in Class 8 trucks that never need to sleep, never exceed their hours of service, and never, ever, sue for overtime. Cargo, unlike passengers, does not tweet. Cargo does not call its congressman. Cargo does not retain a personal-injury attorney who advertises on bus shelters. Cargo arrives, or it does not, and the insurance adjuster handles the rest. This is not a trivial advantage.

Evidence Anchors

Alphabet 10-K (FY, 2025); Waymo blog, "$16 Billion to Scale Waymo." February 2, 2026 • S&P Global Mobility, Autonomous Ride-Hailing Market Assessment (December 2025) • NHTSA PE 25012 filings: INOA-PE25012-19171 (Oct 2025), INIM-PE25012-30897 (Dec 2025) • Swiss Re—Waymo Actuarial Safety Study (December 2024, 25.3M autonomous miles) • Tesla Q4 2025 Earnings Call Transcript (January 28, 2026); Electrek fleet tracking (December 2025) • Tesla CEO Performance Award proxy filings (2024–2025)

CHAPTER 3

The Long Haul

Autonomous Freight and the First Billion

The field does not remember who shouted loudest at planting. It remembers who watered.

— Kuttanad farming proverb

In the paddy fields of Kuttanad—the rice bowl of Kerala, where the land lies below sea level, and farming is an act of defiance against geography itself—the harvest does not arrive with drama. There is no single moment of triumph. The water is pumped. The bunds are maintained. The seedlings are transplanted by hand, row by patient row. And then, months later, the grain appears—not as a revelation but as an accumulation. The farmer who waited, who prepared the field while others chased quicker returns, eats first.

This is the autonomous trucking industry in 2026. While the world fixates on the robotaxi theatre— the $126 billion Waymo valuation, the Tesla earnings-call incantations, the Zoox bidirectional fever dream—a quieter revolution is unfolding on Interstate 45 between Dallas and Houston, on the I-10 corridor from Fort Worth to Phoenix, and in the Permian Basin oilfields of West Texas. Class 8 trucks are hauling commercial freight without human drivers. They are being paid for it. They are doing it safely. Moreover, they are doing it in the segment of American transportation where the economics are most obviously, immediately, and overwhelmingly favorable: long-haul freight. In this nearly trillion-dollar market, the single largest operating cost—the human being behind the wheel—is also the single largest constraint on utilization.

For the Gordon Gekko investor scanning the American AV landscape for the first dollar of genuine, scalable, recurring revenue that is not subsidized by a parent company's balance sheet or sustained by narrative immunity, autonomous trucking is not a sideshow. It is the beachhead.

3.1 The Economics of Autonomous Freight

The American trucking industry peaked at $1.004 trillion in revenue in 2023 before a freight recession pulled it down to $906 billion in 2024—still, by any standard, one of the largest service industries on earth. Trucks move 72.6 percent of domestic freight tonnage. The industry employs 3.5

million drivers, embedded within a broader trucking workforce of 8.4 million people. It is, in the most literal sense, the circulatory system of the American economy.

The economics of that circulatory system are defined by one brutal structural fact: driver compensation accounts for 35-44% of total per-mile operating costs. The American Transportation Research Institute's 2025 operational cost survey pegs total cost per mile at $2.26, with driver wages and benefits combining to roughly $1.00 per mile. On a 1,500-mile long-haul route, driver compensation thus represents $1,500 to $1,800 per trip. Eliminate the driver—or, more precisely, eliminate the driver on the highway portion and retain them for the complex first and last miles—and you unlock savings of 25 to 42 percent per mile, depending on route length and configuration. McKinsey's September 2024 analysis projects total cost of ownership reductions of up to 42 percent on routes exceeding 1,500 miles.

However, the cost savings are only half the equation. The other half is utilization—and the utilization story is where the economics shift from attractive to obscene. Federal Hours of Service regulations mandate that a truck driver may drive no more than eleven hours within a fourteen-hour on-duty window, after which a mandatory ten-hour rest period is required. This means that a human-driven Class 8 truck sits idle for roughly 40 percent of every twenty-four-hour cycle—a capital asset worth $150,000 to $200,000, generating precisely zero revenue while its operator sleeps in a bunk the size of a coffin at a truck stop off Interstate 20. In what other trillion-dollar industry would investors tolerate a 40 percent idle rate on their primary capital asset? In commercial aviation, a 40 percent idle rate would trigger a shareholder revolt. In manufacturing, it would trigger a bankruptcy filing. In trucking, it is considered normal because the constraint is biological: the human body requires sleep, and no amount of shareholder pressure has yet repealed that particular regulation.

An autonomous truck does not sleep. It does not pull into a truck stop for a meal, a shower, or a phone call home. It does not accumulate fatigue, distraction, or the existential dread that accompanies 600 miles of I-10 through West Texas at two in the morning. An autonomous truck can operate around the clock, limited only by maintenance schedules and refueling stops—roughly doubling the asset utilization of a human-driven equivalent. Double the utilization at 25–42 percent lower per-mile cost, and the compounding effect on fleet economics is not incremental. It is transformational.

The industry's labor dynamics amplify the opportunity—and illuminate its politics. The American Trucking Associations' headline figure of 78,000 unfilled driver positions has become contested even within the ATA itself; at the October 2025 Management Conference, chief economist Bob Costello pivoted to what he called a "quality problem," not a quantity problem, while FreightWaves and the National Academies have called the "shortage" framing a myth designed to suppress wages. The truth is structural: long-haul trucking offers a lifestyle so demanding—weeks away from home, sedentary work conditions, median pay of roughly $55,000—that turnover rates at large carriers routinely exceed 90 percent annually. The industry does not have a shortage. It has a retention crisis disguised as a shortage. Moreover, autonomous trucks solve the retention crisis not by making the job more attractive but by eliminating the job in the segment where retention is worst: the long, monotonous, interstate haul. The Teamsters read the same McKinsey reports. They know that autonomous freight does not eliminate the urban driver, the dockworker, or the last-mile specialist—but it does eliminate the long-haul seat, which is the seat their members least want to occupy. The question is whether their political capital outlasts the technology's timeline. History suggests the timeline wins. It always does. However, history also suggests that the timeline is longer than the VCs promise and shorter than the unions hope.

3.2 The Transfer Hub Model

The genius of autonomous trucking—the reason it will likely generate meaningful revenue before robotaxis do—lies not in a technological breakthrough but in an operational simplification so elegant that it borders on the obvious. The industry refers to it as the transfer hub model. A Theyyam devotee might call it *prakrithi yukthy*—nature's logic: do not fight the terrain you cannot conquer; go around it.

The model works as follows. A human driver operates the truck through the complex first mile: navigating the warehouse loading dock, merging onto city streets, maneuvering through construction zones, stopping for a school bus, handling the ten thousand micro-decisions that make urban driving the hardest unsolved problem in artificial intelligence. The truck reaches a transfer hub—a designated facility at the edge of the interstate on-ramp—where the human parks, the autonomous system activates, and the truck proceeds onto the highway. Three hundred, six hundred, a thousand miles later, the truck arrives at a second transfer hub near its destination, where a different human driver takes over for the last mile of urban delivery. The autonomous system handles only the highway segment: limited-access, lane-marked, predictable, and—critically—constituting 80 to 90 percent of the total mileage on a typical long-haul route.

This is the American flywheel in its most efficient form. By constraining the operational design domain to interstate highways—the simplest driving environment, with no pedestrians, no cyclists, no unprotected left turns, no double-parked delivery vans—the transfer hub model reduces technical complexity by an order of magnitude while capturing the vast majority of the economic value. It is the equivalent of a restaurant that serves only its three best dishes: the menu is short, but the kitchen runs smoothly.

Aurora: The First Mover

Aurora Innovation completed its first commercial driverless freight delivery on April 27, 2025, sending a Class 8 truck from Dallas to Houston along I-45. This 280-mile corridor passes through exactly the kind of flat, well-marked, limited-access highway that makes autonomous freight engineers sleep soundly and urban robotaxi engineers weep with envy. By February 2026, Aurora had expanded to ten driverless routes spanning Texas, New Mexico, and Arizona, including a 600-mile Fort Worth–to–El Paso run and a 1,000-mile Fort Worth–to–Phoenix corridor.

The operational numbers are modest in absolute terms but remarkable in their trajectory. As of February 11, 2026: 250,000 fully driverless miles with zero Aurora Driver-attributed collisions. A fleet of approximately thirty trucks, of which roughly ten run fully driverless. Customers include FedEx, Schneider, Werner, and Uber Freight. Revenue for 2025: $3 million. Revenue target for 2026: $14–16 million, a 400 percent year-over-year increase, with 200-plus driverless trucks deployed and a Transportation-as-a-Service revenue run-rate approaching $80 million by year-end. Aurora holds $1.5 billion in liquidity, projected to sustain operations through the second half of 2027.

A note of scholarly rigor: Aurora's frequently cited figures of "10,000-plus customer loads" and "3 million autonomous miles" refer to the cumulative supervised pilot phase, which spanned more than four years and included safety drivers. The actual fully driverless operation began at approximately 1,200 miles upon commercial launch and has grown to 250,000 miles. A supervised mile and a driverless mile are, from an operational, regulatory, and insurance perspective, fundamentally different achievements. Conflating them is like counting rehearsals as performances—technically true, spiritually dishonest.

The skeptic's objection deserves inhabitation. Aurora is a SPAC-era company with $3 million in 2025 revenue, a quarterly cash burn of $190–$220 million, and a market capitalization sustained by forward projections. At that burn rate, $1.5 billion in liquidity is not a runway—it is a cliff with a view, and the view is approximately seven quarters long. Kodiak went public at a $2.5 billion valuation with 10 trucks. The Cruise precedent demonstrated how a single catastrophic incident—not even a fatality, but a pedestrian dragging and a cover-up—can annihilate a decade of operational credibility in 72 hours. What happens when an Aurora truck jackknifes on I-10 in a dust storm? What happens when a Kodiak vehicle carrying frac sand collides with a passenger vehicle outside Midland? The insurance architecture, the regulatory response, and the narrative-immunity dynamics are entirely different for freight companies than for Tesla. Freight companies cannot fall back on cult-like shareholder devotion. They must rely on safety records, and those records, at 250,000 driverless miles, are still in their statistical infancy. To put it in the language of clinical trials: the sample size would not meet an FDA Phase I standard. The bet is sound. The margin for error is tissue-thin.

Kodiak: The Permian Basin Play

Kodiak Robotics went public via a SPAC on September 25, 2025, at a valuation of approximately $2.5 billion. The company has 10 driverless trucks in operation, has logged more than 5,200 hours of paid driverless service, and has driven 3 million autonomous miles. Its primary customer is Atlas Energy Solutions, which has placed a binding order for 100 autonomous trucks to haul frac sand in the Permian Basin—a use case so specific, so geographically contained, and so economically compelling that it approaches the Platonic ideal of an autonomous freight deployment: fixed routes, known loads, predictable terrain, a client willing to pay for 24/7 utilization, and cargo that will never, under any circumstances, file a personal injury lawsuit. The Permian Basin is, for autonomous trucking, what Phoenix was for Waymo: a proving ground so forgiving that success there is almost a prerequisite and failure there is almost disqualifying. At CES 2026, Kodiak announced a strategic partnership with Bosch to scale mass production. Plans call for hundreds of trucks by the end of 2026. Additional freight customers include J.B. Hunt, Werner, and C.R. England.

Gatik: The Middle Mile

If Aurora and Kodiak are playing the long-haul game, Gatik has staked its claim on the middle mile— the 200-to-400-mile routes that connect distribution centers to retail stores, operating on a fixed-route, high-frequency basis that resembles a bus schedule more than a freight dispatch. The company claims to be the first in North America to operate fully driverless trucks at a commercial scale, having completed 60,000 driverless delivery orders without incident as of January 2026. Contracted revenue stands at $600 million from multiyear, non-cancellable commitments with Fortune 50 retailers, including Walmart, Kroger, and Tyson Foods. Gatik operates medium-duty trucks across Dallas–Fort Worth, Phoenix, and Northwest Arkansas, with routes spanning up to 400 miles. A partnership with Isuzu Motors aims to mass-produce autonomous medium-duty vehicles by late 2027.

The Gatik model is interesting for a reason that extends beyond logistics: it demonstrates that autonomous freight is not a single market but a spectrum of use cases, each with its own economics and amenable to different levels of technological maturity. The middle mile does not require the heroic engineering of a 1,000-mile interstate crossing. It requires consistency, reliability, and the humble discipline of doing the same route perfectly, a hundred times a week—the paddy farmer's virtues, not the hunter's.

3.3 The Five Advantages That Will Make Trucking the First Billion-Dollar AV Market

The structural advantages of autonomous trucking over autonomous ride-hailing—from an investment thesis perspective—are so comprehensive that they deserve articulation, if only because the venture-capital imagination has spent the past decade mesmerized by robotaxis and largely ignoring the freight opportunity hiding in plain sight.

First, cargo does not sue. This is not a trivial observation. Cargo does not tweet. Cargo does not call its congressman. Cargo does not retain a personal-injury attorney who advertises on bus shelters. Cargo does not write a one-star Yelp review or appear on local news in a neck brace describing its "emotional distress." Cargo arrives, or it does not, and the insurance adjuster handles the rest. The single greatest regulatory and legal impediment to robotaxi deployment is passenger liability: who is responsible when an autonomous vehicle carrying a human being is involved in a collision? The answer involves insurance law, product liability doctrine, negligence standards, state-by-state variations in tort reform, and a litigation industry that generates billions in annual fees by answering precisely this type of question. An autonomous truck hauling forty thousand pounds of consumer electronics has none of these problems. The shipper's concern is whether the goods arrive undamaged and on time, not whether the truck's decision algorithm adequately weighed the ethical implications of swerving versus braking. Fleet operators make rational economic decisions. They do not write letters to their congressman after a minor fender-bender.

Second, there is no consumer acceptance barrier. Robotaxi deployment requires persuading millions of individual consumers to entrust their lives to an AI-driven vehicle—a psychological threshold that, as the Cruise pedestrian-dragging incident demonstrated, can be shattered by a single viral video. Autonomous trucking requires persuading a few hundred fleet managers that the total cost of ownership is lower and that delivery performance is at least comparable to that of conventional trucks. Fleet managers read spreadsheets, not Twitter. ROI calculations, not sentiment, govern their adoption decisions. No fleet manager has ever cancelled a purchase order because of a TikTok. The same cannot be said of consumer demand for robotaxi services.

Third, the operating environment is dramatically simpler. Interstate highways represent the most structured, predictable, and well-mapped driving environment in the United States. Lane markings are standardised. Speed limits are consistent. Pedestrians and cyclists are prohibited. Traffic signals are absent. The operational design domain of highway trucking is so constrained that it is closer to rail than to urban driving—and rail, as any transportation economist will tell you, automated itself decades ago.

Fourth, the addressable market is enormous and immediate. McKinsey's September 2024 analysis projects the global autonomous heavy-duty trucking market at approximately $616 billion by 2035, with the US portion at $178 billion, China at $327 billion, and Europe at $112 billion. US adoption is projected at 13 percent of heavy-duty trucks by 2035—the fastest rate globally. Even at single-digit penetration, the revenue opportunity dwarfs the current robotaxi market. Waymo's annualized revenue of $350 million is impressive for a robotaxi operation; it is a rounding error in trucking.

Fifth, the regulatory landscape is more favorable. Autonomous trucks operate primarily on interstate highways, which are federally regulated. The fifty-state patchwork that plagues robotaxis—the theme of Chapter 5—is less obstructive for freight because the operational domain is the federal highway system, not the municipal street grid. Texas, the epicenter of autonomous trucking deployment, has been particularly accommodating, though a new state law enacted in February 2026 now requires Level 4 certification for fully driverless commercial operations.

The combined effect of these five advantages is that autonomous trucking occupies the sweet spot of the technology-readiness-meets-market-readiness matrix. It does not require Level 5 ubiquity. It does not require managing consumer sentiment. It does not require litigating passenger injury in fifty jurisdictions. It requires a truck that can remain in its lane on I-10 for 600 miles without colliding with other vehicles, and a business model that charges per mile less than a human driver. That is a solvable problem. It is, arguably, already solved.

For investors, the arithmetic is stark. Waymo has spent $27.1 billion in lifetime funding to reach $350 million in annualized revenue—a capital efficiency ratio that would make a petroleum-exploration company flinch. Aurora has spent a fraction of that and, if its 2026 projections materialize, will achieve an $80 million revenue run-rate with $1.5 billion in remaining liquidity. Kodiak went public at $2.5 billion with binding orders from blue-chip carriers. Gatik has $600 million in contracted, non-cancellable revenue from Fortune 50 retailers. These are not moonshot bets on a distant technological frontier. These are businesses with identifiable customers, signed contracts, and revenue trajectories that a discounted-cash-flow model can actually discount. The first billion in autonomous-vehicle revenue may not come from the company with the largest market capitalization or the most impressive demo reel. It may come from the company that figured out the most boring, most repeatable, most economically rational application of the technology—and freight, for all its unglamorous particularity, is exactly that.

3.4 Two Civilizations, Two Freight Models

Before leaving the truck cab for the safety and regulatory chapters that follow, it is necessary to plant a seed that will germinate in Act II. Everything described in this chapter—the transfer hub model, the human-first-mile architecture, the hub-and-spoke expansion pattern—is a distinctly American solution to a distinctly American problem. It is a solution designed for an infrastructure environment in which the road is dumb, the vehicle must be smart, and the transition between human and machine must be managed at physical facilities, because the road itself offers no assistance.

China's autonomous trucking landscape follows a fundamentally different pattern—and understanding that difference is essential for any investor modelling the global freight automation market. Where America builds transfer hubs at interstate on-ramps—physical facilities where human drivers hand off to autonomous systems like relay runners passing a baton—China is building V2X-equipped smart highways that communicate directly with autonomous trucks, providing real-time traffic data, weather alerts, road surface conditions, and cooperative perception from roadside sensors. Where American companies must solve the first-mile/last-mile problem by handing the wheel to a human, Chinese smart infrastructure extends the autonomous operating domain deeper into urban and peri-urban environments. The truck does not need to be as smart when the road shares the cognitive load. The American approach concentrates all intelligence in the vehicle. The Chinese approach distributes intelligence across the system. Both work. They produce different cost structures, different scaling curves, and—crucially—different export models for the rest of the world.

This last point deserves emphasis, because it will become Act II's central strategic insight on the global stage. The American freight model exports *vehicles*: Aurora's truck, Kodiak's platform, deployed on existing highway infrastructure wherever it exists. The Chinese freight model exports *infrastructure*: V2X corridors, roadside perception units, cooperative driving systems—entire intelligent highway packages that a host country purchases, installs, and operates with Chinese technology embedded in the asphalt. When Saudi Arabia, the UAE, or a Belt and Road partner in Southeast Asia decides to automate its freight corridors, the American pitch is "buy our trucks." The Chinese pitch is "let us build your highway." The second pitch creates deeper lock-in, longer revenue streams, and—as Chapter 10 will chronicle—a geopolitical footprint that extends far beyond the vehicle itself.

McKinsey projects China's autonomous trucking market at $327 billion by 2035—nearly double the US figure—and that projection assumes a manufacturing cost structure that benefits from the same industrial-scale deflation that produces BYD's $7,800 electric car. The American trucking companies profiled in this chapter—Aurora, Kodiak, Gatik—are impressive by any standard. However, they are building single-vehicle intelligence for a road network designed in the 1950s. Their Chinese counterparts are building system-level intelligence for a road network being redesigned in the 2020s. The difference is not one of degree. It is one of the civilizational architectures.

In the Four Temples Framework, autonomous trucking represents the most promising pathway for American companies to fill the "Industrialiser" cell in the US AV temple. Aurora, Kodiak, and their peers are not passenger-vehicle OEMs. They do not compete with Tesla or BYD for consumer market share. However, they are developing manufacturing-scale autonomous platforms for commercial deployment—and in doing so, they are the closest American equivalent to the Chinese model of embedding autonomy in purpose-built vehicles at industrial scale. They are Farmers in a landscape dominated by Hunters, and the Farmer, as the Kuttanad proverb teaches, is the one who eats first. Whether this equivalence holds or the Chinese infrastructure advantage proves decisive is a question that Act II will begin to answer, and Act III will model in investment terms.

For now, the long haul has begun. The first billion in autonomous-vehicle revenue will not arrive in a sleek robotaxi gliding through San Francisco's Mission District. It will arrive in an eighteen-wheeler rolling through the West Texas night, carrying consumer electronics from a Dallas distribution center to an El Paso warehouse, at seventy miles per hour, without a soul aboard, billed at $1.40 per mile, and delivering a margin that no human driver—however skilled, however devoted, however willing to spend three weeks away from home—can match. The gods of Silicon Valley may have decreed that the future of transportation is a robotaxi summoned by smartphone. The gods of logistics—quieter, less photogenic, infinitely more patient—have decreed otherwise.

The paddy farmer harvests while the hunter is still stalking. However, before we follow the freight to its destination, we must confront what the autonomous vehicle—truck and taxi alike—is really for. Forty thousand Americans die on the roads every year. Each one is a tomb. Chapter 4 will count them.

Evidence Anchors

Aurora Driverless Safety Report (2025). Aurora IR press releases (May, Oct 2025; Feb 11, 2026) • NHTSA ADS Report to Congress (July 2025); ATRI Operational Costs Report (2025, 2024 data) • WEF Autonomous Vehicle Roadmap, trucking use case (April 2025) • McKinsey "Autonomous Driving's Future: Convenient and Connected," trucking segment (September 2024) • ATA American Trucking Trends 2025; Kodiak SEC filings (September 2025); Gatik press release (January 2026)

CHAPTER 4

40,000 Tombs

Safety, Disruption, and the American Case

Every system is perfectly designed to get the results it gets.

— W. Edwards Deming (attributed)

In the village temples of northern Malabar, when a community member dies, the body is carried to the cremation ground along a path lined with coconut-oil lamps. The lamps are not for the dead; the dead are past needing light. They are for the living—so that those who remain can see the path clearly, can count their steps, can know exactly how far they have walked and how far they have yet to go. The lamps do not reduce the grief. They make the grief *visible*.

This chapter is a row of lamps.

In 2023, 40,901 Americans died in traffic crashes. In 2022, the figure was 42,721. The 2024 preliminary estimate of 39,345 was greeted in transportation-policy circles as good news—the first time the count fell below 40,000 since 2020—which tells you everything you need to know about the psychic numbness that descends upon a society that has normalized a body count equivalent to a mid-size American city being emptied every year. By the National Safety Council's broader criteria, which include non-traffic motor-vehicle deaths, the 2023 figure was 44,762. Millions more are injured annually—2.4 million in police-reported incidents, more than 5 million by the NSC's medically consulted standard. NHTSA's comprehensive cost study pegs direct economic damages at $340 billion per year; total societal harm, including quality-of-life losses, reaches $1.4 trillion. Adjusted for inflation to 2025, those figures become approximately $429 billion and $1.77 trillion, respectively.

Forty thousand tombs, every year, are dug by a system that is—per Deming's axiom—perfectly designed to produce them.

4.1 The Safety Evidence

The moral case for autonomous vehicles does not require speculation about a technologically utopian future. It requires reading existing data. The most rigorous evidence comes from the Swiss Re–Waymo actuarial partnership, which began in 2022 and has produced two landmark studies that, in a rational world, would have ended the debate about whether autonomous vehicles are safer than human drivers.

The first study, published in *Heliyon* in September 2023, analyzed 3.8 million fully autonomous Waymo miles against a benchmark of 600,000 insurance claims and 125 billion human-driven miles. It found 76 percent fewer property-damage claims and zero bodily-injury claims. The second study, released in December 2024 and covering 25.3 million fully autonomous miles across Phoenix, San Francisco, Los Angeles, and Austin, confirmed and extended the findings: 88 percent fewer property-damage claims and 92 percent fewer bodily-injury claims. In absolute terms, Waymo generated 9 property-damage claims and 2 bodily-injury claims across that distance; human drivers would have been expected to generate 78 and 26, respectively. The comparison held even against newer ADAS-equipped vehicles (model years 2018–2021): 86 percent fewer property-damage claims, 90 percent fewer bodily-injury claims.

A distinction that most industry commentary collapses—and that this book insists on maintaining—is the difference between **safety performance** and **safety proof**. Safety performance is what the vehicle does on the road: crash avoidance, claim reduction, injury prevention. Safety proof is the institutional architecture that verifies, certifies, and communicates performance to regulators, insurers, and the public who must trust it. Waymo has both. Its performance is measured in 25.3 million driverless miles. Swiss Re validates its proof—the reinsurer of reinsurers—using insurance-claims methodology calibrated by zip code, fault allocation, and vehicle age. Tesla, as of February 2026, has neither: its supervised rides have crash rates many times the human average, and it has no third-party actuarial validation whatsoever. Chinese OEMs are building proof through an entirely different channel—state-administered testing protocols and municipal pilot-zone data—which Act II will chronicle. The investor who conflates performance and proof will misread every valuation in this book.

The methodological innovation is as important as the finding. These studies do not rely on crash counts—a metric vulnerable to definitional inconsistencies—but on *liability insurance claims*, which represent actual financial harm that an insurer was compelled to pay. The benchmark is calibrated by zip code and responsibility allocation, meaning the comparison accounts for where Waymo operates and who is at fault. Swiss Re does not publish actuarial studies as marketing exercises. It publishes them because its clients—the insurance companies that would bear the financial consequences of autonomous-vehicle failures—need to accurately price risk. When the reinsurer of reinsurers tells you the technology is 88 percent safer, the appropriate response is not skepticism. It is urgency. Eighty-eight percent fewer claims. Ninety-two percent fewer injuries. The reinsurer has spoken. The regulators are still reading.

Separately, Waymo has simulated 72 fatal and severe crash scenarios drawn from real-world NHTSA reconstructions. These are not hypothetical exercises; they are detailed digital re-creations of actual fatality events, run through the Waymo Driver's perception and decision-making pipeline to determine whether the autonomous system would have avoided or mitigated the crash. This is the equivalent of asking whether the technology, had it been present at the scene of 72 real deaths, could have prevented them, and the methodology represents the most sophisticated counterfactual safety analysis ever attempted for a commercial autonomous-driving system. While the full results remain proprietary, the implications are not subtle: each positive result is a life that would have been saved.

The *ullil kaanal* demands that we state what these numbers mean in human terms—that we hold the lamp closer to the path. If autonomous vehicles with Waymo-level safety performance replaced human drivers across the United States today, approximately 35,000 to 37,000 of the annual 40,000 traffic deaths would not occur. Three million injuries would be reduced to a few hundred thousand. $429 billion in annual crash costs would shrink by an order of magnitude. Every year that the United States delays full autonomous deployment is a year in which the equivalent of a small city dies. The regulatory paralysis chronicled in Chapter 5 is not merely an economic inefficiency. It is, measured in bodies, a catastrophe administered in slow motion by well-meaning bureaucrats, litigious interest groups, and a Congress that has failed to pass a comprehensive autonomous-vehicle law in nine years of trying.

A caveat, because scholarship demands it: Waymo operates exclusively in urban and suburban environments with mostly dry, sunny weather. Rural driving—which accounts for 41 percent of US traffic fatalities despite carrying far less traffic—does not appear in the Swiss Re data. Winter driving, mountain highways, and unpaved roads: all absent. The safety case is overwhelming for the environments where Waymo currently operates. Extending it to the full American driving landscape requires technological progress that has not yet been demonstrated. The lamps illuminate the path already walked. The path ahead remains dark.

And yet. The environments where Waymo *does* operate—dense urban cores with pedestrians, cyclists, construction zones, double-parked delivery vehicles, and the full menagerie of American driving chaos—are precisely the environments where human drivers are most dangerous. The 40,000 annual deaths are not evenly distributed across geography; they cluster at intersections, in metropolitan areas, during nighttime hours, and among impaired or distracted drivers. The technology does not need to solve every road in America to save the majority of the lives currently being lost. It needs to address the roads with the highest death tolls. Furthermore, on those roads, the evidence already shows it.

4.2 The Disruption Cascade

The safety case is a moral argument. The disruption cascade is an economic one. Moreover, if the safety case makes autonomous vehicles seem like an unambiguous good, the disruption cascade makes them look like a wrecking ball swung by an angel—virtuous in intent, devastating in impact, and aimed at an ecosystem of industries whose combined lobbying budget ensures that the wrecking ball will be delayed, diverted, and litigated at every swing. The lamps that illuminated the dead now illuminate something equally uncomfortable: the living, whose livelihoods depend on the dying.

Begin with the direct labor displacement. The United States has approximately 1.5 to 2 million active rideshare drivers (Uber and Lyft combined, with significant overlap) and 3.5 million truck drivers, embedded in a broader trucking workforce of 8.4 million. Full autonomous deployment does not eliminate all of these jobs simultaneously—the transfer hub model of Chapter 3 preserves first-mile and last-mile human drivers, and the multi-decade deployment timeline means displacement is gradual rather than sudden—but the trajectory is unmistakable. When Uber's CEO publicly targets 100,000 autonomous vehicles on the platform by 2027, the rideshare driver does not need a PhD in labor economics to read the writing on the dashboard. The gig economy, that great American innovation in labor-rights avoidance, will have completed its final evolution: from "you are not an employee, you are an independent contractor" to "you are not an independent contractor, you are a software update." The app that once liberated the worker from the boss has now liberated the boss from the worker—a plot twist that would make a Dickens novel blush. *For the investor, the rideshare labor pool is not an asset to protect; it is a cost line to automate. Every Uber bull case implicitly contains a bear case for 2 million gig workers. Price those accordingly.*

Now follow the money downstream. The US automobile insurance industry generates more than $350 billion in annual gross written premiums—a figure that has grown substantially in recent years as premiums have risen to offset higher repair costs and medical inflation. If autonomous vehicles reduce claims by 88 percent, as the Waymo data suggests, the insurance industry does not shrink by 88 percent—premiums would restructure around product liability, fleet coverage, and cybersecurity risk—but the contraction would be severe enough to reshape the sector. State Farm, GEICO, Progressive, Allstate: these are not startup disruptors that pivoted from a garage. They are pillars of the American financial establishment, employers of hundreds of thousands of people, and campaign donors of exquisite bipartisan generosity. They will not go quietly. *For the investor: traditional personal-auto insurers face a structural headwind that no premium increase can offset. The winners are fleet insurers, product-liability specialists, and the cybersecurity firms that will underwrite the algorithmic risk. Watch the reinsurance layer—Swiss Re is already positioning.*

The parking industry, valued at roughly $121 billion and encompassing somewhere between 700 million and 2 billion spaces, depending on how aggressively you count residential driveways, faces a different kind of obsolescence. Autonomous vehicles do not need to park near their destination; they can reposition to cheaper lots, circulate to the next rider, or return to a charging depot. The commercial parking garage—that concrete monument to the American automobile's insatiable demand for idle real estate—becomes a stranded asset. Municipal parking revenue—meters, garages, fines—erodes accordingly. Moreover, municipal fine-and-fee revenue, which the Tax Policy Center estimates at $12.9 billion annually, faces a more existential threat: autonomous vehicles do not speed, run red lights, park illegally, or accumulate traffic violations that constitute a meaningful portion of local government funding. When the vehicle obeys every law perfectly, the fine becomes uncollectable—and the budget line that depended on the citizen's predictable lawbreaking disappears. It is a fiscal model built on sin, and the sinners have been replaced by saints made of silicon. *For the investor, urban real estate adjacent to parking infrastructure becomes a redevelopment opportunity. The Muni-bond analyst should be stress-testing fine-dependent revenue assumptions now, not in 2030.*

The Accident Industry

Zoom out further, and the full perversity of the incentive structure becomes visible. Here, the lamps gutter—not from wind, but from the breath of those who profit from the darkness. What this book calls the *accident industry*—the constellation of businesses whose revenues depend, directly or indirectly, on the continued occurrence of automobile crashes—exceeds $1 trillion in annual economic activity. This includes auto-body repair, towing services, emergency-room trauma care, orthopedic surgery, physical rehabilitation, personal-injury litigation, expert-witness fees, accident-reconstruction consultancies, traffic-court administration, and the portion of the auto-insurance industry devoted to claims processing. It includes the manufacturers of guardrails, crash barriers, and highway signage. It includes municipal employees who issue parking tickets and state troopers who issue speeding citations.

None of these industries consciously conspires to perpetuate traffic deaths. Nevertheless, each of them benefits economically from the current system—and each has, at minimum, a structural incentive to slow the adoption of a technology that would reduce their revenue. This is not a conspiracy. It is something worse: a system so perfectly aligned with its own dysfunction that it requires no conspiracy at all—just inertia, quarterly earnings reports, and the quiet understanding that no industry ever lobbies for its own obsolescence. The personal-injury bar alone generates an estimated $40–50 billion annually in the United States. That is not a lobby. That is a standing army—with the best suits, the largest campaign contributions, and a professional interest in ensuring that the negligent human driver remains behind the wheel for as long as legislatively possible. Trial lawyers are among the most generous political donors in the country, and their interest in preserving a tort system built around human-driver negligence is not subtle. When autonomous vehicles eliminate the negligent human driver, the negligence claim evaporates—replaced, potentially, by product-liability claims against manufacturers, but under a legal framework that is far less favorable to plaintiff attorneys and far less lucrative per case.

The Gordon Gekko investor should study the accident industry not with outrage but with clinical interest. These trillion-dollar revenue streams will not disappear overnight; they will erode over decades, creating both losers and winners. *The losers: traditional auto insurers, personal-injury law firms, auto-body chains, towing companies, and any business model predicated on the 40,000-death status quo. The winners: fleet insurers and product-liability underwriters, cybersecurity firms pricing algorithmic risk, autonomous-vehicle maintenance networks, and the urban-redevelopment plays that emerge when parking garages become stranded assets.* The disruption cascade is not a wall of water. It is a slow tide. However, the tide is rising, and the sandcastles are already showing cracks.

4.3 The Disruption Asymmetry: US vs. China

Everything described above—the safety evidence, the disruption cascade, the accident-industry lobby—is a distinctly American problem set, shaped by distinctly American institutions: a tort system that incentivizes litigation, a federalist regulatory structure that fragments authority, organized labor with constitutional protections, and a campaign-finance architecture that gives economic incumbents veto power over technological change. The American system is not incapable of managing disruption—it managed the automobile's displacement of the horse, the computer's displacement of the typist, and the internet's displacement of the travel agent—but it manages disruption slowly, litigiously, and with enormous friction.

China's disruption calculus is fundamentally different. Where the United States faces organized-labor opposition to autonomous trucking, China's All-China Federation of Trade Unions is a Party organ that implements policy rather than resists it. Where American autonomous-vehicle deployment is constrained by fifty-state tort law and a plaintiff's bar with $40 billion in annual revenue, China's civil litigation system produces negligible class-action risk and awards damages at a fraction of American levels. Where American regulators must navigate a federal-state-municipal maze in which a vehicle legal in San Francisco may be illegal in Sacramento, China's three-tier regulatory architecture—MIIT national standards, ministerial coordination, and municipal pilot zones—functions as a unified industrial-policy instrument. Where the American insurance industry has $350 billion in annual premiums and the institutional weight to slow any technology that threatens those premiums, China's state-directed insurance sector treats autonomous-vehicle adoption as a policy objective to be facilitated, not a revenue stream to be protected.

The implications are structural, not ideological. This is not a judgment about which system is "better"—the American system's protections for workers, consumers, and plaintiffs exist for reasons rooted in democratic accountability, and the Chinese system's efficiency comes at costs that this book does not minimize. The point is narrower and more analytical: when measuring the speed at which autonomous vehicles will be deployed at scale, and the friction costs that will slow that deployment, the institutional architectures of the two countries produce radically different timelines. America debates. China deploys. America litigates. China legislates. America studies the disruption. China manages it.

This does not mean China is immune to public backlash. The Xiaomi SU7 crash of March 29, 2025, proved otherwise with devastating clarity. Three university students died when the vehicle, operating in Navigate on Autopilot mode at 116 kilometers per hour on the Dezhou–Shangrao Highway near Tongling, Anhui Province, struck a concrete guardrail in a construction zone. A fire broke out after impact. Xiaomi disclosed that the vehicle's AEB system did not activate because the obstacle type—a water-filled barrier—was not in its recognition library. Within one week, 12 million Weibo posts had been generated. Baidu searches for "self-driving car safety" surged 220 percent. Xiaomi's stock fell 6.3 percent. Multiple Chinese OEMs paused or revised the rollout of autonomous driving features.

However, the asymmetry that defines the civilizational contrast at the heart of this book is the regulatory response. In the United States, a comparable incident—Cruise's October 2023 pedestrian-dragging in San Francisco—triggered permit revocations in one state, an NHTSA investigation, a company collapse, and a corporate exit from the robotaxi market, with no national policy response and no systemic reform. The system punished the company. It did not fix the system.

In China, MIIT initiated a comprehensive review of autonomous-driving regulations within weeks. New testing protocols were drafted. OEM accountability standards were revised. The response was swift, systemic, and—critically—*generative*: it produced new regulatory infrastructure rather than merely punishing the offender. China treated the Xiaomi crash as an engineering problem to be solved at the system level. America treated the Cruise crash as a liability event to be adjudicated at the company level. One approach builds capacity. The other builds case law. This asymmetry—between a system that constructs and a system that litigates—is the structural foundation of everything that follows in Act II.

The Tombs and the Temple

Forty thousand tombs. Every year. Dug by distraction, impairment, fatigue, inexperience, rage, and the irreducible fragility of human attention applied to a two-ton machine travelling at highway speeds. The technology to prevent the vast majority of these deaths exists. It has been demonstrated, measured, actuarially verified, and commercially deployed. It is currently operating in six American cities, with 88% fewer claims and 92% fewer injuries. The reinsurer of reinsurers has certified its safety. The actuarial tables are unambiguous.

Moreover, it is being delayed by an incentive structure that profits from the status quo, a regulatory apparatus that cannot act, a Congress that has failed to pass a unified law in nine years, and a political system that treats 40,000 annual deaths as an acceptable cost of personal mobility—an externality so familiar it has become invisible, like the carbon in the atmosphere or the sugar in the cereal. In Kerala, the Theyyam performer channels the deity to heal the community's wounds, to make the invisible visible, to force the congregation to see what it has trained itself not to see. In America, the wounds are measured in actuarial tables, the deity has been retained as an expert witness by both sides, and the congregation is watching its phones.

Somewhere in midtown Manhattan, a fund manager—call him Marcus, because we will meet him again—reads these numbers in a research note and reaches not for his conscience but for his Bloomberg terminal. The 40,000 deaths register not as a tragedy but as a $429 billion annual misallocation—which is, in the language of his profession, a market inefficiency. Marcus does not mourn the dead. He prices the friction that kills them. Moreover, in that friction, he sees alpha. We will revisit Marcus's portfolio logic in Chapters 11 and 12, where his confidence will encounter the Māyā Meter and the Four Temples—and where the reader will discover whether the alpha was real or whether Marcus, too, was seeing Māyā.

Chapter 5 will examine the regulatory architecture that produces this paralysis—the fifty veils, the partisan gridlock, the BIS iron curtain that cleaves the autonomous world in two. However, the reader should carry the weight of this chapter's numbers through what follows. Every month of regulatory delay costs approximately 3,400 lives and roughly $36 billion in societal harm. Each year of gridlock excavates another 40,000 tombs and misallocates $429 billion that should be directed toward the technology, the infrastructure, and the regulatory clarity that would prevent them. The debate about autonomous vehicles is not a technology debate, a policy debate, or an investment debate, though it is all of those things. It is, at its foundation, a moral reckoning—and for the investor, a moral reckoning with a price tag. The capital is available. The technology is proven. The only thing standing between the present and 35,000 fewer annual deaths is institutional friction—and institutional friction, for the contrarian who can see through it, is another name for *opportunity*.

The reckoning is overdue. The lamps are lit. Count the steps.

Evidence Anchors

NHTSA Standing General Order Summary Page; NHTSA Traffic Safety Facts (2023, 2024 preliminary) • Waymo Safety Impact Data Hub (September 2025); Waymo–Swiss Re Actuarial Studies (2023, 2024) • NHTSA DOT HS 813 403: The Economic and Societal Impact of Motor Vehicle Crashes (2019 data, pub. 2023) • Safety Case for ADS, Journal of Safety Research (2026); NSC Injury Facts (2023 data) • CnEVPost, Fortune Asia: Xiaomi SU7 Crash reporting (April 2025); Global Brands Magazine Weibo analysis

CHAPTER 5

The Fifty Veils

America's Regulatory Purdah and the Race with China

Each elder guards their own gate. None guards the village.

— Malayalam governance proverb (*Avar avarude vaathil nokkum; graamam nokkaan aaru?*)

In traditional Kerala society, *purdah* was not practiced in the Mughal sense—there were no zenanas, no latticed screens, no segregated quarters. However, there was a different kind of veiling: the elaborate caste protocols of *teettu* and *Pulappedi* that dictated who could approach whom, at what distance, through which intermediary, and with what ritual preparation. A Namboodiri Brahmin walking down a village lane required a Nair to maintain sixteen paces of distance, a Thiyya thirty-two paces, and an Avarnan to remove himself from the road entirely. The rules were internally consistent, locally enforced, and—to anyone standing outside the system—perfectly, magnificently insane. Each rule served a purpose. The collective effect was paralysis.

The American autonomous-vehicle regulatory framework is the *teettu* of the twenty-first century. Not a system but a caste system—fifty levels of purity, each requiring its own rituals of propitiation, each with its own priesthood, each with the power to excommunicate any vehicle that fails to observe the prescribed distance. Fifty states, each with its own statutes, executive orders, and administrative interpretations. Thousands of municipalities, each with authority over streets, curbs, traffic signals, and operating permits. A federal government that has the constitutional authority to establish vehicle safety standards but has failed, across three administrations and nine years, to enact a comprehensive autonomous-vehicle law. A Bureau of Industry and Security that, with a single rule, has permanently severed the American AV ecosystem from the Chinese one. Moreover, beneath all of this, an accretion of local zoning ordinances, municipal operating permits, first-responder memoranda of understanding, and neighborhood association objections that would make a Kafkaesque bureaucracy blush with recognition.

The result is a system in which a vehicle certified safe in Arizona may be illegal in California, and a vehicle that operates commercially in Texas may face criminal penalties in New York. A vehicle that has demonstrated 88 percent fewer insurance claims than human drivers may not be permitted to pick up a fare in the city where its engineers live. Every wall in the maze was built on purpose. The maze itself serves no one.

Consider a concrete example, because abstraction is the maze's best camouflage. A Waymo Jaguar I-PACE, fully certified by NHTSA, operating legally under Arizona's permissive executive order, picks up its last paid rider in Tempe at 11:47 p.m. The rider asks to go to Needles, California—a three-hour drive west on I-10. The vehicle cannot comply. California requires a separate DMV Autonomous Vehicle Deployment Permit, a drivered-testing permit, and compliance with the state's vehicle code. This process involves roughly as much paperwork as adopting a child. Suppose instead the rider asks for Las Vegas. Nevada requires its own autonomous-vehicle testing license, a $5 million insurance bond, and a letter of intent filed with the Department of Motor Vehicles. Same vehicle. Same safety record. Same 88 percent claim reduction. Three states, three entirely different legal realities, three separate priesthoods demanding three separate acts of propitiation. The vehicle that passed every test in Arizona is, for regulatory purposes, an unvetted stranger the moment it crosses a state line. In Kerala, the *teettu* at least applied consistent rules by caste. America's *teettu* applies different rules by postcode.

5.1 The Three-Tier Maze

The First Veil: Federal Innovation Rhetoric, Institutional Atrophy

On April 24, 2025, Transportation Secretary Sean P. Duffy announced the Department of Transportation's "Innovation Agenda," anchored by NHTSA's Automated Vehicle Framework. The framework articulated three principles: prioritize safety, unleash innovation, and enable commercial deployment. Two initial actions followed: a streamlined crash-reporting order and an expanded Automated Vehicle Exemption Program now covering domestically produced vehicles—previously, the AVEP had been restricted to imports, a restriction so arbitrary it suggested the original drafters believed autonomous vehicles were, like Scotch whisky, inherently a foreign product.

The framework's stated ambition—a single national standard to prevent a "harmful patchwork" of state laws—is laudable. Its institutional capacity to deliver that ambition is another matter. Between February and July 2025, NHTSA underwent a workforce reduction of approximately 28 percent—from 772 employees to a target of 555—as part of the broader Trump 2.0 deregulatory posture. Three of seven staff members investigating autonomous-vehicle technology were fired in the initial round. The broader Department of Transportation lost roughly 4,100 employees. Consumer advocates observed, with some justification, that reducing the safety regulator's headcount while simultaneously accelerating the technology it was supposed to regulate was the bureaucratic equivalent of firing the lifeguards during a tsunami.

The conflict-of-interest dimension is impossible to ignore. NHTSA's Preliminary Evaluation PE 25012—an active investigation into Tesla's Full Self-Driving system covering 80-plus incidents and 2.9 million vehicles—was being conducted by an agency whose workforce was being reduced under the auspices of DOGE, an efficiency initiative led by Elon Musk, who is simultaneously the CEO of the company under investigation. If a screenwriter submitted this plot to a studio, it would be rejected as too implausible for satire. However, it is the actual governance structure of the world's autonomous-vehicle safety regulator, as of February 2026. In any other country, this would be a scandal. In America, it is Tuesday.

The maze persists not because its architects are incompetent but because three structural forces converge to make it self-reinforcing. First, campaign-finance architecture: the accident industry's $1 trillion in annual economic activity generates lobbying budgets that ensure every proposed reform faces organized opposition from trial lawyers, insurers, and municipal revenue offices whose funding depends on the status quo. Second, liability distribution: federalism allows each jurisdiction to externalize risk onto its neighbors. If your state's lax regulation produces an accident, the victim's state bears the tort cost, creating a simultaneous race-to-the-bottom in permissiveness and race-to-the-top in self-protection. Third, local veto points: every level of government can block what no single level of government can advance, and the autonomous-vehicle context has more veto points per mile than any regulatory domain in American history. This is not dysfunction. This is a system—per Deming—perfectly designed to get the results it gets.

The Second Veil: Fifty Laboratories, Zero Coordination

More than 29 states, plus the District of Columbia, have enacted AV-related legislation, with some analyses counting 35 when executive orders are included. The variance is staggering. Arizona operates under a permissive executive order that requires neither a state permit nor a pre-deployment safety filing—the Wild West of autonomous-vehicle testing. California requires a DMV Autonomous Vehicle Deployment Permit, a drivered-testing permit, and compliance with the state's vehicle code—a regulatory apparatus so layered that obtaining approval to test a self-driving car in San Francisco involves roughly as much paperwork as adopting a child. Texas threaded a middle path, welcoming autonomous trucking on its interstates while enacting, in February 2026, a Level 4 certification requirement for paid driverless rides—triggered, not coincidentally, by Tesla's robotaxi crashes in Austin. Twenty-five states introduced new AV-related bills in 2025 alone, each legislative session producing new requirements, exemptions, and contradictions.

The core problem is not that individual state approaches are unreasonable. Many are thoughtful and evidence-based. The problem is that there are fifty of them, and they are mutually incompatible. A Waymo vehicle certified in California must separately meet the requirements of every new state it enters. A Zoox robotaxi with an NHTSA demonstration exemption still requires state-level authorization. An Aurora truck operating driverlessly on I-10 in Texas must contend with different rules when it crosses into New Mexico. The operational burden is not fatal—companies are navigating it—but it imposes friction costs that slow deployment, increase legal overhead, and create a structural disadvantage relative to competitors operating in countries with unified national frameworks. Countries like, for instance, the one described in Act II. The American regulatory landscape is, in effect, fifty separate conversations about the same technology, conducted in fifty different dialects, with no interpreter and no shared dictionary—and each conversation concluding, independently, that more study is needed.

The Third Veil: The Municipal Layer No Analyst Sees

Beneath the state layer lies a tier that rarely appears in policy analysis but is operationally decisive: municipal authority. Cities control streets, curbs, traffic signals, loading zones, and operating permits. When Cruise deployed in San Francisco, it was the city—not the state or the federal government—that managed which streets were accessible, where vehicles could idle, how incidents were reported, and how the company communicated with the fire department. When residents of the Chandler, Arizona neighborhood where Waymo first tested its vehicles began slashing tires, throwing rocks, and pulling guns on the driverless cars—documented incidents, all of them—it was the local police department that had to respond, without any federal or state protocol for how to handle a human-on-robot conflict.

Municipal authority is the hidden veil—invisible in federal legislation, absent from most state statutes, and absolutely determinative of whether an autonomous vehicle can actually operate in any given location. A company can secure a California DMV permit, an NHTSA demonstration exemption, and a favorable safety interpretation, and still be unable to deploy if the city council objects to robotaxis occupying curb space near a school. The genius of the American system is that every level of government has a voice. The curse of the American system is that every level of government has a veto. Moreover, in the autonomous-vehicle context, the veils multiply until the vehicle—however safe, however certified, however actuarially validated—cannot move.

5.2 The SELF DRIVE Act: Gridlock as Performance Art

Into this three-tier maze, in February 2026, Congress introduced the SELF DRIVE Act of 2026—formally, the "Safely Ensuring Lives Future Deployment and Research In Vehicle Evolution Act," which is either a heroic attempt at a meaningful acronym or evidence that congressional staffers are paid by the letter. The bill represents the third attempt at comprehensive federal AV legislation. The first, in 2017, passed the House *unanimously*—a bipartisan miracle so rare it should have been preserved in amber—only to die in the Senate, strangled by the trial lawyers' lobby and preemption concerns. The second, in 2021, went nowhere. Congress has now spent nine years failing to pass a law that everyone agrees is necessary. This is not gridlock. This is performance art.

The subcommittee markup on February 10, 2026, forwarded the bill to the full Energy and Commerce Committee by a roll-call vote of twelve yeas to eleven nays—a razor-thin, party-line margin that lost key Democratic backing over concerns about safety deregulation. The Democrats who voted no were not unreasonable; their concerns about an understaffed NHTSA being tasked with overseeing a massive new regulatory mandate were legitimate. However, legitimacy and progress are different things, and the result was the same: a bill that everyone agrees is necessary, advanced by a margin that everyone agrees is insufficient, toward a floor vote that nobody expects to happen. GovTrack estimates a 5% chance that the bill will advance past committee. For context, the average American's lifetime probability of being struck by lightning is roughly one in fifteen thousand. The SELF DRIVE Act has better odds—but not by the margin that a civilization racing for technological supremacy ought to find comfortable.

The juxtaposition with China is instructive to the point of being painful. While the United States Congress debated whether an autonomous-vehicle bill could survive a subcommittee vote, China's State Council, MIIT, and municipal governments were coordinating the rollout of autonomous-vehicle pilot zones across twenty-plus cities, standardizing V2X communication protocols, issuing the country's first Level 3 conditional driving permits, and deploying Baidu Apollo robotaxis at commercial scale. The American system produces a twelve-to-eleven vote on a bill with a 5 percent survival rate. The Chinese system produces infrastructure, standards, and deployed fleets. The American system has checks and balances. The Chinese system has checklists and timelines. The reader may draw their own conclusions about which approach is better suited to winning a trillion-dollar technology race—bearing in mind that the American approach has its own virtues, including the virtue of not arresting citizens who draw unflattering conclusions about their government's transportation policy.

5.3 The BIS Connected Vehicle Rule: The Iron Curtain

If the SELF DRIVE Act represents domestic gridlock, the Bureau of Industry and Security's Connected Vehicle Rule represents something else entirely: a deliberate, strategic, permanent severance of the American and Chinese autonomous-vehicle ecosystems. Published in the Federal Register on January 16, 2025, and effective March 17, 2025, the rule is the single most consequential regulatory action in the global AV landscape. It is not a trade restriction. It is a technological divorce.

The rule prohibits the import and sale of connected-vehicle hardware and software designed, developed, manufactured, or supplied by entities with a nexus to the People's Republic of China or Russia. The phased implementation: Model Year 2027 for software prohibitions (which also bar manufacturers with a PRC or Russian nexus from selling connected vehicles in the United States), Model Year 2030 for hardware prohibitions, with annual Declarations of Conformity and a ten-year record-keeping requirement.

Read that again. After Model Year 2027, no Chinese-developed autonomous-driving software may operate in any vehicle sold in the United States. After Model Year 2030, no Chinese-manufactured connected-vehicle hardware may be installed in any vehicle sold in the United States. Chinese robotaxi companies are functionally impossible to test on American roads. Baidu Apollo, which operates the world's largest autonomous ride-hailing fleet—more than 700 robotaxis across multiple Chinese cities, with cumulative ride volumes that rival Waymo's—cannot deploy a single vehicle in America. Pony.ai, which was listed on the Nasdaq in November 2024 and trades in U.S. dollars on U.S. exchanges for U.S. investors, cannot operate its core product in the country where it is publicly traded. The metaphysical absurdity of this—that American investors can buy shares in a company whose product is banned from American roads—deserves a moment of silent appreciation. This is not trade policy. This is cognitive dissonance codified into law. WeRide, Momenta, Huawei's ADS 3.0—all permanently excluded from the world's most lucrative per-ride market.

For the Kerala reader, the analogy is immediate: this is *excommunication*. Not the temporary displeasure of a regulatory setback, but the permanent exclusion of an entire civilization's technology from the American temple. The BIS rule does not merely restrict Chinese AV companies from competing in the US market. It ensures that the two largest autonomous-vehicle ecosystems on earth will develop along parallel, incompatible technological trajectories—different software stacks, different hardware architectures, different communication protocols, different data standards. Two rivers that will never merge.

The geopolitical logic is straightforward. Connected vehicles are rolling surveillance platforms: they know where their passengers go, what routes they take, what conversations occur within the cabin, and what infrastructure they map along the way. The national-security argument for excluding Chinese-connected technology from American roads is genuine and serious. Nevertheless, the economic consequences are equally serious. Chinese AV companies, permanently barred from the American market, will redirect their competitive energy toward the rest of the world—Southeast Asia, the Middle East, Latin America, Africa, and the non-aligned nations that constitute the majority of the global vehicle market. The BIS rule does not eliminate Chinese competition. It redirects it. Moreover, in redirecting it, it creates a bifurcated global market in which American AV companies must compete, eventually, against Chinese rivals who have honed their technology across billions of miles of deployment in dozens of countries—countries where the price of a robotaxi ride matters more than the nationality of the software that drives it.

This is the essential context for Act III's investment analysis. The BIS rule means that the American and Chinese AV industries are not competing for the same market. They are competing for different markets—the US domestic market (closed to Chinese players) and the global market (open to both). *For the investor: American AV companies enjoy a protected domestic moat but face Chinese competition everywhere else. Chinese AV companies lose the richest per-ride market but gain uncontested access to the fastest-growing ones.* Marcus—the fund manager we met in Chapter 4, the one who prices friction as alpha—has built his entire model on US-addressable market assumptions. The BIS rule indicates that his TAM is correct for domestic positions but structurally incomplete for global positions. He has not yet priced the redirect. By Chapter 11, he will have to. *The supply chain reroutes accordingly—Hesai's LiDAR, RoboSense's sensors, Horizon Robotics' chips will find new pathways to non-US markets, and American component suppliers face a choice between domestic captivity and global irrelevance. The investor who models the US-only TAM for American AV companies is modelling correctly. The investor who models US-only TAM for Chinese AV companies is modelling a fantasy.* Act III will price this bifurcation.

5.4 The Empty Stall in the American Temple

Act I ends not with a summary but with a provocation.

The United States has solved Level 4 reliability. Waymo has delivered 20 million fully autonomous rides across six cities, with 88% fewer insurance claims than human drivers. Aurora has completed 250,000 miles of driverless trucking with zero at-fault collisions. The technology works. The safety data is overwhelming. The engineering achievement is genuine, historic, and worthy of admiration.

The United States has not solved the Level 4 affordability problem.

Waymo's 5th-generation vehicle costs approximately $175,000 per unit. The 6th-generation Zeekr RT platform will reduce that to roughly $75,000—a remarkable improvement and still a luxury-class price point. BYD's Seagull, the best-selling electric vehicle in the world's largest car market, launched at approximately $9,550 and was reduced to $7,800 in April 2025. It is not available in the United States, because a 100 percent tariff makes it uncompetitive—but in the rest of the world, where tariffs are lower, and price sensitivity is higher, it is redefining what a car costs.

One miracle scales upward: more sensors, more compute, more safety, more capability, higher price. The other miracle scales outward: fewer components, simpler architecture, ruthless manufacturing deflation, lower price, more buyers, more miles, more data. The American automotive industry, trained for a century to maximize profit per unit—to sell the $60,000 pickup truck, the $80,000 SUV, the $100,000 electric vehicle—is structurally incapable of producing the second miracle. Detroit knows how to make vehicles expensive. It does not know how to make vehicles cheaply.

Furthermore, before the American reader objects that cheapness is not the American way—that quality commands a premium, that you get what you pay for, that the market speaks—consider that BYD's Seagull scored four stars in Euro NCAP safety testing, offers a range of 300 kilometers, and includes features that American manufacturers charge $30,000 or more to provide. This is not cheap in the pejorative sense. This is manufacturing excellence of a kind that Henry Ford would recognize and that Henry Ford's corporate descendants have forgotten.

This is not a criticism; it is a description of a profit-maximization culture that has served American shareholders extraordinarily well for a hundred years. However, it is a culture that leaves an empty stall in the American temple. Furthermore, the empty stall has consequences that extend beyond national vanity. If no American company can produce an autonomous-capable vehicle at a price point below $75,000, then the global market for autonomous transportation—the billions of people in Southeast Asia, South Asia, Latin America, and Africa who cannot afford a $175,000 Waymo Jaguar but who need safe, affordable mobility—will be served by someone else. The BIS rule ensures that no one else will compete in America. It does not guarantee that someone else will not win elsewhere.

In the Four Temples Framework, Waymo occupies the Pure-Play Operator stall. Tesla aspires to the Industrialiser stall but has not earned it—it manufactures at scale, but its autonomous capability remains supervised, geographically constrained, and under federal investigation. Uber occupies the Platform stall with characteristic asset-light elegance. The Industrialiser—the company that manufactures autonomous-capable vehicles at price points accessible to mass markets, that embeds the technology as standard equipment rather than a $12,000 option, that treats autonomy as a feature of the vehicle rather than a service layered on top—does not exist in America. There is no American BYD. No American Momenta is licensing its AV stack across a dozen OEMs simultaneously. No American Huawei is building the *Shenqi*—the "spirit vessel"—of an autonomous-driving ecosystem that integrates software, hardware, and cloud infrastructure into a single exportable platform.

The empty stall is not an accident. It is the structural consequence of an industrial ecosystem optimized for a different goal. American venture capital funds Pure-Play Operators and reward them with valuations of $126 billion. American equity markets reward Aspirational Industrialisers with narrative-immune market caps. American platform companies are world-class at demand aggregation. However, manufacturing affordable, autonomous-capable vehicles at mass scale for global markets—the thing that actually determines who wins the trillion-dollar race—requires a different kind of industrial capacity, a different cost culture, a different relationship between government and industry, and a different tolerance for margins that would make a Detroit CFO physically ill. The empty stall is the structural vulnerability that Act II will diagnose, and Act III will price.

The *ullil kaanal*—the inner seeing—has shown us the American river in its fullness: its technological brilliance, its operational pioneers, its billion-dollar graveyards, its moral urgency, its regulatory paralysis, and its yawning structural gap: five chapters, five veils drawn aside. The question is no longer whether America can build autonomous vehicles. It can. The question is whether America can build them cheaply enough, deploy them broadly enough, and govern them coherently enough to win a global race against a competitor that has answered all three questions differently.

To answer, we must cross the river.

ACT I TRANSITION BRIDGE
The Gilded River: What We Know, What We Do not, What We Must Ask

The American flywheel is turning. Waymo delivers ~400,000 paid rides per week across six cities, funded by $27.1 billion in lifetime capital, valued at $126 billion. Aurora hauls commercial freight driverless across 10 routes in 3 states. The technology is proven. The safety data is overwhelming. The first billion in AV revenue is within sight.

The American temple has empty stalls. The US has one Pure-Play Operator (Waymo), one Aspirational Industrialiser (Tesla), one Platform (Uber), and zero Mass-Market Industrialisers. No American company manufactures autonomous-capable vehicles priced below $75,000. The BIS Connected Vehicle Rule has permanently severed the American and Chinese AV ecosystems, creating two parallel technological civilizations.

The regulatory purdah persists. Fifty states, no unified federal law, a 12–11 subcommittee vote on a bill with a 5 percent survival probability, and a safety regulator whose workforce has been cut 28 percent while investigating the CEO who oversees the cuts. Meanwhile, 40,000 Americans die on the roads every year.

Five questions for Act II:

1. How did China build a regulatory machine that creates markets rather than merely permitting them?

2. Who are the Chinese Industrialisers, and how do they manufacture autonomy at one-tenth the American price?

3. What does the Chinese AV supply chain—$200 LiDAR, $7,800 vehicles—mean for global competition?

4. How does the Belt and Road become an autonomous-vehicle deployment corridor?

5. Is the Chinese model exportable—and if so, to whom?

If the answers to these five questions align with the data, then the market has mispriced not just a handful of Chinese companies but an entire civilizational approach to autonomous mobility.

The Gilded River has shown us its depths. Now we cross to the other bank—where the water runs turbid, the boatmen have been reading different currents all along, and Marcus's Bloomberg terminal is about to encounter data points that do not fit his model.

Evidence Anchors

BIS Connected Vehicles Final Rule, 15 CFR Part 791 (Federal Register, January 16, 2025) • U.S. DOT Automated Vehicle Framework and Innovation Agenda (April 24, 2025) • AVEP Domestic Exemptions Guidance: NHTSA Third Amended SGO 2021-01 • SELF DRIVE Act of 2026, H.R. 7390 (February 5, 2026); Subcommittee markup vote (February 10, 2026) • NHTSA staffing data: Reuters/CNBC (July 17, 2025); Foley & Lardner analysis (November 2025)

ACT II

THE TURBID RIVER

CHAPTER 6

The Permission Temple

How China Built the Regulatory Machine

In the temple, every pillar bears two loads.

— Kerala temple architecture proverb

The great temples of Kerala—Padmanabhaswamy, Guruvayur, Vadakkunnathan—share a structural principle that distinguishes them from the cathedrals of Europe and the mosques of the Middle East. In a Kerala temple, no element serves a single purpose. The *chuttambalam*, the covered ambulatory around the sanctum, is simultaneously a prayer path, a ventilation corridor, an acoustic chamber that amplifies the priest's chants, and a structural buttress that prevents the inner walls from buckling under the weight of the *gopuram*. The pillars of the *mandapam* bear the roof, channel rainwater, and provide surfaces for sculptural narrative, and mark the ritual boundaries between the sacred and the profane. Nothing is decorative. Everything is load-bearing. The genius is not in any single element but in the integration—the recognition that in a monsoon climate where resources are scarce, every pillar must bear two loads.

China's autonomous-vehicle regulatory architecture is a temple. Moreover, it is built on the same principle.

On December 26, 2025—eleven days after MIIT granted China's first national market-access permits for Level 3 autonomous driving—forty-six Changan Deepal SL03 vehicles equipped with L3 conditional automation systems began fleet operations on designated highway sections in Chongqing. Not test runs. Not demonstration laps for visiting journalists. Fleet operations: paying customers, commercial routes, autonomous driving at speeds up to 50 kilometers per hour on congested expressways in a city whose mountainous terrain and multi-layered highway interchanges have earned it the nickname "magical 8D city." Eleven days. From national regulatory clearance to vehicles on roads carrying passengers. The reader who has just finished Chapter 5—the Fifty Veils, the twelve-to-eleven subcommittee vote, the 5 percent survival probability, the nine years of congressional failure—should allow that number to settle. Eleven days. In the time it takes the American Congress to schedule a hearing, China deployed a fleet.

This is the Chinese answer to the Fifty Veils—not fifty states groping in fifty directions, but a single architect building a structure where every pillar serves two purposes. The regulatory apparatus does not merely *permit* autonomous vehicles; it also requires them. It *creates the conditions for their industrialization*. The distinction is fundamental. America's regulatory framework asks: "Shall we allow this technology?" China's regulatory framework asks: "How shall we deploy this technology to achieve national strategic objectives?" The first is a gatekeeper. The second is a general contractor. Moreover, the difference between a gatekeeper and a general contractor, compounded over a decade of regulatory decisions, is the difference between Waymo's 2,500 vehicles and China's 35,000 kilometers of AV-ready test roads.

6.1 The Three-Tier Architecture

China's AV regulatory structure operates on three tiers—three pillars, each bearing two loads, each reinforcing the others. Where Chapter 5 gave us three veils concealing paralysis, Chapter 6 gives us three pillars supporting momentum.

The First Pillar: MIIT as Master Architect

The Ministry of Industry and Information Technology sits at the apex, establishing national standards (such as GB/T 40429-2021, which codified the taxonomy of driving automation), managing vehicle market-access permits, and coordinating data-security requirements. MIIT does not regulate in isolation; it orchestrates. When MIIT Vice-Minister Xin Guobin announced in October 2025 that the ministry would formulate a comprehensive development plan for intelligent connected vehicles under the 15th Five-Year Plan (2026–2030), he was not making a policy suggestion. He was issuing a construction order. The plan will cover AI-automotive integration, next-generation chip architectures, and autonomous-driving standard-setting—not as separate initiatives but as interlocking components of a single industrial strategy. More than 60 percent of new passenger vehicles sold in China already feature combined driver-assist functions. The 15th Five-Year Plan will govern the transition from driver-assist to autonomous.

For investors accustomed to reading Chinese industrial policy as state planning's dead hand, a correction is in order: this is not the Soviet five-year plan for tractor production. This is a coordinated technology-deployment roadmap with binding targets, budgetary commitments, and career consequences for officials who fail to deliver. The Soviet plan told factory managers how many units to produce. The Chinese plan is to define the finish line of a competitive ecosystem and then watch the runners race.

The Second Pillar: Ministerial Coordination

Beneath MIIT, a constellation of ministries executes domain-specific regulation. The Ministry of Public Security manages road-testing permits and traffic-safety enforcement—it was MPS that issued 16,000 autonomous-vehicle test licenses and opened 32,000 kilometers of roads for AV testing by August 2024, numbers that have since expanded to more than 35,000 kilometers of test roads and 120 million cumulative test kilometers nationally. The Ministry of Transport governs commercial deployment, including the "AI + Transport" initiative. SAMR manages interoperability standards. The coordination mechanism—ministerial working groups, joint announcements, cross-agency pilot approvals—operates with a frictionlessness that would be comical if it were not, from an American perspective, deeply instructive. When MIIT decided to issue L3 market-access permits in December 2025, it coordinated with seven other departments in a single announcement cycle. In America, coordinating two federal agencies on anything takes longer than the gestation period of an African elephant.

The Third Pillar: Municipal Competition

The third tier is the most distinctive and, for Western analysts, the most counterintuitive. Chinese cities do not merely *comply* with national AV policy. They *compete* for AV investment by creating the most favorable regulatory environments. The central government sets the destination; the cities race to arrive first, each hoping that early regulatory leadership will attract the companies, the talent, and the investment that follow. The dynamic is not top-down command. It is a top-down direction with bottom-up competition—centralized strategy, decentralized execution. A paradox that confounds Western analysts trained to see centralization and competition as antithetical.

The temple's three tiers function as a single organism. MIIT provides the architectural blueprint. The ministries build the load-bearing walls. The cities pour the foundation and compete for the honor of hosting the largest congregation. For the investor, the critical insight is that this architecture produces not just speed. Still, *competitive pricing of regulatory access*—cities underbid each other on bureaucratic friction the way American states underbid each other on corporate tax rates, except the commodity being discounted is not tax burden but time-to-deployment. The municipality that offers the fastest permitting, the densest V2X infrastructure, and the most accommodating test-road network wins the company—and the company's data, talent, and supply chain follow. This is industrial policy operating through market incentives, which is precisely the combination that Western analytical frameworks have no category for.

6.2 The December 2025 Watershed and the 15th Five-Year Plan

On December 15, 2025, MIIT granted China's first national market-access permits for Level 3 autonomous driving. The two approved vehicles—Changan Automobile's Deepal SL03 and BAIC's Arcfox Alpha S—received not test permits, not demonstration licenses, not conditional exemptions, but *national product regulatory clearances* for L3 conditional automation. The distinction is everything. A test permit permits a company to conduct experiments. Product regulatory clearance allows a company to sell its products.

The operational parameters were precise and conservative: the Deepal SL03 was approved for single-lane autonomous driving on congested highways and urban expressways at speeds up to 50 km/h, initially on designated sections of road in Chongqing. The Arcfox Alpha S was approved for up to 80 kilometers per hour on designated sections in Beijing. By December 20, Chongqing's traffic management bureau had issued China's first L3 license plate—"Yu AD0001Z"—to a Changan vehicle. By December 26, forty-six vehicles had begun large-scale pilot operations. The speed of execution—eleven days from national regulatory clearance to fleet deployment—is not a data point. It is a diagnosis.

Changan's L3 system had undergone more than five million kilometers of real-world testing in Chongqing, covering 191 scenario categories, exceeding national standards by 49 percent, with extreme conditions accounting for 36 percent of total testing. The liability framework is explicit: when L3 is activated within its operational design domain, the automaker bears liability for collisions caused by the system. This is not ambiguity. This is accountability.

Anchor this in the 15th Five-Year Plan, and the strategic coherence becomes unmistakable. MIIT's January 2026 inter-ministerial work meeting framed 2026 as the opening year of the plan and declared that China's intelligent connected vehicle sector is entering "a significant opportunity period." The Energy-Saving and New Energy Vehicle Technology Roadmap 3.0 sets explicit targets: L4 fully popularized by 2040, L5 entering the market by 2040, and vehicle-road-cloud integration achieving comprehensive coverage. Industry projections anticipate that L2 combined driver-assistance will become standard equipment on new vehicles by 2026, with penetration exceeding 70 percent.

China is now the only country, along with Germany and Japan, to have formal L3 approval frameworks for passenger vehicles. However, neither Germany nor Japan has accompanied its framework with a five-year industrial plan, a network of municipal proving grounds, and a supply chain capable of producing autonomous-capable vehicles at prices that make American engineers choke on their lattes.

6.3 The City-Level Proving Grounds

The national statistics are staggering in aggregate: 35,000 kilometers of AV-ready test roads, 16,000 test licenses issued, more than 120 million cumulative test kilometers, 17 national ICV testing zones, and vehicle-road-cloud integration pilots in 20 cities. However, aggregate statistics obscure the competitive intensity of the city-level ecosystem. Each major city is building its own AV temple, and each is architecturally distinct.

Beijing is the regulatory pioneer: its demonstration zone, launched September 2020, now covers 600 square kilometers of intelligent roadside infrastructure, with thirty-three companies operating approximately 900 vehicles that have accumulated more than 32 million test kilometers—over a quarter of the national total. In April 2025, Beijing's new AV regulations provided the country's most explicit municipal framework for Level 3 and above, including annual inspection systems that acknowledge what regulators elsewhere have been slow to grasp: that an autonomous system is not a static product but an evolving intelligence that must be continuously validated.

Wuhan is the scale leader: Baidu Apollo Go operates more than 400 fully driverless robotaxis across a service area exceeding 3,000 square kilometers—China's first city to offer 24/7 commercial autonomous ride-hailing. While Waymo serves 400,000 weekly rides across six American cities, Apollo Go in Wuhan alone operates at a geographic scale that dwarfs any single American metro.

Shenzhen is the legislative vanguard, having enacted China's first comprehensive ICV regulation in August 2022—three full years before most Chinese cities had frameworks and a regulatory achievement that placed it ahead of every American city except, arguably, San Francisco. **Guangzhou** is the infrastructure showcase: seventeen companies have logged more than 24.4 million autonomous kilometers, supported by 78,000 5G base stations, 530 V2X units, 897 roadside sensors, and 419 edge computing stations. **Shanghai** has expanded its test-road network to more than 750 kilometers and is executing an action plan for autonomous-vehicle development through 2027.

The competitive dynamic among these cities is Darwinian. Cities that attract AV companies attract engineers, supply chains, testing infrastructure, and data ecosystems that generate further competitive advantage. The municipal official in Guangzhou who deploys 78,000 5G base stations is not fulfilling a bureaucratic obligation. He is building a moat—a moat made of roadside sensors and edge-computing stations rather than water, but a moat nonetheless. Moreover, he is doing it because the municipal official in Wuhan built one first.

6.4 The Data Iron Curtain and the Galapagos Effect

China's data-localization requirements form the fourth wall of the Permission Temple—and it is the wall that Western companies find most impenetrable. Under regulations tightened further in 2025–2026, autonomous-driving data collected in China must remain in China. Training datasets, algorithmic features, high-definition mapping data, and the vast troves of sensor data generated by millions of vehicles on Chinese roads cannot be exported without regulatory approval that is, in practice, rarely granted. The MIIT's Guidelines for the Security of Cross-Border Transfer of Vehicle Data, released in early 2026, specifically target autonomous-driving training datasets, forcing foreign companies to build entirely duplicative AI infrastructure within China.

Tesla, characteristically, has responded by building a dedicated AI training center in China—an investment that acknowledges the data regime's reality while simultaneously demonstrating its cost. Every Western company that wishes to compete in the Chinese AV market must now maintain parallel computing infrastructure: one set of servers for Chinese data, another for the rest of the world. The capital expenditure required to maintain this duplication is substantial and structural— it does not diminish with scale. It increases.

The biological metaphor is the Galapagos Islands. Chinese autonomous-vehicle technology is evolving within a connected habitat—a rich, vast (120 million cumulative test kilometers and counting), and entirely enclosed data ecosystem. The species that evolve within this habitat are optimized for Chinese driving conditions: the density of Chinese urban traffic, the behavior patterns of Chinese pedestrians and the swarms of e-bike riders that constitute a rolling obstacle course of uniquely Chinese character, the specific road geometries of Chinese highways and mountainous expressways, and the V2X communication protocols that are standard in Chinese infrastructure and nonexistent on American roads. These species may prove spectacularly capable within their habitat. They may also prove maladapted for export—just as the Galapagos finch's beak, perfectly evolved for its specific seed, is useless on the mainland.

The BIS Connected Vehicle Rule of Chapter 5 mirrors this from the other side. America has built its own Galapagos—a regulatory island where Chinese AV technology cannot land. The result is two enclosed evolutionary environments, each producing autonomous-driving intelligence optimized for its own terrain, each blind to the other's data, each developing along trajectories that may prove irreconcilable. The Galapagos Effect is not Chinese or American. It is bilateral. For the global automotive industry, this means autonomy will not converge on a single technological standard. It will bifurcate into two, with the rest of the world forced to choose between them or adapt both, at enormous cost.

Unless the habitat itself is exported, this is the Belt and Road thesis of Chapter 10: that Chinese AV technology will travel not on its own merits alone but on the back of Chinese infrastructure investment—the V2X communication protocols, the 5G base stations, the smart-highway systems, and the vehicle-road-cloud integration platforms already being deployed along Belt and Road corridors in Southeast Asia, the Middle East, and Africa. The Galapagos finch does not fly to the mainland. The mainland is terraformed to accommodate the finch. However, that is a story for later.

6.5 The Trust Dividend

Eighty-five percent of Chinese consumers say they are comfortable with autonomous driving that does not require human supervision. Thirty-nine percent of American consumers say the same. This is not a footnote. It is a 46-point structural advantage in adoption velocity.

The gap extends beyond autonomous vehicles. The 2025 Edelman Trust Barometer found a 40-point chasm in AI trust between China and the United States. BCG's global automotive survey confirmed it: 61 percent of Chinese consumers are open to riding in a fully autonomous taxi, compared with 34 percent in the US. Every metric, from every source, in every year, tells the same story: Chinese consumers are ready for autonomy. American consumers are not.

The implications for deployment economics are severe. In America, the AV company must spend marketing dollars to overcome fear, PR dollars to manage the viral amplification of every incident, government-affairs dollars to navigate community opposition, and legal dollars to defend against litigation. In China, the AV company spends engineering dollars to improve its capabilities. American companies fight on two fronts simultaneously—the technology and trust fronts. Chinese companies fight on one.

Now connect this to valuation—and to the fund manager whose cognitive errors we have been tracking since Chapter 4. Marcus, the reader will recall, first appeared, pricing 40,000 American traffic deaths at $429 billion in annual misallocation—seeing alpha in institutional friction. In Chapter 5, we noted that his US-only TAM model had not yet priced the BIS rule's global redirect. Here, in the Permission Temple, Marcus encounters the data point that should have restructured his entire thesis—and misreads it completely.

In March 2025, Marcus reads a Financial Times headline: "China Tightens Rules on Autonomous Vehicles After Fatal Crash." Marcus sells his Pony.ai position at $4.20 and rotates into additional Tesla exposure, reasoning that Chinese regulatory risk has just increased. Three months later, MIIT issues L3 market-access permits. Pony.ai rallies 35 percent. Marcus's Pony.ai proceeds, now in Tesla, declines as the NHTSA investigation deepens. Marcus has traded a 46-point consumer-acceptance advantage for narrative immunity. He has sold the farmer and bought the hunter. He did so because every instinct trained by twenty years of reading Western financial media told him that "tightening" equals "bearish." The *ullil kaanal* would have told him the opposite.

The capital markets have answered: America deserves the higher terminal multiple. ARK Invest prices American robotaxi at 60 percent of Tesla's expected value. Wall Street assigns Waymo a $126 billion valuation. Chinese AV companies—operating in a market with double the consumer acceptance, a unified regulatory framework, and state-directed infrastructure investment—trade at a fraction of American multiples. Pony.ai's market cap on Nasdaq is ~$5 billion. The market values Baidu's AV division at roughly the same amount as Waymo's single fundraising round.

The market has answered. The *ullil kaanal* suggests the market is wrong.

6.6 The Tighten-and-Release Rhythm

Western investors who read China's 2025 regulatory tightening as "cracking down on AV" committed a familiar analytical error. The same error produced the "China is uninvestable" thesis of 2021, which was followed by one of the largest tech-sector rebounds in emerging-market history. The error is to confuse accountability with hostility, to mistake the monsoon for the flood.

The Xiaomi SU7 crash of March 29, 2025—three students killed, 12 million Weibo posts, a 6.3 percent stock drop—triggered a regulatory response that was sweeping in scope and precise in application. MIIT proposed to ban misleading marketing terminology for driver-assistance features (e.g., no longer calling L2 "autopilot" or "full self-driving"). It required pre-approval for all driving-related over-the-air software updates. It drafted mandatory L2 safety requirements to establish a floor below which no manufacturer's system could fall. In February 2026, MIIT released draft L3/L4 safety rules requiring "human-driver-equivalent safety" as the minimum threshold and mandating driver-training prerequisites before L3 activation.

The pattern is rhythmic and, once understood, predictable. It is not a reaction. It is an operating cadence—a deliberate regulatory design pattern: permit, then scale, then incident, then tighten standards, then resume expansion on firmer ground. This is the regulatory equivalent of the Kerala monsoon metaphor that has governed this book's narrative. The rains come hard. They flood the paddy. The fields are saturated. And then the grain grows taller than it could have grown in any drought. China is hardening L2 safety standards at a mass scale precisely to protect the L3/L4 deployment runway. The tightening is not the reversal. It is the preparation.

The comparison with America's regulatory response is instructive. After the Cruise pedestrian-dragging incident, America revoked one company's permit in one state. After the Xiaomi SU7 crash, China overhauled the marketing, update, and safety standards for the entire industry. America punished the company. China upgraded the system. The Western investor who reads Chinese tightening as bearish is the one who sells monsoon futures because it has started raining. The correct trade is the opposite: the tightening means the next expansion cycle will be built on bedrock, not sand.

For the Gordon Gekko investor, the analytical framework is: watch the permit-tighten-expand cycle, not the headlines. When MIIT tightens, it is not retreating. It is reloading.

The Temple Stands

The Permission Temple is complete. Three pillars—national architect, ministerial builders, competing municipal congregations—operating as a single organism. The December 2025 watershed: not test permits but product clearances, national in scope, eleven days from approval to fleet deployment. The 15th Five-Year Plan: a codified national mandate with intelligent connected vehicles at its center. City-level proving grounds that have accumulated 120 million test kilometers across 35,000 kilometers of roads. A data-localization regime that creates a Galapagos of autonomous-driving intelligence—enclosed, rich, and potentially exportable. A consumer population where 85 percent are ready to ride. Moreover, a regulatory rhythm that Western investors consistently misread as hostility when it is, in fact, husbandry.

For the investor, the regulatory P&L reads as follows. Capex: China's unified framework eliminates the duplicative legal, compliance, and lobbying costs that American companies bear across 50 jurisdictions—a structural savings McKinsey estimates at 15–25 percent of total deployment costs. Time-to-scale: eleven days from permit to fleet, versus nine years of congressional failure. Risk premium: the tighten-and-release cycle produces not unpredictability but a predictable cadence that can be modelled, hedged, and traded. The American regulatory system produces uncertainty. The Chinese regulatory system produces volatility—and volatility, unlike uncertainty, has a price and can be arbitraged.

Chapter 5 showed the American regulatory purdah: fifty veils, no national standard, a 12–11 vote on a bill with a 5 percent survival probability. Chapter 6 shows the Chinese answer: a single temple where every pillar bears two loads. The contrast is not subtle. It is architectural.

However, a temple without worshippers is merely a building. Chapter 7 will fill the Permission Temple with its congregation—the Four Dragons of Chinese AV innovation: the National Champions, the Pure-Play Scalers, the Manufacturing Giants, and the Software Stack Integrators. The regulatory machine has been built. We now meet the companies it was designed to serve.

Evidence Anchors

Beijing AV Regulations (effective April 1, 2025); Beijing Demonstration Zone data (Xinhua, June 2025) • MIIT L3 Market Access Permits (December 15, 2025): CnEVPost, Reuters, SCIO • Changan L3 Pilot Operations: ECNS (December 31, 2025); CarnewsChina (January 14, 2026) • 15th Five-Year Plan ICV announcements: MIIT Vice-Minister Xin Guobin (October 2025); MIIT inter-ministerial meeting (January 2026) • Consumer Acceptance: Rest of World/Automobility 85%/39% survey (2023); Edelman Trust Barometer (2025); BCG Global Automotive Survey (November 2025) • Draft L3/L4 Safety Rules: Reuters (February 2026); Guangzhou AV data: CarnewsChina (August 2025)

CHAPTER 7

The Four Dragons

A Taxonomy of Chinese AV Strategy

The kingfisher does not boast of catching fish. It boasts of knowing where the fish swim.

— Kerala backwater proverb

In the ecology of Kerala's backwaters, survival belongs not to the single dominant species but to the system. The kingfisher needs the fish. The fish needs the plankton. Plankton need nutrients from paddy runoff. The paddy needs the monsoon. No element thrives in isolation. The backwater ecosystem is resilient precisely because it is not a monoculture—it is a structured ecology of interdependent archetypes, each optimized for a different niche, each feeding the conditions that sustain the others.

Western investors analyze the Chinese autonomous-vehicle ecosystem the way a tourist looks at the backwater: they see water. They see Baidu and conclude "China's Waymo." They see BYD and conclude "China's Tesla." They view the forest as a collection of individual trees rather than as a system whose competitive advantage lies in the connections among them. This is an error that will incur costs.

The Chinese AV ecosystem is not a monolith. It is a structured ecology of four archetypes—what this book calls the **Four Dragons** of Chinese AV strategy. Where America's temple has one altar and one god (Waymo), China's temple has four altars, four dragons, and a congregation that worships at all of them. Together, they form a system more resilient, more commercially advanced, and more globally exportable than any single company's strategy in the West.

7.1 The National Champion: Baidu Apollo Go

Baidu Apollo Go is the closest Chinese analogue to Waymo—and the comparison simultaneously illuminates and obscures. Both operate autonomous ride-hailing fleets at a commercial scale. Both have accumulated billions of kilometers of autonomous driving data. Both are subsidiaries of larger technology conglomerates whose shareholders periodically question why their companies are spending billions on a business that has not yet generated meaningful profits. The resemblance ends there.

The numbers, first. Apollo Go has completed more than 17 million cumulative rides across 22 cities worldwide, including domestic hubs (Beijing, Shanghai, Wuhan, Shenzhen, Hong Kong) and international pilots (Abu Dhabi, Dubai, Switzerland). As of October 31, 2025, the service delivers more than 250,000 fully driverless rides per week—matching Waymo's reported paid weekly ride volume. The fleet has driven more than 240 million autonomous kilometers with no major accidents resulting in human injury or death. The safety metric is striking: one airbag deployment per 10.14 million kilometers of operation, which Baidu claims surpasses both human-driver averages and Waymo's published figures.

Now the number that separates Baidu from Waymo, like a cleaver separates bone from meat: vehicle cost. Baidu's sixth-generation RT6 robotaxi costs approximately 204,600 yuan (approximately $28,600) to manufacture. Waymo's 5th-generation Jaguar I-PACE, festooned with a hundred-thousand-dollar sensor stack, costs approximately $175,000. The 6th-generation Zeekr RT platform will reduce that to roughly $75,000. Even at that reduced price, Waymo's vehicle is two-and-a-half times the cost of Baidu's. The RT6 achieves its cost structure by leveraging China's electric-vehicle supply chain, Baidu's in-house sensor systems, and a purpose-built platform designed for autonomous operation rather than adapted from a luxury consumer vehicle.

Unit economics have broken even in Wuhan, Apollo Go's flagship city, where the service covers more than 3,000 square kilometers. Baidu CEO Robin Li confirmed this during the Q2 2025 earnings call, noting that Wuhan's taxi fares are 30 percent cheaper than in China's Tier 1 cities—meaning that breakeven was achieved at the *bottom* of the fare structure, not the top. The implication for higher-fare markets—Dubai, London, San Francisco—is arithmetic: if the economics work at $0.55 base fares in Wuhan, they will work spectacularly in markets where average ride-hailing fares are three to five times higher.

The international expansion strategy is accelerating. Dubai issued a trial permit in September 2025. Lyft announced plans to deploy Apollo Go RT6 vehicles in London from 2026. Uber has explored Apollo Go partnerships for Germany. The pattern is unmistakable: Baidu is not waiting for the BIS Connected Vehicle Rule to lift. It is going around it—deploying in every lucrative market the rule does not cover. Robin Li projected at the 2025 Baidu World Conference that, by 2030, the operating cost of robotaxis could drop to approximately $0.25 per mile, leading to a five- to sevenfold surge in global ride-hailing demand. Note the frame: Li is not describing Chinese adoption. He is describing *global* adoption—and positioning Apollo Go as the platform best equipped to serve it, with vehicles at one-sixth the cost of Waymo's and fares that undercut every human-driven taxi service worldwide.

How Western analysts misread this archetype: they call it "China's Waymo" and price it accordingly—at a fraction of Waymo's valuation, reflecting the "China discount." However, Baidu is not Waymo at Chinese prices. It is Waymo-level safety at one-sixth the vehicle cost, in a market with double the consumer acceptance, backed by a regulatory architecture that coordinates rather than constrains, and expanding internationally into every market the BIS rule has not sealed. The Western analyst who calls this "China's Waymo" has already mislabeled the trade. The correct label is: Waymo's economics, without Waymo's structural disadvantages. Marcus, our fund manager from Chapters 4 through 6, would recognize the pattern—he has been mislabeling Chinese assets since March 2025, and the mislabeling has cost him 35 percent on Pony.ai alone. The label is the first casualty of the China discount. The portfolio is the second.

7.2 The Pure-Play Scalers: Pony.ai and WeRide

If Baidu is the national champion—the state-supported leviathan with the deepest resources and the broadest domestic footprint—then Pony.ai and WeRide are the expeditionary forces: leaner, faster, more internationally diversified, and more creatively financed.

Pony.ai: The Dual-Listed Sprinter

Pony.ai's Q3 2025 revenue reached $25.4 million, a 72 percent year-over-year increase. The fleet numbered 1,159 vehicles, of which 667 were the cost-optimized Gen-7 platform, whose bill of materials cost has been reduced by 70 percent relative to previous generations. The Gen-7 has achieved citywide unit economics breakeven in Guangzhou at an operational tempo of 23 orders per vehicle per day. That figure—23 orders per vehicle per day—is the metric that matters. It means each robotaxi generates revenue nearly every waking hour, approaching utilization rates that make autonomous ride-hailing economically superior to human-driven alternatives.

Pony.ai's capital-markets strategy is an innovation in itself. The company listed on Nasdaq in November 2024 and subsequently completed a Hong Kong dual listing, raising a combined $1.06 billion. The dual listing is not vanity—it is infrastructure. Nasdaq provides access to American institutional capital, where AV narratives command premium multiples. Hong Kong provides access to Asian and Middle Eastern sovereign wealth, where exposure to China is not a liability but a thesis. The company plans to triple its fleet to 3,000 vehicles by the end of 2026. International deployments span Luxembourg, Seoul, Singapore (via ComfortDelGro), Dubai, and Uber partnerships for multiple markets.

WeRide: The Swiss Army Knife

If Pony.ai is the sprinter, WeRide is the Swiss Army Knife—a company whose competitive advantage lies not in any single vehicle type but in its diversity of form factors: robotaxis, robobuses, robovans, and robostreet sweepers. In America, this would be called "lack of focus." In China, it is called "maximizing addressable market." One of these perspectives will prove more profitable.

Q3 2025 revenue reached $24 million—a 144 percent year-over-year increase—with gross margins of 32.9 percent, up 26.4 percentage points year-over-year. The company operates more than 1,600 autonomous vehicles in 11 countries, is licensed in 8 markets, and plans to expand to 15 cities across the Middle East and Europe. Its cash position of $764 million provides substantial runway. The landmark was the November 2025 launch of Uber's driverless robotaxi service in Abu Dhabi—the first fully driverless service outside the US and China to operate on Uber's platform. The significance is structural: it proves that Chinese AV technology can integrate with Western ride-hailing platforms in third-country markets, a template for global expansion that does not require building a consumer brand from scratch.

The Pure-Play Scalers answer a question that the National Champion cannot: what does Chinese AV look like in markets where Baidu's brand has no recognition and China's state support carries political baggage? The answer: it looks like a Pony.ai vehicle on Singapore's ComfortDelGro platform, or a WeRide robobus shuttling tourists at a Zurich airport, or an autonomous street sweeper cleaning Riyadh's boulevards at 3 a.m. It looks *local*—which is precisely the point. The technology is Chinese. The branding is neutral. The revenue is denominated in dirhams, Swiss francs, and Singapore dollars. The BIS rule bars these companies from doing business in America. It does not bar them from the other 7.8 billion people on the planet.

How Western analysts misread this archetype: they see "Chinese startup, sub-$5B market cap" and apply emerging-market-startup risk premia. However, Pony.ai and WeRide are not startups in any meaningful sense. They are global autonomous-vehicle platforms with dual-listed liquidity, Fortune 500 partnerships, and fleets tripling annually. The risk is execution. The misread is categorisation—pricing a global platform as a local startup because the headquarters is in Guangzhou rather than Mountain View.

7.3 The Industrialisers: BYD and XPeng

This is the archetype that fills the empty stall in the American temple. The Industrialiser does not operate ride-hailing fleets. It does not sell autonomy-as-a-service. It *manufactures* autonomy as a feature—embedded in vehicles, standard across model lines, available at price points that make Waymo's per-vehicle cost look like a rounding error. The Industrialiser is the farmer, not the hunter. Furthermore, the farmer's harvest is measured not in trophies but in acres irrigated.

BYD God's Eye: The Paradigm Shift

On February 10, 2025, BYD Chairman Wang Chuanfu stood before an audience in Shenzhen and made an announcement that sent Hong Kong-listed EV stocks tumbling: BYD's advanced driver-assistance system, branded "God's Eye," would be integrated across the company's *entire* vehicle lineup—21 models, from the premium Yangwang U9 supercar to the entry-level Seagull hatchback, priced at 69,800 yuan ($9,550)—*at no additional cost to consumers*. Li Auto, XPeng, and Geely shares fell 6%, 9%, and 10%, respectively, within 24 hours. The market understood immediately what Wang was saying: the era of autonomous driving as a premium option is over. It is now a seatbelt. It is now an airbag. It is now standard.

God's Eye operates in three tiers. **God's Eye A** (DiPilot 600) is the premium variant: three LiDAR sensors, city and highway NOA. **God's Eye B** (DiPilot 300) uses a single LiDAR, covering upper-range models with full city and highway NOA. **God's Eye C** (DiPilot 100) is the revelation: a purely vision-based system at 100 TOPS of computing power, using 12 cameras, 5 millimeter-wave radars, and 12 ultrasonic radars to deliver highway NOA for vehicles priced under $10,000. The hardware cost of God's Eye C is approximately RMB 2,800—roughly $385—which is seven times cheaper than a typical LiDAR-based ADAS system.

The scale is continental. As of early 2025, more than 4.4 million BYD vehicles were equipped with L2- and above smart-driving systems, with a cumulative total of 3.7 billion assisted-driving kilometers. BYD's 2024 ADAS training mileage was 72 million kilometers *per day*—a data flywheel of staggering proportions. BYD employs 110,000 engineers, 5,000 dedicated to intelligent-driving R&D. The entire system is built on BYD's Xuanji Architecture, integrating central processing, cloud AI, vehicle-side AI, 5G connectivity, satellite networks, and—in a move that caused Silicon Valley to collectively choke on its artisanal coffee—the DeepSeek R1 large language model.

Wang Chuanfu does not speak of killing the competition. He speaks of irrigating the valley. "Good technology should be available to everyone." In six words, he articulated the thesis that separates the Industrialiser from every other archetype. Waymo makes autonomy extraordinary. Tesla makes autonomy aspirational. BYD makes autonomy *ordinary*. Moreover, the ordinary, deployed at scale across a company that sold 4.3 million vehicles in 2024 and is projected by JPMorgan to reach 6 million by 2026, is the force that reshapes the global automotive industry. The hunter takes one deer. The farmer irrigates the valley.

The competitive impact was immediate. Within twenty-four hours of the God's Eye announcement, Chinese OEMs scrambled to match BYD's offer—price cuts, feature upgrades, accelerated autonomous-driving rollouts. A price war had been running in China's EV sector for eighteen months; BYD had just opened a second front—a *technology* war in which the weapon was not lower prices but higher capabilities at the same price. When the largest manufacturer in the world's largest market decides that advanced driver assistance is no longer a revenue stream but a customer-acquisition tool, every competitor must either match or die. In the Theyyam tradition, the deity descends not to reward the congregation but to transform it. God's Eye is BYD's descent.

XPeng VLA 2.0: The Intelligence Exporter

Where BYD democratizes autonomy through manufacturing scale, XPeng democratizes it through algorithmic innovation—and then exports the algorithm. XPeng's VLA 2.0 (Vision-Language-Action) architecture, presented at AAAI 2026, represents the frontier of end-to-end autonomous driving: a unified neural network that processes raw sensor data directly, bypassing the modular perception-planning-control pipeline that characterized first-generation autonomous systems.

The hardware is equally provocative. XPeng's in-house Turing AI chip delivers 2,250 TOPS of computing power—three times NVIDIA's Orin, the standard chipset for Western AV developers. The training dataset comprises approximately 100 million video clips. The system is designed not merely for XPeng's own vehicles but for export: Volkswagen is the first customer, licensing XPeng's autonomous-driving platform for its Chinese operations, and XPeng is open-sourcing elements of its technology stack to attract global partners.

XPeng Vice Chairman Brian Gu has described the ambition in terms that will resonate with any investor who followed the DeepSeek shock of January 2025: this is the automotive industry's DeepSeek moment—Chinese AV systems outperforming Tesla's Full Self-Driving on Chinese roads at a fraction of the cost, with fewer computational resources, and with architectures designed from inception for export and licensing rather than proprietary lock-in. Just as DeepSeek demonstrated that Chinese AI labs could achieve frontier performance without access to the most advanced NVIDIA chips, XPeng's Turing chip demonstrates that Chinese automotive engineers can design silicon that surpasses Western benchmarks at lower price points. The sanctions were supposed to starve the ecosystem. Instead, they fertilized it. If BYD is the farmer irrigating the valley, XPeng is the agronomist developing the seed that grows in any soil—and then exporting the seed to farmers in Stuttgart, Wolfsburg, and Tokyo.

How Western analysts misread this archetype: they price God's Eye as "cheap ADAS"—a low-margin feature bolted onto budget cars. However, God's Eye is not a cheap ADAS. It is a data monsoon: 72 million kilometers of real-world training data per day, feeding algorithms that improve across 4.3 million vehicles simultaneously. The analyst who prices the irrigation canal as a ditch will miss the harvest.

7.4 The Eyes of the Dragons: Hesai's Quiet Dominance

No analysis is dominated by a single; the Four Dragons are complete without examining the sensor ecosystem that gives them eyes. Moreover, that ecosystem is dominated by a single species: Hesai Technology.

Hesai holds 33 percent of the global automotive LiDAR market by revenue, according to Yole Group's 2025 report—the number-one position for four consecutive years. In the Level 4 robotaxi segment, Hesai's dominance is commanding: ~65 percent market share, supplying nine of the world's top ten robotaxi operators, including Zoox, Aurora, Baidu, Didi, Pony.ai, and WeRide. Read that list again. Hesai supplies both Chinese and American L4 operators. It is the common denominator of global autonomous driving.

In September 2025, Hesai became the first LiDAR company in the world to exceed one million units in annual production. Its fully automated production lines produce one LiDAR unit every 20 seconds—planned capacity: 2 million units for 2025, with deliveries projected at 1.2-1.5 million units. The company has secured design wins with 24 OEMs across 120 vehicle models globally. Q3 2025 revenue reached RMB 795.4 million ($111.7 million), with shipments of 441,398 units—a 229 percent year-over-year increase.

The cost trajectory is the story within the story. A decade ago, a robotaxi-grade LiDAR cost $100,000 or more. Velodyne's HDL-64E, mounted on Google's early self-driving prototypes, retailed for $75,000. Today, Hesai's ADAS-grade units are estimated at $150–200 per unit at scale—a 500-fold reduction in cost over a decade. This is not a manufacturing improvement. It is a manufacturing revolution, driven by vertical integration (Hesai independently develops all seven key LiDAR components), proprietary manufacturing systems, and the kind of relentless cost engineering that China's industrial ecosystem applies to everything from solar panels to lithium batteries.

Hesai is the only publicly listed LiDAR company to achieve full-year non-GAAP profitability—accomplished in 2024, with Q3 2025 net income reaching RMB 256 million ($36 million). The company's Hong Kong dual listing raised an additional $614 million.

Now consider the Western contrast, because it is there that the *ullil kaanal* finds its sharpest focus. Luminar Technologies, once valued at $12 billion and positioned as Hesai's American rival, filed for Chapter 11 bankruptcy in December 2025. Ouster, the other publicly traded American LiDAR company, shipped approximately 7,200 units in Q3 2025—against Hesai's 441,398 in the same quarter. The ratio is 61 to 1. This is not a competitive landscape. It is an extinction event.

The Western LiDAR industry has been subjected to the same industrial-scale deflation that destroyed Western solar-panel manufacturers, Western battery producers, and Western drone companies before it. The pattern is identical: a Chinese manufacturer achieves production volumes that drive unit costs below the level at which Western competitors can survive, then uses those lower costs to capture market share, which drives further volume, which drives further cost reductions, in a spiral that the Western competitor cannot escape regardless of the quality of its technology. Luminar's technology was, by many accounts, excellent. Its factory could not match Hesai's—one LiDAR every 20 seconds, one million units per year, and a trajectory toward two million units per year. Hesai produces LiDAR the way BYD produces cars: at volumes and price points that make Western competition structurally unviable.

How Western analysts misread this: they see "Chinese LiDAR company" and apply the BIS-ban risk premium. However, the BIS rule targets connected-vehicle hardware in vehicles sold in the US—it does not target sensor components sold to American AV companies. Hesai supplies Zoox, Aurora, and other American operators today. The analyst who assumes Hesai is locked out of the American market has not read the rule. The analyst who understands that Hesai is the pick-and-shovel play of autonomous driving—profiting regardless of which robotaxi operator wins—has read the chapter.

7.5 The Stack Integrators: Huawei, Momenta, DeepRoute, Didi

The Stack Integrator is the archetype with no American equivalent—and its absence is the structural vulnerability the Four Temples Framework diagnoses. The Stack Integrator does not manufacture vehicles. It does not operate fleets. It builds the autonomous driving technology stack—the software, algorithms, cloud infrastructure, and, in some cases, the chips—and licenses it to multiple OEMs simultaneously. It is the Android of autonomy: the platform that enables an ecosystem rather than a product that dominates a market.

Huawei ADS: The Spirit Vessel

Huawei's Advanced Driving System is the most consequential autonomous-driving platform that most Western investors have never valued. ADS now powers more than one million vehicles across 28 models from five brands—AITO, Luxeed, Avatr, Deepal, and Arcfox. Cumulative assisted-driving distance exceeds 4 billion kilometers. ADS 4.0, the latest iteration, targets highway L3 capability.

Huawei does not sell cars. It sells the intelligence that makes cars autonomous—and then it sells the cloud infrastructure that trains that intelligence, the telecommunications hardware that connects the intelligence to the road, and the chips that process it in real time. The integrated offering—ADS software, Ascend AI chips, HarmonyOS cockpit, Huawei Cloud, 5G infrastructure—constitutes what Huawei internally calls the *shenqi*, the "spirit vessel": a complete, exportable, vertically integrated autonomous-driving ecosystem.

There is no American equivalent. NVIDIA sells chips. Qualcomm sells chips. Google sells software. Amazon sells cloud. No American company sells it all as a single, integrated platform that an OEM can adopt wholesale and deploy within a single development cycle. The closest American analogue would be if Google simultaneously offered Waymo's software stack, designed the TPU chips to run it, provided Android Automotive for the cockpit, hosted the training infrastructure on Google Cloud, and built the 5G base stations that connected the vehicle to the road. That company does not exist in America. It exists in Shenzhen, is called Huawei, is under US sanctions, and is growing faster than any sanctioned entity in modern economic history has any right to. The sanctions were supposed to cripple Huawei's chip capabilities. Instead, they motivated Huawei to build its own. The spirit vessel, denied foreign components, grew its own organs.

Momenta, DeepRoute, and Didi: The Specialist Triad

Momenta has achieved something remarkable: it has convinced both Chinese *and* Western OEMs to trust a Chinese startup with their autonomous-driving future. The partner list reads like a roll call of the global automotive aristocracy: Mercedes-Benz, BMW, Toyota, Honda, Nissan, General Motors, Audi, Volkswagen. Over 160 vehicle models have selected Momenta's intelligent-driving solutions. CEO Cao Xudong notes that winning major foreign carmakers requires five to seven years of stringent validation—making Momenta's client roster not merely a business achievement but a moat built on accumulated credibility—valuation: $6 billion. For the thesis, Momenta matters because it is the proof that Chinese AV software can pass Western automotive-grade validation. This credential dissolves the "cheap Chinese tech" narrative at the OEM procurement level.

DeepRoute.ai has carved a focused niche: third-party Navigate on Autopilot. With more than 200,000 production vehicles equipped and an estimated 40 percent share of China's third-party NOA market, DeepRoute demonstrates that not every Stack Integrator needs to be a platform hegemon. Sometimes the right strategy is depth, not breadth—owning a specific capability and executing it better than anyone else. For the thesis, DeepRoute is important because it demonstrates that the middleware layer is monetisable—a revenue stream that is invisible to analysts who model only the OEM and the fleet operator.

Didi brings something unique to the archetype: the demand-data-distribution trinity. As China's dominant ride-hailing platform, Didi possesses what no pure-technology company can replicate: hundreds of millions of rides' worth of demand patterns, routing data, pricing elasticity, and operational intelligence. Its R2 robotaxi, delivered in January 2026, achieves a 74 percent cost reduction relative to previous generations—designed not for demonstrations but for commercial fleet deployment at scale. When Didi deploys its own robotaxis, it does not need to build demand from scratch. It already has the passengers, the routes, the data, and the app installed on hundreds of millions of phones. The trinity is complete—and it is a trinity that neither Waymo (which lacks a ride-hailing platform) nor Uber (which lacks proprietary AV technology) can fully replicate. For the thesis, Didi matters because it is the only entity on Earth that simultaneously owns the demand platform, autonomous technology, and fleet economics. This vertical integration collapses the entire value chain into a single company.

How Western analysts misread this archetype: they model Huawei as a "chip company under sanctions" and apply a sanctions-risk discount to the entire entity. However, ADS is not a chip business. It is a full-stack ecosystem—software, cloud, chips, telco, cockpit—that OEMs adopt wholesale. The analyst who models the trunk is missing the forest. The correct model: platform economics with switching costs that increase with each OEM integration, in a market where 60% of new vehicles already feature smart-driving features.

The Ecosystem as Strategy

The Four Dragons are not competitors. They are symbiotes.

Baidu's Apollo Go generates the ride-hailing data that trains the algorithms. BYD's God's Eye generates the manufacturing-scale driving data—3.7 billion kilometers and counting—that feeds the cloud-training infrastructure. Huawei's ADS provides the software stack that enables OEMs who lack in-house capability. Momenta licenses its technology to foreign OEMs, extending the reach of the Chinese algorithm into global markets through vehicles that do not carry Chinese brands. WeRide and Pony.ai demonstrate the technology's international exportability. Hesai supplies the LiDAR that gives all of them perception. Moreover, the Permission Temple of Chapter 6—the regulatory architecture—provides the framework that coordinates their collective advancement.

The American ecosystem has Waymo. It has Tesla's aspiration. It has Uber's platform. It has Aurora's trucks. These are impressive individual achievements. However, they are not a system. They do not feed each other. Waymo's data does not improve Tesla's algorithms. Tesla's manufacturing does not reduce Waymo's vehicle cost. Aurora's trucking routes do not expand Uber's ride-hailing coverage. They are individual trees in a forest that lacks a canopy.

The Chinese ecosystem is the canopy. Moreover, the canopy in the monsoon determines whether the forest survives the storm or whether the trees stand naked in the rain, each absorbing the full force of the downpour alone.

For the Gordon Gekko investor, the Four Dragons demand a portfolio framework, not a stock-picking checklist. Each archetype carries a moat, a dependency, a failure mode, and a leading indicator:

The National Champion (Baidu): *Moat is data volume and state coordination. Dependency is continued municipal support and international market access. Failure mode: geopolitical lockout from Gulf and European markets, or a catastrophic safety incident at international scale. Leading* indicator: quarterly international ride volume—when Baidu's non-China rides exceed 10 percent of total, the global thesis is confirmed.

The Pure-Play Scalers (Pony.ai, WeRide): *Moat is international diversification and platform-agnostic deployment. Dependency is third-party platform partnerships (Uber, ComfortDelGro, Lyft). Failure mode: platform partners build or buy their own AV capability, disintermediating the scalers. Leading indicator: number of platform partnerships signed—each new partnership raises switching costs and validates the model.*

The Industrialisers (BYD, XPeng): *Moat is a manufacturing-scale data flywheel and cost culture. Dependency is consumer EV demand continuing its trajectory. Failure mode: a global EV demand plateau that slows the data flywheel, or regulatory barriers to Chinese vehicle exports in key markets. Leading indicator: God's Eye activation rate—the percentage of BYD owners who actively use the system tells you whether the data monsoon is real or theoretical.*

The Stack Integrators (Huawei, Momenta, Didi): *Moat is OEM integration depth and switching costs. Dependency is OEM's willingness to outsource autonomy rather than build in-house. Failure mode: major OEMs (Toyota, VW) reverse course and insource, collapsing the licensing model. Leading indicator: new OEM design wins per quarter—each win deepens the moat and extends the revenue tail by three to five years.*

When you invest in Waymo (through Alphabet), you are betting on one company in one archetype in one country, constrained by one regulatory patchwork, dependent on one vehicle platform at $75,000–175,000. When you invest in the Chinese AV ecosystem, you are betting on four archetypes operating as a system, coordinated by a unified regulatory framework, supplied by the world's cheapest and most scalable sensor manufacturer, deploying across the world's largest automotive market with 85 percent consumer acceptance, and expanding internationally into every market the BIS rule has not closed. The American bet is a bet on a company. The Chinese bet is a bet on a civilization.

Chapter 8 will look beneath the canopy—at the infrastructure that feeds it, the vehicle-road-cloud integration that gives it a nervous system, and the civilizational architecture that separates China's "smart road, smart car" from America's "dumb road, smart car"—and price the difference.

Evidence Anchors

Baidu Q2 (2025). Earnings Call; Apollo Go Baidu World Conference (November 2025); CNBC (November 3, 2025) • Pony.ai Q3 2025 Financials; NASDAQ/HKEX Dual Listing (November 2024/2025) • WeRide Q3 2025 Financials; Abu Dhabi Uber Launch (November 2025); HK Prospectus (October 2025) • BYD God's Eye Launch (February 10, 2025): Fortune Asia, CnEVPost, CarnewsChina • XPeng VLA 2.0 / FastDriveVLA (AAAI, 2026); Turing chip specifications; VW partnership • Huawei ADS 4.0: 1M+ vehicles, 4B km; Momenta: 160+ models, $6B valuation • Didi R2 Robotaxi (January 2026): 33 sensors, Orca platform, 74% cost reduction • Hesai: Yole Group Lidar for Automotive 2025; Q3 2025 financials; 1M unit milestone (October 2025) • Luminar Chapter 11 filing (December 2025): Ouster Q3 2025 shipments

---

CHAPTER 8

The Nervous System and the Neuron

China's Vehicle-Road-Cloud Integration vs. America's Smart Car, Dumb Road

The canal does not carry water for one field. It carries water for every field it passes.

— Kerala irrigation proverb

In the rice paddies of Kuttanad, irrigation is not a private investment. The canals that bring monsoon water to the fields are shared infrastructure—built by the community, maintained by collective labor, serving every farmer whose land borders the channel. The alternative is for each farmer to dig their own well. Some farmers can afford deep wells. Most cannot. The deep-well farmers harvest abundantly; the rest watch their paddies crack in the sun. The canal system costs more to build than any single well. However, it makes *every* field productive—and the cumulative harvest dwarfs anything the well-farmers can achieve alone.

China is building the canal. America is digging wells.

This is the chapter's thesis, and it rests on a distinction that will determine who wins the trillion-dollar autonomous-vehicle race: the difference between a **nervous system** and a **neuron**. America's approach to autonomous driving places all intelligence in the vehicle—each car a self-contained neuron, carrying $175,000 of redundant sensors to navigate roads that offer nothing in return. China's approach distributes intelligence across a system—vehicles, roads, cloud platforms, 5G networks, high-definition maps, and cybersecurity protocols functioning as an integrated nervous system, where perception is shared, computation is offloaded, and the cost of intelligence is amortized across every vehicle that passes. The American neuron is brilliant. The Chinese nervous system is cheaper. Moreover, cheaper, deployed at scale across the world's largest automotive market, is how you win.

Consider two intersections. The first is in Beijing's Yizhuang demonstration zone: a four-way junction equipped with LiDAR, millimeter-wave radar, cameras, and an edge-computing unit that fuses all sensor data within 200 milliseconds and broadcasts it to every vehicle within range. A Baidu Apollo Go robotaxi approaches the intersection. Before it arrives, the road has already told it: there is a delivery scooter in the blind spot behind the parked truck, a pedestrian stepping off the curb on the far side, and the traffic signal will turn red in eight seconds. The robotaxi's onboard sensors confirm what the road already knows. Redundancy is shared. Perception is cooperative. The vehicle does not need to see everything, because the road sees what it cannot.

The second intersection is in San Francisco's Mission District. A Waymo Jaguar I-PACE approaches, bristling with twenty-nine cameras, six LiDAR units, and a radar suite that costs more than most Americans' houses. The road offers nothing—no data, no warning, no cooperative perception. The vehicle must perceive everything itself, because the infrastructure was designed in 1956 and has not been upgraded to communicate with anything more sophisticated than a timer-controlled traffic light. The Waymo vehicle is a marvel of engineering, carrying $175,000 in sensors to compensate for roads that provide no intelligence. It is a deep well, brilliantly dug, on a farm that has no canal.

8.1 The Architecture: Six Elements, One System

The official Chinese term *chē lù yún yītǐhuà* (车路云一体化) translates as "Vehicle-Road-Cloud Integration"—a three-element phrase that understates a six-element reality. MIIT guidance documents for pilot cities define the technical framework as: **vehicle** (carrying C-V2X on-board units and automated driving systems), **road** (equipped with intelligent roadside infrastructure—RSUs, LiDAR, cameras, radar, and edge computing at intersections), **cloud** (hosting data fusion, collaborative decision-making, and traffic management platforms), **network** (5G and LTE-V2X communications), **map** (high-definition mapping and Beidou positioning), and **safety** (encrypted communications, certificate management, cybersecurity protocols). Every element is load-bearing. Every element is government-coordinated. Moreover, the integration between them—the recognition that a road that talks to a vehicle reduces what the vehicle must carry, while a cloud that trains on data from millions of vehicles improves what the road can see—is the architectural principle that separates a nervous system from a collection of neurons.

The standardization effort is enormous: by September 2024, China's National Technical Committee of Auto Standardization had published 70 standards, conducted 40 validation tests, and embedded C-V2X into China's vehicle safety rating system (C-NCAP 2024)—creating a market pull for OEM adoption that America's voluntary approach cannot match. MIIT allocated the 5905–5925 MHz band for C-V2X direct communication in 2018—a clean, uncontested spectrum decision that contrasts starkly with what happened on the other side of the Pacific. However, that is a story for Section 8.3.

8.2 Twenty Pilot Cities and an $84 Billion Investment Wave

On July 3, 2024, five Chinese ministries jointly designated 20 cities as Vehicle-Road-Cloud Integration pilot zones. The geographic breadth is deliberate: cold-weather northeast cities (Changchun, Shenyang), mining regions (Ordos), megacities (Beijing, Shanghai, Guangzhou, Shenzhen), and tourist corridors (Hainan). The pilot period runs from 2024 to 2026, with plans to expand to 50 cities by 2026.

The investment scale requires a moment of silence. Industry estimates place cumulative planned and approved project budgets at over 600 billion yuan ($84.3 billion) by the end of 2024. The city-level commitments are staggering—and they read less like municipal budgets than like the infrastructure equivalent of an arms race in which the weapons are concrete, fiber optics, and edge-computing stations: Wuhan, $2.34 billion—covering a unified ICV service platform, 15,000 smart parking spaces, and smart road renovation. Beijing, $1.4 billion—covering 6,050 intersections across 2,324 square kilometers. Changchun, $12.7 billion in three-year infrastructure in partnership with FAW Group. Shanghai, $32.4 billion in new ICV projects. Nanjing, an intelligent upgrade of 3,700 intersections by 2026. This is not venture capital. This is not a research grant. This is the state treating roads as infrastructure, the way the Interstate Highway System treated roads—except this time, the roads have eyes, ears, and the computational capacity to think.

Funding flows through multiple channels: ultra-long-term special treasury bonds (central government, capped at 15 percent of project cost), local government special bonds (the primary vehicle), and SOE self-funding. The central government allocated roughly 100 billion yuan ($14 billion) via ultra-long-term bonds in 2024 alone. The China Society of Automotive Engineers projects that the total ICV ecosystem will reach 2.58 trillion yuan by 2030 and that a full national buildout will cost 2.7 trillion yuan ($376 billion)—comparable to China's high-speed rail investment. If that comparison does not register, consider: China's high-speed rail network, at 45,000 kilometers, is longer than the rest of the world's combined. When China builds infrastructure at this scale, the world's experience suggests it finishes the job.

As of mid-2025, deployment figures confirm the ambition: 35,000 kilometers of test and demonstration roads are open nationwide, 11,000 RSUs are deployed across pilot cities, and over 3 million vehicles are fitted with 5G and C-V2X technology. In 2024, approximately 500,000 Chinese passenger cars were shipped with factory-installed C-V2X—a 2.21 percent assembly rate projected to reach 8 percent by 2028. By contrast, the United States received its first FCC-certified C-V2X roadside unit in January 2026. The gap is not six years. It is a geological epoch in technology time.

8.3 How the FCC Handed China a Six-Year Head Start

This section tells the story of how the United States' own regulatory agency, through a single spectrum decision, gifted China a lead in vehicle-to-everything infrastructure that may never be closed. It is, in the tradition of this book's satirical register, a story so absurd that the writers' room of Veep would reject it for being too on the nose.

In 1999, the FCC reserved 75 MHz of spectrum in the 5.9 GHz band exclusively for transportation safety—the radio frequencies that would enable vehicles to communicate with roads, other vehicles, and pedestrians. For twenty years, this spectrum sat waiting for V2X technology to mature. Then, on November 18, 2020, FCC Chairman Ajit Pai decided the band had been "underused" and reallocated the lower 45 MHz to unlicensed Wi-Fi. The remaining 30 MHz was retained for transportation, with a mandated switch from the older DSRC standard to C-V2X technology.

The "underuse" argument deserves a moment of sustained incredulity. After all, it is the regulatory equivalent of demolishing a hospital because not enough people are currently sick. The spectrum was reserved for a technology that was still maturing—that was, by design, the entire point of reserving it. Declaring it underused was akin to criticizing a savings account for not generating sufficient spending. The spectrum was infrastructure-in-waiting. The FCC converted it to infrastructure-for-streaming. To put it in terms the American consumer might understand: the FCC reallocated the spectrum America needed for its roads to talk to its cars so that America's cars could more efficiently stream *The Office* in higher resolution from their driveways. Somewhere in Shenzhen, an MIIT official read the ruling, set down his tea, and permitted himself a smile that has not yet faded.

The opposition was nearly universal. The US Department of Transportation argued V2X could save lives and that reallocation would cause harmful interference, citing over $800 billion in annual crash costs. ITS America's CEO called it "reckless." The American Association of State Highway and Transportation Officials opposed it. All 50 state DOTs opposed it. The National Transportation Safety Board opposed it. NXP Semiconductors opposed it, citing a billion-dollar prior investment. The Motor and Equipment Manufacturers Association opposed it, noting the automotive industry had committed to deploying 5 million ITS radios. The American Trucking Associations opposed it. A more comprehensive coalition of opposition would be difficult to assemble outside of a war. The D.C. Circuit upheld the ruling unanimously in August 2022. The spectrum was gone.

The regulatory aftermath was devastating. Because the original FCC rules were DSRC-based, C-V2X operations required individual waivers—creating years of uncertainty. Toyota halted its V2X deployment plans. OEMs delayed. Infrastructure operators refused to install roadside units without OEM commitment. Final C-V2X rules were not adopted until November 21, 2024. The first FCC-certified C-V2X roadside unit arrived in January 2026—nearly eight years after China's MIIT cleanly allocated spectrum and Chinese companies began commercial deployment.

The irony is architectural. Chairman Pai argued the spectrum had been "underused." By 2026, China's use of equivalent spectrum is so extensive that 11,000 roadside units are broadcasting cooperative perception data across 35,000 kilometers of roads to 3 million equipped vehicles. America's spectrum was not underused. It was underfunded, undercoordinated, and then withdrawn. The FCC's decision was not merely a regulatory error. It was the single most consequential act of unforced V2X self-sabotage in the history of American transportation policy. China's MIIT allocated spectrum. America's FCC allocated spectrum to Wi-Fi. One decision built a nervous system. The other built faster downloads at Starbucks.

8.4 What the Road Sees That the Car Cannot

The academic literature is clear on the direction, if imprecise on the magnitude: vehicle-to-everything infrastructure materially reduces what each vehicle must carry to achieve equivalent safety. Roadside sensors see around parked trucks, behind buildings, and into blind spots that are fundamentally unsolvable by vehicle-only approaches. Shanghai's citywide sharing of traffic signal phase and timing data eliminates the need for vision-based signal recognition entirely—a simple example of infrastructure offloading vehicle-side computation. Roadside cameras alert vehicles to oncoming traffic 150–200 meters away, within 200 milliseconds. Construction zone warnings, vulnerable-road-user detection, and real-time HD map maintenance are all demonstrably offloadable to infrastructure.

The specific magnitude of hardware reduction varies by deployment context—no single authoritative study quantifies it precisely as "30 percent fewer sensors"—and this chapter will not claim otherwise. However, the direction is unmistakable, and the economic logic is powerful: offloading perception tasks from the vehicle to the road reduces the sensor stack every vehicle must carry. In a fleet of 10,000 vehicles, that reduction compounds. In a fleet of 3 million C-V2X-equipped vehicles, it transforms the entire cost structure of autonomous deployment.

For the investor, the arithmetic is as follows. A smart intersection with full sensor coverage and edge computing costs approximately $69,000–139,000. If 10,000 vehicles pass daily over a 10-year lifespan, the per-vehicle-passage cost is fractions of a cent. Meanwhile, each vehicle in a self-reliant fleet carries its own redundant sensing—Waymo's platform at $175,000, Baidu's RT6 at $28,300. The American model duplicates perception in every car. The Chinese model permeates every road. One is a well for every farmer. The other is a canal for every field. The canal costs more to build. The canal makes every field productive. Moreover, the cumulative harvest—measured in cost per autonomous mile—favors the canal by an order of magnitude as fleet size grows. The investor who models only per-vehicle economics is modelling the well. The investor who models system-level economics is modelling the canal. They will arrive at different valuations, and only one will be correct.

8.5 Shanghai's Digital Twin: A City Cloned for Autonomous Driving

In the Theyyam tradition, the deity does not visit the temple. The deity *becomes* the temple—inhabiting the performer, the space, and the ritual —until the boundary between representation and reality dissolves. Shanghai has done something analogous with its infrastructure. It has not merely mapped itself for autonomous vehicles. It has cloned itself.

The Beijing-based company 51World created a complete virtual replica of Shanghai in Unreal Engine—all 3,750 square kilometers—with over 20 landmark structures individually modelled and the remainder algorithmically generated from satellite, drone, and sensor data. The companion platform, 51Sim-One, is described as the world's first L3–L4 autonomous driving simulation platform, with partners including BMW, Daimler, and Audi. On December 31, 2024, Shanghai launched a high-level autonomous driving pilot zone featuring a closed-loop data service toolchain—collection, cleansing, labelling, testing, application—that integrates citywide vehicle-collected training data with real-time roadside sensor data to create virtual dataset segments through world models for full-scenario simulation. A fleet of 100 data-collecting vehicles, targeting 500, aims to generate 10 million driving clips annually.

Shanghai's Jiading district, home to the first National ICV Pilot Demonstration Zone since 2016, has opened its entire road network—1,117 kilometers of roads with approximately 9,100 testing scenarios, 300 smart intersections, and 356 kilometers of high-precision road network. The district has accumulated 10.79 million kilometers of autonomous driving distance, making it the leader in China. Shanghai was also the first Chinese megacity to share citywide traffic signal phase and timing data directly with vehicles, thereby eliminating the need for onboard camera-based signal recognition. The city has cloned itself, and the clone is learning to drive.

8.6 America's V2X Void

The scale gap between US and Chinese V2X deployment is now a chasm. The US has a low number of RSUs scattered across state-level pilot programs, near-zero OEM mass production of V2X-equipped vehicles for the domestic market, and $60 million in federal V2X grants awarded in June 2024 to three projects—Arizona's 750-RSU deployment in Phoenix, Texas A&M's Houston-area project, and Utah's three-state Connected West Project. ITS America's industry proposal calls for equipping 250,000 of America's 330,000 signalized intersections over 10 years at an estimated cost of $6.5 billion—less than the budget of a single Chinese pilot city.

The USDOT released its National V2X Deployment Plan in August 2024, targeting 50 percent coverage of the National Highway System by 2029–2031—but the plan is aspirational and legally non-enforceable. Structural factors explain the divergence: the US fragments authority across the FCC (spectrum), NHTSA (vehicle safety), FHWA (highway infrastructure), and thousands of state and local DOTs—with no single entity capable of coordinating a national rollout. NHTSA never finalized its proposed V2X mandate for vehicles. The USDOT has identified a 27,000-person shortfall in engineers qualified for V2X deployment. China coordinates through a 20-plus-ministry committee under MIIT's leadership, issues binding policy directives, and funds deployment through sovereign bonds. The result: China's 2018 spectrum allocation enabled commercial deployment that same year. America's 2020 spectrum disruption will not produce its first certified hardware until 2026.

Important tensions exist within the Chinese framework, and the *ullil kaanal* demands they be named. A revealing quote from a Beijing Yizhuang insider captures the political economy: "Most automakers are very hesitant to participate... they do not want their investors to know that their AVs depend on anything other than the vehicle; they tell investors it is smart enough to drive on its own." Pause on this, because it is the chapter's most important revelation—and it applies to both sides of the Pacific. The American AV industry's entire valuation premise rests on the vehicle-as-neuron model: each car a self-sufficient intelligence, needing nothing from the road. To admit that roads *could* contribute intelligence is to admit that the $175,000 sensor stack is partially redundant—and redundancy, in a $126 billion valuation, is not a feature. It is a write-down. The reluctance to acknowledge infrastructure dependence is not unique to China or the United States. It is structural: every company that has told its investors "our car drives itself" has a financial incentive to ensure the road never gets a word in edgewise.

The commercial sustainability of government-led infrastructure investment remains uncertain, with Caixin, Yicai, and multiple Chinese industry observers noting unclear business models and strained local fiscal budgets. The full national buildout—2.7 trillion yuan for 5.4 million kilometers of roads—is achievable but massive even by Chinese infrastructure standards. The nervous system is being built. Whether it can sustain itself beyond government subsidies, extend beyond pilot zones, and meet safety requirements at a national scale remains an open question.

A Nervous System vs. Individual Neurons

The US-China V2X divergence goes beyond a technology gap—it reflects fundamentally different theories of how autonomous mobility should be organized. America defaulted to the neuron model: each vehicle a self-contained intelligence, carrying redundant sensors to navigate unchanged infrastructure. China is building the nervous system model: distributed perception embedded in roads and intersections, coordinated through cloud platforms, reducing what each vehicle must carry.

China: 11,000 RSUs, 35,000 kilometers of instrumented roads, 3 million C-V2X vehicles, 20 pilot cities expanding to 50, $84 billion in committed investment, a city that has cloned itself in Unreal Engine. United States: a low thousand of RSUs, $60 million in federal grants, its first certified C-

V2X hardware arriving in January 2026, and an aspirational plan targeting 50 percent intersection coverage by 2031. The structural factors—fragmented US governance, the FCC's spectrum disruption, absence of a vehicle mandate, and market-driven rather than state-directed deployment—are not easily reversed.

Whether China's vehicle-road-cloud approach ultimately proves superior depends on execution. However, the strategic asymmetry is already locked in. China is building an $84 billion infrastructure platform that, if successful, will make every vehicle on its roads cheaper and more capable—a shared cognitive resource that no amount of individual vehicle intelligence can replicate. The canal has been dug. The water is flowing. The question is not whether the fields will be irrigated. It is whether America's deep-well farmers can harvest enough, fast enough, to compete with a system that irrigates every field at once.

For the investor, the nervous-system model creates a different cost curve than the neuron model. Every RSU deployed reduces the marginal cost of the next autonomous vehicle on that road. Every C-V2X vehicle deployed increases the data flowing to the cloud that trains the next generation of roadside algorithms. This is a network effect—the same force that made Google, Facebook, and Amazon unstoppable—applied to physical infrastructure. America's AV companies are pricing individual vehicle intelligence. China's AV ecosystem is pricing system-level intelligence. The investor who understands the difference will make different bets than the investor who does not.

Chapter 9 will examine the supply chain that feeds the nervous system—the LiDAR cost curve that dropped 1,000-fold in a decade, the compute chips designed in Shenzhen to run the algorithms, and the manufacturing base that produces autonomous-capable vehicles at prices the American industry cannot approach. The canal has been dug. Now we examine what grows.

Evidence Anchors

MIIT Vehicle-Road-Cloud Integration Pilot Cities Circular (工信部联装函〔2024〕181号, July 2024) • Caixin Global: "$84 billion industry estimate" (November 2024) • Wuhan 17B yuan commitment (June 2024); Beijing 9.9.4B yuan (mid-2024); Shanghai 32.4B yuan ICV projects • NTCAS SC34: 70 standards, 38 studies (September 2024); C-NCAP 2024 C-V2X integration • FCC First Report and Order, ET Docket No. 19-138 (November 18, 2020); D.C. Circuit ruling (August 2022); Second Report and Order (November 21, 2024) • USDOT National V2X Deployment Plan "Saving Lives with Connectivity" (August 2024) • ITS America: 250,000 intersections / $6.5B proposal • 51World Shanghai digital twin; Jiading 10.79M km • SAE International Journal (August 2025): cooperative perception via monocular cameras • IEEE Survey: Infrastructure Assisted Autonomous Driving (2025) • Wiley Journal of Advanced Transportation: Beijing deployment analysis (2024)

CHAPTER 9

The Supply Chain Moat

When Hardware Becomes a Weapon

He who controls the granaries controls the kingdom.

— Kautilya, *Arthashastra* (c. 300 BCE)

There is a passage in the *Arthashastra*—Kautilya's ancient treatise on statecraft, the text that taught Indian kings how to build empires while their Greek contemporaries were still debating the Forms— that advises: *"He who controls the granaries controls the kingdom."* In the autonomous vehicle industry, the granaries are the supply chains, and China controls them with a thoroughness that would make Chandragupta Maurya weep tears of proud recognition.

China's autonomous vehicle cost advantage stems not from any single innovation but from an integrated supply chain ecosystem that reduces costs at every layer—sensors, compute, vehicle platforms, and manufacturing labor—with the relentless logic of water finding the lowest point. A Theyyam performer does not dazzle through the brilliance of a single ornament but through the total ensemble: the headgear, the face paint, the costume, the drumming, the ritual fire, the centuries of accumulated knowledge that bind the performer to the divine. Remove one element, and you still have spectacle. However, when every element aligns, you have something beyond human—an *Ullil Kaanal*, an "inner seeing," that transcends the sum of its parts. China's supply chain moat operates on the same principle: total integration, where the whole is so much greater than the parts that competitors attempting to match any single element fundamentally misunderstand what they are competing against.

The transformation is best captured in the LiDAR cost curve—the single most dramatic illustration of how a manufacturing civilization turns exotic technology into a commodity input and, in the process, buries the Western companies that invented the damn thing.

9.1 The LiDAR Cost Curve: From Laboratory Jewel to Industrial Commodity

Let us begin with a number that should be tattooed on the forehead of every Western automotive executive: **$150,000.** That was the approximate cost of a Velodyne HDL-64E spinning LiDAR unit in 2012—the sensor that sat atop Google's first self-driving Prius like a mechanical tiara, rotating sixty-four laser beams to paint the world in three-dimensional point clouds. It was exquisite technology. It was also, per unit, more expensive than the car it was bolted to.

Now consider another number: **$150.** That is the approximate unit cost of a RoboSense MX solid-state LiDAR sensor in 2025: same core function—three-dimensional environmental perception via time-of-flight laser ranging. One-thousandth the price. This is not Moore's Law. Moore's Law, at its most aggressive doubling cycle, would have reduced the price by roughly 32x over thirteen years. The LiDAR cost curve has achieved **1,000x** compression in the same period. This is what happens when a manufacturing civilization applies the full weight of its industrial logic to a sensor that the rest of the world still treats as a specialty component.

The LiDAR Cost Curve (2012–2025): 2012: $150,000 (Velodyne HDL-64E, mechanical spinning) → 2015: $75,000 (Velodyne VLP-16 "Puck," smaller form factor) → 2020: $10,000+ (first solid-state designs; Chinese entrants scale) → 2022: $2,000 (Hesai, RoboSense achieve mass volume) → 2023: $800 (chipification accelerates; ASIC integration) → 2024: $400 (ADAS deployments drive scale; Chinese firms hold ~89% market share) → 2025: <$200 (RoboSense MX enables mass-market; Hesai ATX at half AT128 cost)

Hesai's company profile was detailed in Chapter 7, where we examined market structure—who dominates, and by how much. Here, we examine the force that Hesai rides—not the company, but the cost dynamics that make its dominance structurally irreversible. Chinese firms now dominate the global automotive LiDAR supply market with the quiet totality of a monsoon season—you can debate whether it should have happened, but you cannot debate that it has. The top four Chinese manufacturers account for approximately 89 percent of the global automotive LiDAR market. Hesai became the first LiDAR company worldwide to surpass 1 million units in annual production. Its Gen4 chip architecture introduced 3D stacking technology, enabling single-board integration of 512 channels. RoboSense sold 544,200 units in 2024, with its MX-series sensors using purpose-built ASICs rather than expensive FPGAs to keep unit costs below $200. The dominance is as complete as it is unremarked upon in Western financial commentary.

Meanwhile, on the other side of the Pacific, on December 15, 2025, the epitaph was delivered. **Luminar Technologies filed for Chapter 11 bankruptcy protection**—the once-lionized American LiDAR pioneer, valued at $3.4 billion during its 2020 SPAC debut, brought low by the slow-motion collapse of its Volvo partnership, an SEC investigation, serial executive departures, and, most damningly, an inability to achieve the manufacturing scale that its Chinese competitors had mastered years earlier. Luminar's bankruptcy filings disclosed assets of $100–500 million against liabilities of $500 million–$1 billion. The company that was supposed to make LiDAR standard on every Volvo could not survive long enough to see its sensors reach mass production. Hesai reported record profits five weeks before Luminar filed for Chapter 11. The symmetry is too perfect for fiction. It is not a coincidence. It is an epitaph.

Kautilya's granary, the first: the grain is LiDAR. China controls 89 percent of the harvest. The Western granary is empty, and the last Western farmer has just declared bankruptcy.

9.2 Vehicle-Level Cost Comparisons: The Arithmetic of Inevitability

If the LiDAR cost curve is the opening movement, vehicle-level cost comparisons are the full symphony—and the music is playing in a key that Western automotive executives cannot comfortably hear.

The Investor's Cost Table: Autonomous Vehicle Platform Comparison (2025–2026)

Waymo (Zeekr/Jaguar I-PACE): $150,000–$175,000. Purpose-built, maximum sensor redundancy; 29 cameras, 6 LiDARs, radar suite; proprietary compute.

Baidu Apollo RT6: ~$28,300. Purpose-built robotaxi; 38–40 sensors; 1,200 TOPS compute; detachable steering wheel.

Didi R2 (with GAC Aion): 74% cost reduction vs. Gen-1. 33-sensor suite; 2,000+ TOPS Orca platform; 24/7 driverless design.

Pony.ai Gen-7 ADK: 70% BOM reduction vs. Gen-6. 100% automotive-grade components; 10-year/600K-km design life; unit economics breakeven achieved.

WeRide (OEM platforms): ~$40,000. Multi-domain: robotaxi, robobus, robovan, robosweeper.

BYD Seagull + God's Eye C: ~$9,550 (total vehicle). ~$385 incremental ADAS hardware cost; L2+ across 21 models.

Study this table as you would study a battlefield map, because that is what it is. Waymo at $175,000. Baidu at $28,000. BYD at $9,550. One of these numbers is not like the others. One of these numbers will win. When LiDAR costs $150 rather than $75,000 and a purpose-built robotaxi costs $28,000 rather than $175,000, the calculus for deploying autonomy across millions of vehicles fundamentally changes. Waymo's vehicle costs roughly 6x what Baidu's Apollo RT6 costs. This is not a rounding error. This is the difference between a fleet of 2,500 vehicles and a fleet of 15,000 at the same capital outlay. When the break-even utilization requirement falls by 84 percent, the question shifts from 'can we afford to deploy?' to 'can we afford not to?'

The BYD Seagull entry at the bottom of the table deserves special attention, because it is not merely a data point—it is a category error made visible. This is a complete, road-legal electric vehicle with L2+ autonomous driving capability—the *entire car*—for $9,550. The incremental cost of the God's Eye C ADAS hardware package is approximately $385. Three hundred and eighty-five dollars. For context, a single Luminar Iris sensor—the flagship product of the company that just filed for bankruptcy—was priced at approximately $1,000 per unit at volume, and that is just one component of a much larger perception stack. BYD's entire autonomy hardware package costs less than a single unit of the sensor that bankrupted Luminar. The analyst who files BYD under "budget automaker" and Luminar under "innovation" has confused the product's price with the value of the strategy.

Operating costs in China are correspondingly compressed: Baidu's Apollo Go fares run 30 percent cheaper than Tier-1 city taxis, with base fares as low as $0.55 per ride. Industry estimates project that autonomous ride costs will fall to $0.20–0.40 per mile by 2030. At those price points, autonomous mobility becomes cheaper than car ownership for most urban consumers—a threshold that, once crossed, cannot be uncrossed. The river does not flow uphill.

Kautilya's granary, the second: the vehicle platform is the irrigation system. China's EV manufacturing base—BYD alone at 4.3 million vehicles annually—makes the canal that Chapter 8 described. The water (autonomy) flows cheaply because the canal (manufacturing) was already built for another purpose (electrification). America has no canal. It digs wells, one $175,000 vehicle at a time.

9.3 The Chip War Within the AV War

If LiDAR is the eye and the vehicle platform is the body, compute silicon is the brain—and it is here that the American policy establishment has chosen to fight its most consequential battle. The logic of semiconductor export controls is straightforward: deny China access to advanced AI chips, and you deny its AV industry the computational horsepower needed for autonomous driving inference. The logic is clean. The reality is a graduate seminar in unintended consequences.

When the Biden administration tightened semiconductor export restrictions in October 2022 and again in October 2023, the explicit objective was to prevent Chinese access to chips with performance above a specified threshold for AI training and inference. The controls achieved their immediate tactical objective: they made it more difficult and more expensive for Chinese firms to obtain NVIDIA A100 and H100 GPUs. What the controls did *not* do was make China abandon the race. Instead, they accelerated domestic substitution with a ferocity that even the architects of the controls may not have anticipated. Washington spent a decade designing export controls. Beijing spent a decade designing around them. The American strategy was a wall. The Chinese strategy was water.

The response is captured in a Chinese phrase that deserves a place in every investor's lexicon: 以软补硬 (*yǐ ruǎn bǔ yìng*)—"using software to supplement hardware." Algorithmic innovation to overcome material constraints. This is the same intellectual instinct that produced DeepSeek's MLA architecture, which delivered frontier AI performance with one-eleventh the training compute of Meta's Llama. As RAND's *Full Stack* report observed, Chinese policymakers responded to export controls by pursuing an "autonomously controllable" AI hardware and software ecosystem—Xi Jinping himself emphasized "self-reliance" at an April 2025 Politburo meeting on AI.

Three Chinese players have emerged as the primary beneficiaries of this forced self-reliance. **Horizon Robotics** is China's dominant automotive AI chip company: over 40 percent of the Chinese OEM ADAS market, partnerships with more than 40 global OEMs, including all of China's top ten automakers, design wins across 400 vehicle models, and cumulative shipments surpassing 10 million units in 2025—the first Chinese smart driving chip company to reach this milestone. Its flagship Journey 6P delivers 560 TOPS on TSMC's 7nm process. In October 2024, Hong Kong's IPO valued it at over $11 billion. **Huawei's Ascend series** represents the most direct response to the NVIDIA embargo—the Ascend 910C delivers approximately 60 percent of the H100's inference performance, a gap that algorithmic optimization can partially bridge, and its significance lies not in matching NVIDIA benchmark-for-benchmark but in existing at all. When an embargo is designed to create absence, the mere fact of presence is a strategic statement. **XPeng's Turing chip** may be the most provocative: 2,250 TOPS of computing power—roughly three times the NVIDIA Orin that anchors most Western AV compute stacks. Volkswagen has signed on as Turing's first external customer, marking the first deployment of a Chinese autonomous-driving chip in non-Chinese-brand vehicles. The student has begun to teach. The tributary has become the river.

The *ullil kaanal* demands, here as in Chapter 8's V2X caveat, that genuine uncertainty be named alongside genuine momentum. The direction of China's chip self-sufficiency is unmistakable; the timeline is not. Horizon's Journey 6P benchmarks have not been independently verified at production scale by any third-party organization equivalent to MLPerf or SPEC. Huawei's Ascend 910C performance figures are self-reported and have not been subjected to the kind of rigorous, adversarial benchmarking that NVIDIA's products routinely undergo. XPeng's 2,250 TOPS claim for the Turing chip is an architectural specification, not a demonstrated real-world inference throughput—and the gap between specification and deployed performance has swallowed more than one chip company's ambitions. The automotive chip sector's reliance on mature-node fabrication (14nm–28nm) is real and commercially significant, but the most demanding AV inference tasks— real-time VLA processing at highway speeds, multi-modal sensor fusion under adversarial conditions—may yet require sub-7nm capability that Chinese foundries cannot currently deliver at yield rates competitive with TSMC. The investor who dismisses China's chip progress is ignoring 10 million shipped units. The investor who assumes the timeline is fixed ignores the verification gap. Both errors cost money; the second costs more slowly, which makes it more dangerous.

The aggregate trajectory is unmistakable. China's government has instructed domestic automakers to increase local chip procurement to 20–25 percent by 2025, with industry targets of 100 percent domestic chip content by 2027. Critically, the automotive chip sector does not require cutting-edge sub-7nm fabrication for most functions—MCUs, power management ICs, and sensor fusion processors operate comfortably at 14nm–28nm nodes, where Chinese foundries such as SMIC are fully competitive. Export controls designed to constrain China's AI capabilities have created market conditions for a parallel Chinese semiconductor ecosystem that, within a decade, may not need American chips at all—at least not for automotive applications, the largest-volume market. *For the investor, the timeline is the trade signal: 2025–2027 is the substitution window during which Chinese chip companies capture domestic market share at accelerating rates. The investor who waits for complete self-sufficiency to be announced has missed the inflection. The granary is already being restocked.*

Kautilya's granary, the third: the seed stock is computed silicon. When the adversary burns the trade routes, you do not mourn the lost caravans. You breed your own seed. Horizon Robotics, Huawei Ascend, and XPeng Turing are the new seed stock—bred under embargo conditions, optimized for Chinese soil, and already being exported to farmers in Stuttgart, Wolfsburg, and Tokyo.

9.4 The Kautilya Principle: He Who Controls the Granaries

To understand the full architecture of China's supply chain moat, it is necessary to see it not as a collection of individual advantages—cheaper LiDAR here, cheaper chips there—but as an integrated system in which each layer reinforces every other. This is the Kautilya Principle applied to industrial strategy: control of the granary is not merely about possessing grain. It is about controlling the land, irrigation, storage, roads to market, and the marketplace itself.

Consider the full vertical integration at work in a Chinese AV deployment. The **sensor layer** is domestically supplied: Hesai and RoboSense for LiDAR (89% global market share), and Chinese suppliers for cameras, radar, and ultrasonics. Unit costs are a fraction of Western equivalents. The **compute layer** is rapidly localizing: Horizon Robotics for ADAS inference (10 million chips shipped), Huawei Ascend for high-performance AI, XPeng Turing for next-generation VLA architectures. The **vehicle platform layer** leverages the world's largest EV manufacturing base: BYD alone delivered over 4.6 million vehicles in 2025, with an incremental ADAS hardware cost of $385 per vehicle. The **infrastructure layer**—documented in Chapter 8—includes the Vehicle-Road-Cloud integration system, which reduces per-vehicle sensor requirements. Moreover, the **data layer** is the final and perhaps most decisive granary. BYD alone generates 160 million kilometers of driving data every day from its 2.3 million God's Eye-equipped vehicles. That is roughly three times

Waymo's *total accumulated autonomous miles since inception*—generated every single day, from vehicles operating in the chaotic, unpredictable, construction-zone-and-jaywalker-infested crucible of Chinese urban traffic.

Each layer feeds the others. Cheap sensors enable cheap vehicles. Cheap vehicles enable mass deployment. Mass deployment generates data. Data improves algorithms. Improved algorithms reduce the computational cost per inference cycle. Lower compute requirements enable cheaper chips. Cheaper chips enable cheaper vehicles. The cycle continues, accelerating with each revolution like a Theyyam dancer's whirling crescendo—each orbit faster and more precise than the last, building toward the moment of divine possession when the mortal performer becomes something else entirely.

Western competitors face a structural bind. They cannot replicate the sensor cost advantage without the manufacturing volume. They cannot achieve the manufacturing volume without the vehicle platform scale. They cannot achieve the platform scale without the EV manufacturing ecosystem. They cannot build the EV manufacturing ecosystem without the battery supply chain. Moreover, they cannot match the battery supply chain without mineral-processing infrastructure. At every layer, the granary is spoken for.

9.5 The DeepSeek Moment: What the West Has Not Yet Internalized

The term "DeepSeek moment" has entered the lexicon of technology competition as shorthand for the instant when an established player realizes that its cost advantage was never an advantage at all— merely a reflection of its own inefficiency. DeepSeek did not outspend OpenAI to beat it. It beat OpenAI by proving that the same outcome could be achieved at a fraction of the cost. The competitive moat evaporated not because someone built a bigger castle, but because someone demonstrated that the moat had been dry all along.

The LiDAR cost curve is the AV industry's DeepSeek moment. Hesai's Q3 2025 earnings—$112 million in revenue, 42.1 percent gross margins, $36 million in net income, 441,398 units shipped, projecting 2–3 million units in 2026—did not merely demonstrate Chinese competitiveness. They demonstrated Chinese *profitability* at price points where Western companies could not even achieve breakeven. Hesai's 42.1 percent gross margin at sub-$200 ASPs represents the same structural impossibility that DeepSeek's R1 model represented for OpenAI: proof that the cost floor your competitors operate on is not the same floor you are standing on.

Luminar's bankruptcy filing, arriving exactly five weeks after Hesai's triumphant Q3 report, is the symmetry that fiction would consider too on-the-nose. One company is reporting record profits. Another filing for Chapter 11. Both are making the same fundamental product. The difference is not technology—Luminar's Iris sensor was, by most technical assessments, a competitive device. The difference lies in the ecosystems in which each company operates. Hesai is embedded in a Chinese supply chain that produces sensors at scale for the EV industry, which manufactures millions of vehicles annually. Luminar was dependent on the Western automotive industry, which still treats LiDAR as an optional accessory that can be dropped as a "cost-cutting measure," which is precisely what Volvo did in September 2025, reducing expected Luminar volumes by 90 percent and triggering the chain of events that led to the courthouse.

The RAND Corporation's June 2025 report, *Full Stack: China's Evolving Industrial Policy for AI*, captured the broader pattern: Beijing is deploying industrial policy tools across the entire AI technology stack, from chips to applications, with Chinese AI models closing the performance gap while adoption grows rapidly across sectors. The LiDAR cost curve is merely the sensor-layer expression of this full-stack strategy. The RAND authors note that while most of this growth is driven by innovation at China's private tech firms, state support has helped enhance the ecosystem. Put differently, the state builds irrigation canals, and private farmers grow rice. The harvest belongs to both.

The implication for investors is not subtle. It is a klaxon. The supply chain moat is not a temporary cost advantage that Western firms will naturally erode as they scale. It is a purpose-built, layer-by-layer, component-by-component, policy-by-policy structural feature of an industrial ecosystem developed over the past decade. It is the granary. Moreover, the granary does not change hands easily.

However, the granary's harvest does not stop at the kingdom's borders. Kautilya's genius was not merely in controlling the grain but in controlling the trade routes that carried it to neighboring kingdoms—and in using that trade to extend influence, secure alliances, and reshape the balance of power across the subcontinent. China's AV supply chain moat is now doing the same. The companies documented in Chapter 7, equipped with the cost structures documented in this chapter, backed by the infrastructure documented in Chapter 8, are heading outward—to Abu Dhabi and Riyadh, to London and Zurich, to Singapore and São Paulo—carrying Chinese autonomous-driving technology along Belt and Road corridors that were built for exactly this purpose. Marcus, the fund manager whose US-only TAM model we have tracked since Chapter 4, has not yet modelled these corridors. His Bloomberg terminal shows the kingdom. It does not show the trade routes. Chapter 10 follows the caravans.

As the Theyyam performer knows, the fire does not ask your permission before it becomes divine. It simply transforms. Moreover, by the time the audience realizes what has happened, the human performer is already gone, replaced by something older, more powerful, and entirely beyond their control.

Evidence Anchors

Hesai Group Q3 2025 Earnings Release (November 11, 2025); Hesai HK Dual Listing (2025) • RoboSense 2024 shipments; MX-series ASIC specifications • Luminar Technologies Chapter 11 Bankruptcy Filing (December 15, 2025) • RAND Corporation, "Full Stack: China's Evolving Industrial Policy for AI" (June 2025) • Congressional Research Service, Semiconductor Export Controls reports • Horizon Robotics IPO Prospectus & IAA Mobility 2025; Journey 6P specifications; 10M+ shipment milestone • Huawei Ascend 910C benchmarks; ADS 4.0 deployment data • XPeng AI Day 2025: Turing chip specifications; VW partnership • U.S.-China Economic and Security Review Commission, chip self-sufficiency projections • Nikkei Asia automotive chip sourcing analysis

CHAPTER 10

The Monsoon Spreads

How Closing the American Door Opened Twenty Others

The procession does not stop because one village refuses the deity. It carries the fire to the next.

— Kerala Theyyam tradition

In the Theyyam tradition, the deity's procession is not confined to a single temple. The performer—face painted, headgear ablaze, possessed by the divine—travels between villages, carrying rituals, authority, and transformative fire to new geographies. The procession does not ask permission. It does not negotiate access. It arrives, and the village is changed.

China's autonomous vehicle industry is now in procession. The temple was built in Chapters 6 through 9: the regulatory architecture, the Four Dragons, the nervous system of vehicle-road-cloud integration, and the supply chain moat. Now the deity travels. Moreover, the deity travels because one very large village—the United States of America—slammed the temple door shut.

Call it the guinea pig gambit. America closed its market to Chinese AV technology through the BIS Connected Vehicles Final Rule. In response, Chinese companies did not retreat. They pivoted—to Abu Dhabi and Dubai, to Riyadh and Doha, to London and Zurich, to Singapore and São Paulo—transforming Belt and Road markets into proving grounds for technology effectively barred from the United States. The guinea pigs are thriving. Furthermore, they are breeding.

A January (2026). A McKinsey survey found that 74 percent of automotive executives now predict a dedicated China tech stack—signaling that the industry expects a permanent bifurcation rather than convergence. Three-quarters of the world's automotive leadership has concluded that the future of autonomous driving will not be one technology but two. The procession has begun. The question is no longer whether it will reach the next village but how many villages it will reach before anyone tries to stop it.

10.1 The Wall

The Bureau of Industry and Security published its Connected Vehicles Final Rule on January 16, 2025, with an effective date of March 17, 2025. Chapter 5 documented the rule's full architecture; here, the essential structural points for understanding the global-expansion story that follows.

The rule prohibits the import or sale of connected vehicles that contain software or autonomous driving systems linked to China or Russia, effective for Model Year 2027. Hardware bans follow with Model Year 2030. Critically, the rule includes an explicit prohibition on commercial ADS services—robotaxi operations by Chinese firms are specifically barred, even if the vehicles are manufactured domestically. Penalties reach $368,136 per civil violation. The Trump administration's "America First Trade Policy" executive order directed Commerce to review whether controls should be expanded further.

The wall is real. It is legally enforceable. Moreover, it has produced exactly the strategic response that a student of Kautilya's *Arthashastra* would have predicted: when the adversary blocks one road, the caravan finds twenty others. Between late 2024 and early 2026—precisely as the BIS rule moved from proposal to implementation—Chinese AV companies announced an avalanche of international partnerships: WeRide-Uber across 15 cities, Baidu-Uber in Asia and the Middle East, Baidu-Lyft across Europe, Pony. ai-Uber in the Middle East, Pony.ai-ComfortDelGro in Singapore, Baidu-PostBus in Switzerland. After GM-backed Cruise shut down in late 2024—eliminating the most advanced American competitor in international markets—Chinese companies faced virtually no overseas competition.

The Carnegie Endowment for International Peace warned in January 2025 that "unduly broad restrictions on Chinese companies' access to data and on Chinese software and connected technology in the United States could have adverse unintended consequences: disrupting ordinary commercial trade… or reducing beneficial innovation because U.S. firms are not exposed to competition from Chinese competitors." The warning is precise in its identification of the mechanism: containment without domestic acceleration produces not security but isolation. The BIS rule removed Chinese competition from American roads. It did not replace that competition with American alternatives. The result is not a protected market. It is a stagnant one—and stagnation, in a technology race, is indistinguishable from retreat.

The irony operates at multiple levels. The same American ride-hailing platforms that are prohibited from deploying Chinese AV technology domestically under the BIS rule are actively enabling its global deployment. Uber has more than 18 AV partnerships and has designated WeRide as its largest autonomous driving investment. Lyft's entire European AV strategy depends on Baidu's RT6 vehicles. The American platforms are not competing with Chinese AV companies. They are *carrying* them—across the Gulf, across Europe, across Southeast Asia—like palanquin bearers who have been told they cannot enter the temple but are happy to carry the deity to the next village.

10.2 The Beachhead: The Gulf as Regulatory Laboratory

On February 6, 2026, WeRide and Uber announced the deployment of at least 1,200 robotaxis across Abu Dhabi, Dubai, and Riyadh—the largest commercial commitment of robotaxis in the MENA region—with completion expected by 2027. The cars are Chinese. The platform is American. The regulatory framework was built by Gulf states that saw an opportunity and moved faster than any Western government. The irony is not lost on anyone except, apparently, the Bureau of Industry and Security. What follows is the operational detail of how three Gulf capitals accomplished in eighteen months what Washington has failed to accomplish in nine years—and did so, in a final flourish of absurdity, using American platforms to deploy Chinese vehicles that American law prohibits on American roads.

Abu Dhabi: Ground Zero

Abu Dhabi leads the Gulf beachhead, with more than 120 Level 4 autonomous vehicles operating without safety drivers as of early 2026. The regulatory architecture involves the Integrated Transport Centre, a Regulatory Sandbox under the General Secretariat of the Cabinet, the Ministry of Interior's committee on advanced driving systems, and the Smart and Autonomous Systems Council. In November 2025, ITC issued the first two commercial operating permits for fully driverless robotaxis—one to WeRide/Uber/Tawasul, another to AutoGo/Baidu Apollo.

WeRide's partnership with Uber launched on December 6, 2024, with safety operators aboard. By November 26, 2025, it became Level 4 fully driverless—making Abu Dhabi the first city outside the United States to host fully autonomous rides on the Uber platform. By February 12, 2026, the service covered approximately 70 percent of Abu Dhabi's core areas, from the Sheikh Zayed Grand Mosque to the Corniche. WeRide now operates more than 200 robotaxis in the region—quadrupled from the December 2024 launch—and reports the service is on track to achieve breakeven unit economics. Uber committed an additional $100 million in equity to WeRide, its largest investment in autonomous driving to date.

Baidu's Apollo Go arrived in parallel. In January 2026, it launched a fully autonomous commercial ride-hailing service on Yas Island, completing the journey from initial deployment to fully driverless commercial service in approximately six months. Phased expansion to Reem Island, Al Maryah, and Saadiyat is planned.

Dubai: The 25-Percent Ambition

Dubai's Law No. 9 of 2023 and its executive regulations created the most explicit municipal AV framework in the Middle East, defining six categories of autonomous vehicles, eight licensing conditions, and 14 operator obligations. Dubai's Smart Self-Driving Transport Strategy aims to have 25 percent of all transportation trips be autonomous by 2030. After GM-backed Cruise shut down in late 2024—following $10 billion in cumulative investment, which buys a great deal of autonomous driving in any country except the United States—Dubai rapidly struck deals with all three major Chinese AV companies: WeRide, Baidu, and Pony.ai.

Baidu received Dubai's first permit for fully driverless vehicle trials in January 2026, opening the Apollo Go Park—a 2,000-square-metre operations center at Dubai Science Park, Baidu's first such facility outside China. On February 10, 2026, Apollo Go launched on the Uber platform in Dubai's Jumeirah area. Pony.ai secured a Dubai testing permit in September 2025, aiming to achieve fully driverless commercial operations by 2026.

Saudi Arabia and Qatar

WeRide became the first company to complete Saudi Arabia's Transport General Authority sandbox process, receiving the kingdom's first permit for robotaxi operations in July 2025. WeRide and Uber launched robotaxi rides in Riyadh in October 2025. Beyond robotaxis, WeRide operates robobuses at King Fahad Medical City and deployed the first monetized autonomous sanitation project in the Middle East. The NEOM Investment Fund injected $100 million into Pony.ai in October 2023, establishing a joint venture to develop autonomous driving services within the $500 billion NEOM megaproject—including plans for a local AV manufacturing and R&D facility. In Qatar, Pony.ai partnered with state-owned Mowasalat to begin testing robotaxis on Doha's public roads, adapting to extreme conditions exceeding 45°C.

The Gulf states have, in less than 2 years, built the most advanced regulatory framework for autonomous vehicles outside the United States and China. Moreover, Chinese companies dominate every market. This is not accidental. When the world's largest autonomous-vehicle ecosystem meets the world's most ambitious regulatory sandbox, the outcome is not a pilot program. It is a proving ground—and the technology being proved is Chinese.

10.3 The Infrastructure: The Road and the Rulebook

The procession does not travel on bare ground. It travels on infrastructure that was built—sometimes decades in advance—to carry exactly this cargo.

The Digital Silk Road

The Belt and Road Initiative reached $213.5 billion in engagement in 2025—the highest level since BRI's 2013 launch and a 75 percent increase over 2024. Cumulative engagement now stands at approximately $1.4 trillion across 150 partner countries. The Digital Silk Road, launched in 2015, has channeled more than $17 billion into digital projects, including at least $7 billion in loans and FDI for fiber-optic cable and telecom networks across approximately 80 countries.

The infrastructure stack is vertical and self-reinforcing. Huawei and ZTE together account for 40 percent of the global 5G market revenue. Huawei operates in over 170 countries, built 70 percent of Africa's 4G networks, and offers products 30–40 percent cheaper than Western alternatives. The BeiDou Navigation Satellite System—with 55 satellites providing global coverage and more accurate positioning within the Asia-Pacific region—serves over 1.1 billion users across 200 countries, with over 30 BRI nations having formally adopted the system. Chinese smart city technology has been exported in 398 documented cases across 106 countries.

This infrastructure creates an integrated stack: Chinese 5G networks provide connectivity, BeiDou provides positioning, Chinese smart city platforms manage traffic, and Chinese autonomous vehicles operate on top—all bound together by Chinese technical standards. For countries that have built their digital infrastructure on Chinese technology, adopting Chinese AV platforms becomes the path of least resistance. The road was built before the vehicles. Now the vehicles are arriving.

The Rulebook: ISO 34505 and the Standards Export Strategy

ISO 34505:2025, published on July 7, 2025, establishes the international standard for evaluating autonomous driving test scenarios and generating test cases. Led by project leader Hang Sun of China's Automotive Technology and Research Centre (CATARC), the standard is the capstone of the ISO 3450x series, which China proposed in April 2018 and has led its development. The five-standard suite (ISO 34501 through 34505) effectively provides the global taxonomy and methodology for testing and validating autonomous vehicles. China wrote the foundational documents.

The standards export strategy operates through multiple channels. Under the China Standards 2035 initiative, Beijing has signed 90 bilateral standardization cooperation agreements with 52 countries. As the Clingendael Institute observed, bilateral agreements create long-term interoperability and dependencies, particularly in developing countries that lack the capacity to develop their own standards. China holds a vice-chair position on the UNECE's GRVA working party, thereby influencing the UN regulatory framework. Domestically, China mandates C-V2X communication rather than DSRC, uses its own automation taxonomy (GB/T 40429-2021) rather than SAE J3016, and maintains a parallel standards ecosystem that feeds into its international strategy.

The strategic logic was made explicit by Cui Dongshu, Secretary-General of the China Passenger Car Association: "Having a voice in standards-setting is strategically important as autonomous driving enters a phase of rapid global growth. It will be helpful for Chinese automakers to go global if we gain a certain advantage in standard formulation." When you write the test, you set the curve. When you set the curve, your students perform best. When your students perform best, the world adopts your curriculum. This is not a technology export. It is *epistemic* export—the export of the framework within which all autonomous driving will be evaluated.

10.4 The Caravan: Seven Million Vehicles and a Global Factory Network

China exported 7.098 million vehicles in 2025, up 21.1 percent year-over-year, consolidating its position as the world's largest auto exporter for the third consecutive year. NEV exports reached 2.615 million units—approximately 37 percent of total exports—doubling from the previous year. Within NEVs, BEV exports grew 66.7 percent while PHEVs surged 230 percent, partly because EU countervailing duties apply only to BEVs. The top export markets shifted: Mexico overtook Russia as the largest destination, the UAE surged to third (up 74.3 percent), and BYD jumped from sixth to second among manufacturers with 1.054 million exports.

The global factory network is the caravan's logistics. BYD's Thailand plant at WHA Rayong 36 Industrial Estate—completed in 16 months with 150,000-vehicle annual capacity, employing 6,900 workers (92 percent Thai nationals)—represents the template for Chinese OEM overseas manufacturing. BYD's global footprint now includes operational plants in Thailand and Uzbekistan, with facilities under construction in Brazil (150,000 capacity at a revamped Ford plant), Hungary ($4.6 billion investment), Indonesia ($1 billion), and Cambodia. Chery operates plants in Brazil and facilities across North Africa. CATL and EVE are building battery factories in Hungary and Portugal. A Rhodium Group analysis found that for the first time since records began in 2014, the Chinese EV supply chain invested more outside China than domestically in 2024.

EU tariffs of 17–35.3 percent on Chinese BEVs, imposed in October 2024, have paradoxically not slowed Chinese sales. Chinese automakers increased European sales by 93 percent within a year of the tariffs, with BYD sales rising 225 percent in some months—most OEMs absorbed the duties rather than raising prices. The tariff response is a miniature of the BIS response: the wall does not stop the caravan. It reroutes it. The vehicles that cannot enter are treated as imports, arriving as locally manufactured products. The technology that cannot enter America arrives in the form of Uber rides in Abu Dhabi. The standards that cannot be imposed arrive in the form of ISO frameworks adopted by 52 countries. The procession continues.

The cost advantage compounds the strategic one. Chinese robotaxi rides cost approximately $0.35 per mile, compared with $2 per mile in the United States. Baidu's Apollo Go overseas GM Halton Niu articulated the unit economics: "Once we can generate profit for every single car in a second-tier city like Wuhan in mainland China, we can generate profits in lots of cities across the world. Scale matters." When your cost base is Wuhan and your revenue base is Dubai, the margins are not merely profitable. They are, to use a term the Theyyam performer would understand, *divine*.

The Guinea Pig Gambit Is Working

The evidence is interconnected and operates at multiple levels simultaneously. At the vehicle layer, China's 7.1 million exports and its expanding factory network create the installed base of hardware. At the infrastructure layer, the Digital Silk Road's 5G networks, BeiDou positioning, and smart city platforms provide the operating environment. At the standards layer, China's leadership of the ISO 3450x series and 90 bilateral standardization agreements establishes the rules. Moreover, at the autonomy layer, WeRide, Baidu, and Pony.ai are deploying robotaxis in markets with no American competition, thereby building operational data and commercial traction that will be difficult to replicate.

The temporal insight is the most important. Abu Dhabi now has 120 Level 4 vehicles operating without safety drivers, with 1,200 committed by 2027. Dubai expects 25 percent of trips to be autonomous by 2030. These are not pilot programs—they are commercial deployments that generate revenue, accumulate data, and establish regulatory precedents that will shape autonomous mobility governance worldwide. Each Chinese robotaxi operating in Abu Dhabi, each BeiDou-enabled vehicle navigating Bangkok, each C-V2X signal transmitted in Riyadh adds another strand to a technology ecosystem that is rapidly becoming self-sustaining—and increasingly difficult for any future policy intervention to unwind.

The *ullil kaanal,* as in every chapter where the thesis accelerates, requires that the failure mode be specified alongside the momentum. Processions can be stopped. The guinea-pig gambit carries a risk that the gambit's architects understand better than their cheerleaders: guinea pigs can become cautionary tales. A serious accident in Abu Dhabi or Dubai—a pedestrian fatality, a multi-vehicle collision at highway speed—would trigger regulatory pauses that Western media would amplify into a narrative of Chinese-AV-failure-abroad, with consequences far exceeding the incident's operational significance. The Gulf deployments, for all their ambition, remain sub-scale: 120 vehicles in Abu Dhabi is not a fleet; it is a demonstration with commercial trappings. Whether these beachheads achieve the density, utilization, and revenue trajectories needed for genuine commercial viability—rather than remaining state-subsidized showcases of regulatory modernity—is a question the next two years will answer, but that the current data cannot. The investor who treats the Gulf as a proven market is front-running the evidence. The investor who dismisses it as a pilot program is ignoring WeRide's breakeven trajectory and Uber's $100 million commitment. As with the chip-timeline caveat of Chapter 9, both errors are available; the disciplined investor makes neither.

As Tesla VP Lars Moravy warned at a February 2026 Senate hearing: "If the US does not lead in autonomous driving development, other nations—particularly China—will shape the technology, standards, and global market." The warning is accurate. It is also late. The procession has already left the village. The fire is already burning in new temples. 74 percent of executives who predict a separate China tech stack are not forecasting a future event. They are describing what is already underway.

The Theyyam performer does not return to the temple that refused him. He carries the divine fire forward, and each new village that receives it becomes part of the procession. The procession grows with each stop. By the time the original village reconsiders, the deity has transformed twenty others—and the question is no longer whether to open the door but whether it matters that the door was ever closed.

Act III opens where the rivers meet. Marcus—the fund manager whose cognitive errors we have tracked from Chapter 4's 40,000 tombs through Chapter 9's granaries—has spent ten chapters modelling two domestic markets. He has priced friction as alpha, miscategorized Chinese tightening as bearish, and built his TAM on US-only assumptions. He has not yet priced the procession. Twenty cities. 1,200 committed robotaxis in the Gulf alone. 7.1 million exported vehicles. Ninety bilateral standards agreements. A $213.5 billion infrastructure network purpose-built to carry this cargo. But before Marcus can compare the two civilizational approaches—American and Chinese, hunter and farmer, neuron and nervous system—he must first understand what is dying. The procession does not merely carry the new technology forward. It cremates the old one. Chapter 11 will take Marcus to the burning ghat, where the 150-year ICE empire meets the embodied-intelligence platform that is dismantling it—not through competition alone, but through a convergence so total that it liquidates the petroleum economy, the supplier web, the dealer network, and the political architecture that sustains all three. Only after he has read the fire will he be ready, in Chapter 12, to stand at the fork where the two rivers diverge and ask the question that every investor, policymaker, and automotive executive must now confront: which architecture will define the next era of global mobility, and where should capital be deployed?

Evidence Anchors

BIS Connected Vehicles Final Rule (90 Fed. Reg. 5360, January 16, 2025) • WeRide-Uber Abu Dhabi: launch December 6, 2024; Level 4 driverless November 26, 2025; 1,200 robotaxi commitment February 6, 2026 • WeRide Q3 2025 financials; 1,600+ global fleet; $764M cash • Baidu Apollo Go: Dubai permit January 2026; Uber launch February 10, 2026; Abu Dhabi Yas Island January 2026; Lyft/FREENOW Europe partnership August 2025; PostBus Switzerland October 2025 • Pony.ai: Nasdaq IPO November 2024; NEOM $100M investment October 2023; six-country network • Abu Dhabi ITC: first commercial driverless permits November 2025 • Dubai Law No. 9 of 2023; 25% autonomous target by 2030 • Saudi Arabia TGA sandbox; WeRide first robotaxi permit July 2025 • ISO 34505:2025 (July 7, 2025); ISO 3450x series (China-led since 2018) • China Standards 2035: 90 bilateral agreements, 52 countries • BRI 2025: $213.5B engagement (Griffith Asia Institute / Green BRI) • Digital Silk Road: $17B+ in digital projects (MERICS) • BeiDou: 55 satellites, 1.1B users, 30+ BRI nations • Vehicle exports: 7.098M (2025); BYD Thailand plant; Rhodium Group FDI analysis • EU tariffs: 17–35.3% (October 2024); 93% sales increase post-tariff • McKinsey Center for Future Mobility: 74% predict dedicated China tech stack (January 2026) • Carnegie Endowment: unintended consequences warning (January 2025) • BloombergNEF: Chinese firms face "little local competition" overseas

---

ACT III

WHERE THE RIVERS MEET

The Investment Playbook

Act III is where the rivers meet—and where the collision becomes visible.

MOVEMENT I: DESCENDS

The Boatman Reads the Burning Ghat

CHAPTER 11

The Burning Ghat
How China's Embodied Intelligence Platform Is Cremating the 150-Year ICE Empire

In the Theyyam, the performer does not become the deity by wearing the mask. He becomes the deity by moving with the mask's logic—by surrendering the body's memory to the body's future. The mask does not conceal. It reveals what the face could never show.

— From the Theyyam traditions of North Malabar

Greed, for lack of a better word, is good. Greed is right. Greed works. Greed clarifies, cuts through, and captures the essence of the evolutionary spirit.

— Gordon Gekko, Wall Street (1987)

11.0 The Burning Ghat: The First Robot, Not the Last Car

I

The Body on the Pyre

In Kerala, when the body arrives at the cremation ground, the boatman who has carried it along the backwater canal does not weep. He has seen this journey a thousand times. He reads the weight of the vessel, the tilt of the current, the way the family huddles on the bank—and from these signs, he extracts information the mourners cannot see. The boatman's knowledge is not mystical. It is hydraulic. He knows which undercurrents will shift the vessel, which eddies will slow it, and precisely where the channel narrows so that only one boat can pass. The mourners see a funeral. The boatman sees a navigational problem.

The internal combustion engine has arrived at its cremation ground. The procession is vast—one hundred and fifty years of capital, forty million jobs, three-quarters of a trillion dollars in annual profit—and the mourners are still arguing about whether the body is actually dead. General Motors calls it "portfolio optimization." Volkswagen calls it "capacity alignment." Stellantis called a $26 billion write-down 'non-cash'—the accounting equivalent of calling a five-alarm fire a thermal reclassification event. The auditors signed off. The stock rose two percent. The language of corporate health has been deployed so aggressively against the symptoms of civilizational illness that the euphemisms themselves have become a secondary infection. The boatman reads the undercurrent beneath the euphemism and sees the vessel listing.

Marcus sits in his midtown Manhattan office, staring at a Bloomberg terminal that cannot decide what to look at. His legacy auto positions are flat. His China exposure is zero. He has a narrative where he needs instruments, sentiment where he needs structure, and opinion where he needs a trade.

This chapter will hand him those instruments—and teach the reader standing behind him to use them.

. . .

II

Embodied Intelligence: The Automobile as the First Robot

The first conceptual error is the most consequential: we are calling the wrong thing by the wrong name.

The Western financial imagination—trained for generations to categorize assets by industry vertical—looks at a BYD Seagull and sees a car. A cheap car, at that. A $9,550 hatchback manufactured in Changsha, sold with a LiDAR suite and autonomous driving software included at no additional consumer cost, and dismissed by Detroit analysts as a loss leader. The dismissal is understandable. It is also the most expensive analytical mistake in the automotive industry's history. The Seagull is not a car. It is the first mass-produced robot.

Beneath the sheet metal of every BYD vehicle equipped with the God's Eye system—and, as of February 2026, that includes vehicles spanning $9,550 to $233,000—there operates a five-layer embodied intelligence stack. The first layer is perception: sensors, cameras, and LiDAR from Hesai or RoboSense, priced at $150–$200 per unit, down from $150,000 a decade ago. The second layer is computation: onboard processors running neural networks trained not only in simulation but also on 160 million kilometers of real-world driving data generated every day by 2.3 million vehicles on Chinese roads. The third layer is energy: a battery pack manufactured by CATL or BYD's own Blade Battery division, drawing on a supply chain in which China controls 77 percent of global cell manufacturing capacity. The fourth layer is connectivity: a vehicle-to-everything (V2X) communication architecture linking the car to 35,000 kilometers of instrumented Chinese roads, cloud computing infrastructure, and a national $84 billion vehicle-road-cloud network purpose-built by MIIT. The fifth layer is the learning loop: every mile driven by every God's Eye vehicle feeds data back into the training pipeline, which improves the next software update, which ships over-the-air to every vehicle in the fleet simultaneously.

This is not an autonomous driving feature bolted onto a car. It is an artificial intelligence platform inhabiting the form factor of an automobile—the way electricity first inhabited the form factor of a lamp before it inhabited factories, cities, and civilizations. The same perception stack guides a Seagull through Shenzhen and a Neolix delivery pod through a logistics park. The same battery chemistry powers vehicles and grid storage. Five industries—autonomous mobility, logistics, robotics, distributed energy, and financial-data rails—are five embodiments of a single intelligence platform, compounding each other's learning curves at a pace that vertical industry analysis cannot capture. Three numbers frame the scale of this misidentification.

1. $13 billion: the cumulative losses Ford has reported on its EV division since 2021, treating the transition as a cost center within an automotive company.
2. $385: the per-vehicle cost at which BYD deploys its God's Eye autonomous driving system, treating the technology as a standard feature of a platform company.
3. $34 trillion: the enterprise value ARK Invest projects for global robotaxi platforms by 2030—a figure carrying the caveats appropriate to promotional research from a fund with concentrated positions, but even conservative institutional estimates imply a TAM multiple times larger than the current automotive profit pool.

. . .

III

The Three Movements: Descends, Ascends, Counts

For the Gekko in the room—and there is always a Gekko, because Gekko reads what the congregation cannot bear to price—the question is architectural. Which Western cash flows are structurally incompatible with a world in which the automobile is a platform, not a product? Which balance sheets were built on the assumption that the internal combustion engine would generate high-margin profits for another two decades? Which pension obligations, dealer franchises, and municipal tax bases were underwritten by a 150-year-old architecture now being metabolized by a different physics entirely?

This chapter answers those questions in three movements, borrowing a structure from the very tradition that illuminates its subject.

Movement I—Descends. The Boatman descends into the burning ghat, reads the undercurrents beneath the ICE empire's last good earnings reports, catalogues the five structural traps that prevent legacy automakers from escaping, and traces the non-linear collapse mechanics that will transform orderly transition into disorderly repricing. This is the autopsy.

Movement II—Ascends. The Theyyam performer ascends from the ashes. We map the embodied intelligence platform's five nodes as an Interdependency Web and subject the thesis to four countercurrents. What survives is the investable thesis.

Movement III—Counts. Gekko counts the wreckage and prices the survivors. We deliver three repeatable frameworks—the Dinosaur Meter for legacy fragility, the Interdependency Web Score for platform strength, and the Quarter-Kelly Sizing for portfolio construction—that the reader can apply to any company, any country, and any allocation decision. This is the trade.

The reader who has traveled the previous ten chapters arrives at this ghat with tools the uninitiated lack.

The boatman reads both currents. The Theyyam performer embodies what he sees. The Gekko who will close Movement III does not moralize about destruction; he prices it. This chapter applies all three lenses—undercurrent, vision, and money—because the demolition derby consuming the global automotive industry cannot be understood through any single lens.

The collapse of the internal combustion engine empire is not a morality tale. It is an accounting event. The birth of embodied intelligence is not a prophecy. It is a balance sheet. The distance between the two is where the capital goes.

> **Integrator:** This chapter is not a eulogy. It is an allocation memo. By its final page, the reader will hold three instruments: the Dinosaur Meter, which scores any legacy automaker on seven fragility factors; the Interdependency Web Score, which maps nations and companies across the five nodes of the embodied intelligence platform; and the Quarter-Kelly Sizing, which calibrates thematic exposure. These are the deliverables. The undercurrent punishes the undecided.

Gekko has three instruments in his case—and the reader will hold them by the final page. The Dinosaur Meter will score Ford at 83.4, Volkswagen at 79.1, and Toyota at 70.6—fragility indices that predict the refinancing wall the bond market is already whispering about. The Interdependency Web Score will show China at 24 out of 25 and Europe at 11—a chasm invisible to the analyst who files BYD under "autos" and calls it a day. The Quarter-Kelly Sizing will cap thematic exposure at 15 percent—the Kuttanad farmer's mathematics applied to portfolio construction, because the farmer who bets the entire paddy on one monsoon is not brave but bankrupt. The reader who wants the instruments immediately may turn to Section 11.12. The reader who wants to understand why they are calibrated as they are should read straight through. Both readers will arrive at the same ghat. The undercurrent does not wait for the slow reader.

The boatman pushes off from the bank. The current is running.

11.1 The Ledger of the Dead: ICE's Last Good Years

I

The Surface Story

The surface numbers still gleam. In the first half of 2025, General Motors reported $4.8 billion in adjusted EBIT from its North American operations, nearly all of it generated by full-size trucks and SUVs powered by internal combustion engines. Ford's Pro division—commercial trucks and vans, overwhelmingly ICE—delivered $2.3 billion in operating profit. Toyota announced record global production. BMW's combustion-powered 3 Series and 5 Series remained the volume foundation of a company trading at fourteen times forward earnings. The surface story, the one that occupies the first slide of every sell-side equity deck, is simple: the ICE profit engine is wounded but working, and the transition to electric vehicles is proceeding at a pace the industry can manage.

Wall Street has a name for this reading. It calls it "cyclical headwinds." The analyst who writes that phrase in a research note is performing the same function as the mourner who calls a terminal diagnosis "a health challenge." The boatman reads the surface and sees the current beneath it, and what the current is saying in 2026 is that the gleaming numbers are the residual glow of a star that has already exhausted its fuel.

The 150-year balance-sheet illusion of the internal combustion engine rests on a single structural assumption: that the profitable vehicle and the technologically advanced vehicle are the same object. For a century and a half, this was true. The Mercedes S-Class, the BMW 7 Series, the Cadillac Escalade—these were simultaneously the pinnacle of engineering and the pinnacle of profitability, because complexity was the moat and the internal combustion powertrain was the complexity.

The embodied intelligence platform has severed that identity. The most technologically advanced vehicle on Earth—a BYD Seagull running God's Eye with real-time V2X connectivity—costs $9,550. The most profitable vehicles in the Western automotive industry—a $65,000 Ford F-150 or a $58,000 Chevrolet Tahoe—are running powertrains whose fundamental architecture has not changed since Nikolaus Otto patented the four-stroke engine in 1876. Technology has shifted the price curve to the left. Profit is stranded on the right.

• • •

II

The Underlying Currents: Policy, Cost Curves, Convergence

The Theyyam performer's inner vision—ullil kaanal—perceives the structural forces that the surface data conceals. Three currents are running beneath the ICE empire's apparent health that will, within three to five years, transform orderly transition into disorderly collapse.

The first current is policy convergence. China has achieved approximately 60 percent penetration of new energy vehicles as of early 2026. Europe has reached roughly 25 percent. The United States trails at approximately 11 percent. Under the IEA's Stated Policies Scenario, by 2030, China reaches approximately 80 percent, Europe approximately 50–60 percent, and the United States approximately 25 percent (IEA Global EV Outlook 2025; BNEF Electric Vehicle Outlook 2025). These are not aspirational targets. They are projections of existing policy trajectories—regulatory mandates, consumer incentives, and manufacturing subsidies that have already been legislated and implemented. The road is built. The vehicles are driving on it.

The second current is cost-curve acceleration. Battery pack costs have declined approximately 90 percent since 2010 and crossed the $100-per-kilowatt-hour threshold in Chinese manufacturing in late 2024. At this price point, the $3,000-to-$5,000 cost gap between electric and combustion powertrains has effectively closed in China and is closing in every market where Chinese manufacturers compete. BYD's Blade Battery, CATL's sodium-ion chemistry, and forthcoming solid-state cells are not incremental improvements. They are cost-curve collapses that eliminate the economic rationale for the internal combustion engine as a mass-market technology.

The third current is platform convergence. ARK Invest's Big Ideas 2026 report identifies a 35 percent increase in "Convergence Network Strength"—the degree to which five technology platforms amplify each other's capabilities. This convergence is mechanical, not theoretical. The same neural network architecture that processes autonomous-driving data also processes logistics-optimization data. The same battery chemistry powers vehicles and grid storage. The same LiDAR sensor costs $150 for a passenger car and $150 for a delivery drone. The platforms are fusing into a single techno-industrial substrate—manufactured, at scale, almost exclusively in China.

• • •

III

Follow the Money: Where the Capital Is Already Moving

Gekko reads capital flows. And the capital flows in the global automotive industry in 2025–2026 are telling a story that equity analysts have not yet written, and credit analysts are beginning to whisper.

Follow the money out of ICE. The Stellantis write-down described in Section 11.0 — $26 billion in goodwill, the largest single impairment in automotive history — was only the most visible capital-flow signal. Ford's Model e division has accumulated $16.7 billion in cumulative EBIT losses since its creation in 2022 through fiscal year 2025 (Ford Q4 2025 earnings, February 10, 2026), losing approximately $64,000 on every electric vehicle sold in 2024, while simultaneously reporting that its ICE division's profitability sustains the company's investment-grade credit rating. General Motors carries $124.7 billion in long-term liabilities, supported by a business model that depends on selling 2.6 million combustion-powered vehicles per year in North America at average transaction prices above $50,000.

Follow the money into the future. Ford's other post-employment benefit obligations are underfunded by $4.4 billion. The Pension Benefit Guaranty Corporation reports a net deficit exceeding $60 billion and a portfolio that includes the obligations of every Tier 1 supplier, every regional assembly plant, and every dealership employee benefit plan in the American automotive ecosystem. These obligations were underwritten by actuarial models that assumed the internal combustion engine would generate cash flows sufficient to fund retirement benefits for workers who would live into the 2060s. The question Gekko asks is whether those cash flows will exist when the vehicles generating them compete against $9,550 robots that do not require pensions.

The pattern is visible in the capex divergence. In 2025, Chinese firms invested more capital in battery manufacturing, autonomous driving research, and EV production capacity than the combined R&D budgets of GM, Ford, Stellantis, and Volkswagen. The capital is voting with its feet—leaving the combustion architecture and flowing toward the embodied intelligence platform, because the cost curves have crossed and the compound returns favor the new physics.

> **Integrator:** The Self-Cannibalization Imperative is the central strategic reality of the Western automotive industry in 2026. Every legacy OEM faces the same impossible choice: destroy your own profitable ICE business to fund a transition where Chinese competitors have a five-year head start and a structural cost advantage—or protect the ICE margins and watch the platform economy pass you by. Ford is attempting the first path and hemorrhaging cash. Toyota is betting on hydrogen. GM is pursuing both paths simultaneously, confusing its capital allocation. The BIS Connected Vehicle Rule, effective March 17, 2025, is the regulatory moat protecting the American market. Whether it is wide enough is the subject of Section 11.7.

11.2 The Five Traps of the ICE Civilization

The boatman knows that a vessel does not sink from a single leak. It sinks because five small leaks conspire at once, each manageable in isolation, each fatal in combination. The internal combustion engine empire is not dying of a single wound. It is trapped in five structural cages, each reinforcing the others, yet invisible to the analyst who examines it in isolation.

I

The Margin Trap: High-Gross, Low-Future

General Motors earns approximately $12,000 in operating profit on a $58,000 Chevrolet Tahoe. The Tahoe requires a 5.3-liter V8 engine, a ten-speed automatic transmission, a separate transfer case for four-wheel drive, an exhaust system engineered to meet emissions standards that required $2 billion in compliance R&D, and a dealer service model that generates more profit from maintenance over the vehicle's life than from the initial sale. This architecture—complex, heavy, maintenance-intensive, margin-rich—is the beating heart of the Western automotive profit model.

The embodied intelligence platform does not attack this model head-on. It makes it irrelevant. A robotaxi fleet does not need a $58,000 premium SUV; it needs a $28,000 purpose-built vehicle that operates twenty hours a day at $0.25 per mile. An autonomous logistics fleet does not need high-margin commercial trucks; it needs autonomous pods that share their perception stack with the robotaxi platform and their battery chemistry with the grid storage system. The profit pool that sustains GM, Ford, and Stellantis—high-margin, low-volume, complexity-dependent—is a pond. The embodied intelligence platform is an ocean. The pond does not survive the ocean's arrival; it is absorbed.

What Wall Street calls "mix enrichment"—the strategy of retreating upmarket into higher-margin vehicles as volume declines—is the last act of a civilization that has confused the quality of its margins with the durability of its market. When autonomous mobility platforms begin capturing the transportation-as-a-service market, the question is not whether premium ICE margins survive. The question is whether the addressable market that generates those margins still exists.

II

The Labor Trap: Jobs Anchored to a Dying Stack

The German automotive industry employs approximately 780,000 workers directly and supports an additional 1.8 million in the supplier ecosystem. Volkswagen's decision to eliminate 35,000 positions and close its first German factory since 1937—a plant in Osnabrück that had operated continuously for eighty-eight years—was not a restructuring. It was a funeral with a press release. Continental has announced 7,150 cuts. Lear Corporation has announced 15,000. Across the European automotive supply chain, an estimated 104,000 jobs were eliminated in 2024–2025—approximately 142 per day, every day, for two years.

The trap is political as much as economic. These are unionized, pension-eligible, community-anchoring jobs concentrated in specific regions—Bavaria, Saxony, the American Midwest, northern France. Their elimination triggers not merely economic pain but political radicalization. In Germany, the correlation between automotive job losses and AfD vote share in affected districts is not subtle. In the American Midwest, the same dynamics that transformed the Rust Belt into a political battleground in 2016 are amplified by EV transition anxiety. The labor trap does not merely strand the workforce; it creates a political constituency whose survival depends on slowing the very transition the cost curves have ordained.

The unfunded pension obligations anchored to these jobs represent the hidden leverage in the system. When ICE cash flows decline, the liabilities do not decline with them—they accelerate. ERISA obligations, PBGC premiums, and state-level public pension exposures to automotive supplier bonds create a cascading mechanism that links factory closures to municipal credit quality. The labor trap is not a human resources problem. It is a credit event waiting for a trigger.

III

The Innovation Sourcing Trap: Tier-1 Cathedrals vs. Integrated Temples

The Western automotive industry is organized as a cathedral: the OEM sits at the apex, and beneath it stretches a vast hierarchy of Tier 1, Tier 2, and Tier 3 suppliers, each one specializing in a component, each one jealously guarding its intellectual property, each one extracting margin from the complexity of the interface between its component and the next. This architecture was brilliantly adapted to the internal combustion engine, where the powertrain alone contained over 2,000 moving parts and the coordination cost justified the cathedral's overhead.

The Chinese embodied intelligence platform is organized as a temple: vertically integrated, ruthlessly consolidated, built for speed. BYD manufactures its own batteries, semiconductors, electric motors, and autonomous driving software. Its vertical integration reaches 75 percent of the vehicle's bill of materials—a figure that would be considered antitrust-adjacent in the Western automotive context and is considered normal operating procedure in the Chinese platform economy. When BYD reduces the cost of its LiDAR integration from $400 to $200, the savings flow immediately to the consumer price without negotiating through four tiers of supplier contracts. When CATL develops a new sodium-ion cell chemistry, it can deploy it across BYD vehicles, grid storage systems, and logistics robots simultaneously because the supply chain is integrated rather than fragmented.

The Western supplier model is not merely less efficient than the Chinese model. It is structurally incompatible with the embodied intelligence platform's operating logic. The platform requires speed—weekly software release cycles. The cathedral requires process—negotiation, validation, and integration across dozens of contractual interfaces. When Bosch, Continental, and ZF report declining margins and announce restructurings, they are not victims of cyclical pressure. They are artifacts of an architectural paradigm that the new physics has made obsolete.

IV

The Dealer Franchise Trap: Distribution Frozen in the Past

There are approximately 16,700 franchised automobile dealerships in the United States, employing over one million people, occupying real estate valued in the hundreds of billions, and protected by state franchise laws that were written in the 1950s to prevent manufacturer abuse and have since become the most effective barrier to automotive innovation in the Western world. The dealer franchise model generates profit from three sources: vehicle sales (declining), financing and insurance products (vulnerable to digital disruption), and after-sales service and parts (dependent on ICE complexity).

The embodied intelligence platform eliminates the third revenue stream entirely. An electric vehicle has approximately 20 moving parts in its powertrain compared to 2,000 in an ICE powertrain. There are no oil changes, transmission services, or exhaust system replacements. The service bay—which generates 40 to 60 percent of dealership gross profit—is a stranded asset when the fleet transitions to electric. Moreover, autonomous fleet operators purchase directly from manufacturers in bulk contracts, with maintenance handled by centralized service centers. The dealer franchise is not merely threatened by the transition. It is architecturally excluded from the post-transition value chain.

The real estate exposure is the hidden detonator. Dealership land and buildings are financed through floorplan credit lines secured by inventory and property values. When service revenue declines and new-vehicle margins compress, the property valuations securing those credit lines decline in tandem, triggering covenant renegotiations or forced sales—in markets where the buyers have the same problem. The dealer franchise trap is not an operational challenge. It is a real estate credit cycle embedded inside an automotive transition.

V

The Shareholder Return Trap: Financial Engineering vs. Re-Engineering

Between 2015 and 2024, General Motors returned approximately $45 billion to shareholders through buybacks and dividends. Ford returned approximately $30 billion. Stellantis returned approximately $18 billion. The combined $93 billion exceeded the total amount these three companies invested in electric-vehicle and autonomous-driving technologies during the same period.

Ninety-three billion dollars. Enough to have built three BYDs from scratch(at BYD's 2024 valuation). Instead, it was converted into share buybacks that briefly inflated stock prices for executives whose compensation was tied to those prices—a circularity so elegant it could teach a graduate seminar in financial self-cannibalism. The auditors signed off. The board approved. The analysts called it "shareholder-friendly." The Boatman calls it what the Kuttanad farmer calls eating the seed corn: a meal that tastes excellent until the next monsoon arrives and the field is bare.

The arithmetic is not subtle. Every dollar returned to shareholders is a dollar not invested in the platform transition. Every buyback that supports the share price in the current quarter is a software engineer not hired, a battery partnership not formed, a data pipeline not built. The shareholder return trap operates through a mechanism that is rational at every individual decision point and catastrophic in aggregate: the institutional shareholder who demands returns today creates the competitive deficit that destroys returns tomorrow.

While Western OEMs were engineering their balance sheets, Chinese manufacturers were engineering their platforms. BYD invested $4.2 billion in R&D in 2024 alone—more than its total shareholder distributions. The Chinese flywheel does not face the shareholder return trap because state-linked investors, which provide patient capital, do not demand quarterly returns. They demand a market position. They are farming, not hunting. And the monsoon of compound learning curves rewards the farmer every season.

> **Integrator:** These five traps are not five problems. They are five padlocks on a single cage. The margin trap prevents the strategic retreat. The labor trap prevents the political authorization. The innovation-sourcing trap undermines operational agility. The dealer franchise trap prevents the distribution transformation. The shareholder return trap prevents capital reallocation. Any one of them is manageable; together, they ensure that the first mass-produced robot will not be built by a Western manufacturer. It will be built by the civilization that organized its entire industrial architecture around speed, integration, and compound iteration—the civilization that built temples, not cathedrals. Each trap has one theoretical escape hatch: the margin trap yields to platformization; the labor trap to transition compacts funded at the speed the cost curve demands; the innovation trap to compute commons and open-architecture partnerships; the dealer trap to fleet-direct distribution; the shareholder trap to patient capital with a ten-year horizon. The investor's task is to monitor which padlocks are opening and which are rusting shut.

11.3 The Funeral Procession: How an Empire Collapses in Real Time

I

The Procession Begins

In Kerala, the funeral procession follows a prescribed route. Each step in the sequence is irreversible. Once the fire is lit, there is no returning the body to the home. The procession has its own momentum, its own physics, its own point of no return.

The Osnabrück plant closed after eighty-eight years of continuous production. Three generations of families had worked there. The children of the workers who built the first Volkswagens in that plant watched their grandchildren's plant close. No Boatman is reading for this. There is no Theyyam vision. There is only the fact of it—eighty-eight years of continuous production, ended in a press release, and the people who made the cars standing in the parking lot with boxes.

The boatman sees the procession. The body is being carried toward the ghat. Each step is irreversible.

• • •

II

The Non-Linear Cliff: When the Math Breaks

The Theyyam performer sees what the mourners cannot: the procession has a cliff.

The ICE automotive industry operates on a minimum viable scale. A combustion engine manufacturing line requires an annual production volume of approximately 250,000 to 300,000 units to cover its fixed costs—the tooling, workforce, quality systems, and supplier contracts priced on volume commitments. A transmission plant requires a similar scale. An exhaust aftertreatment facility, a fuel-injection system line, and a catalytic converter supplier—each node in the ICE supply chain has a minimum volume below which unit economics collapse. The industry has operated above these minimums for so long that the minimums have become invisible, baked into models that assume they will never be tested.

They are about to be tested. The non-linear collapse mechanics work as follows:

When EV penetration in a given market reaches approximately 25–30 percent of new-vehicle sales, the remaining ICE volumes begin to fall below the minimum viable scale for the weakest suppliers. Those suppliers either raise prices to compensate for lost volume—thereby increasing costs for OEMs already under margin pressure—or exit the market entirely, forcing OEMs to source components from a shrinking pool of surviving suppliers at higher cost. This is the first inflection.

When EV penetration crosses approximately 50 percent—a threshold China crossed in mid-2025—the second inflection arrives. Residual values on used ICE vehicles are declining as consumers anticipate further EV penetration. Declining residual values convert leased fleets from assets into liabilities, because the vehicles coming off lease are worth less than the residual values guaranteed in the lease contracts. Floorplan financing costs spike as dealers hold inventory longer. Insurance companies reprice ICE vehicle coverage as the repair ecosystem—parts availability, trained technicians, service bay access—begins to thin.

When EV penetration reaches approximately 70–75 percent, the third inflection occurs, and it is discontinuous. The remaining ICE infrastructure—fuel stations, service networks, parts distributors, vocational training programs—can no longer sustain itself economically. The gasoline station network, which requires minimum throughput to justify land and environmental compliance costs, begins to contract. The contraction reduces the convenience of owning an ICE vehicle, accelerating the shift to EVs, which further reduces throughput, accelerating contraction. The feedback loop is negative for ICE and positive for EV simultaneously, and its velocity increases with each cycle.

China is currently navigating the second inflection. Europe is approaching the first. The United States, shielded by its 100 percent tariff wall and its lower EV penetration rate, is approximately 3 to 5 years behind Europe, meaning the American automotive industry has precisely the time it has historically used to do nothing.

• • •

III

The Valuation Repricing: From Icons to Orphans

The multiples tell a story the equity research industry has not yet processed, because processing it would require reclassifying some of the most iconic companies in American capitalism.

A growth company trades at a multiple that reflects its future cash flow growth. A value company trades at a multiple that reflects current cash flow stability. A run-down company trades at a multiple that reflects declining cash flows and terminal value—the mathematical equivalent of pricing a business consumed by its own cost structure. The internal combustion engine manufacturers, as of February 2026, trade at multiples that imply they are value companies. The bond market, which prices credit risk with a precision that equity markets cannot match, is beginning to whisper that they are runoff companies.

The evidence is in the credit spreads. Ford's long-term bonds traded at a spread of 185 basis points over Treasuries at year-end 2024. By January 31, 2026, the spread had widened to 245 basis points—not a crisis, but a trajectory. GM's credit default swap spreads have followed a similar arc. Stellantis, stripped of its investment-grade halo after the goodwill write-down, is financing at rates that imply a probability of default approximately three times higher than two years ago. The bond market does not yet say these companies are failing. It says the risk of failure is rising at a rate no longer consistent with "cyclical headwinds."

The refinancing wall is the trigger that the credit analysts are watching. Between 2027 and 2030, the Western automotive industry faces approximately $180 billion in maturing debt—bonds, credit facilities, and supplier financing instruments aggregated from Bloomberg debt maturity schedules across Ford, GM, Stellantis, Volkswagen, and major Tier 1 suppliers—that were issued when ICE cash flows were assumed to be permanent, a word that in corporate finance means "until the quarter someone notices they aren't." Each refinancing event will require the borrower to demonstrate that the cash flows supporting the new debt are sustainable. Each credit committee will ask the question that equity analysts have deferred: if EV penetration reaches IEA's projected levels, will this company's ICE-dependent cash flows exist in sufficient quantity to service this debt at maturity?

For some companies, the answer will be yes. Toyota's diversified powertrain strategy, its hydrogen bet, and its balance-sheet fortress—approximately $60 billion in net cash—give it options other manufacturers lack. For others—particularly the European mid-market manufacturers and the American companies whose profitability depends on high-margin combustion vehicles—the refinancing wall will arrive before the transition is complete.

> **Integrator:** Movement I has completed its descent. The five traps are locked. The non-linear collapse mechanics are mapped. The valuation repricing has begun. The ICE empire is not being disrupted—it is being repriced as runoff. The near-term trigger list: profit-per-vehicle compression below $8,000 on ICE flagships; dealer inventory days above 90; supplier credit spreads above 400 basis points; retreat into "high-margin ICE focus," framed as a strategic choice when it is a strategic surrender. When these signals appear in an earnings report, the Dinosaur Meter's score is not a forecast. It is a reading of what has already happened.

END OF MOVEMENT I: DESCENDS

MOVEMENT II: ASCENDS

The Theyyam Sees the Embodied Intelligence Platform

In the Theyyam, the performer does not rise from the ground because he has been lifted. He rises because the deity has entered his body and the body has remembered what it was always meant to be. The rising is not an event. It is a recognition.

11.4 The Embodied Intelligence Platform Takes the Stage

I

From Car to Platform: The Stack That Walks

Movement I concluded at the cremation ground. The body of the ICE empire lies on the pyre, the five traps locked around it. The mourners are still debating whether the fire is real. It is real. But the fire is not the story. What rises from it is.

In the Theyyam ritual, after the elaborate preparation—the costume, the face-painting, the hours of drumming that reorganize the performer's neurology—there is a moment of transformation so total that the congregation does not experience it as performance. The performer's body, which was ordinary a moment ago, becomes the vessel of something larger. The legs that walked to the temple now carry a deity. The arms that hung at the sides now hold divine authority. The same body. Different operating system. The Theyyam performer has not changed the hardware. He has changed the intelligence that inhabits it.

This is the most precise available metaphor for what is happening to the automobile. The hardware—four wheels, a chassis, a passenger compartment, a power source—has not fundamentally changed. What has changed is the intelligence that inhabits it. The Chinese electric vehicle, equipped with the God's Eye system, Baidu's Apollo platform, or Huawei's ADS 3.0, is not a better car. It is a mobile computing platform that perceives its environment, processes that perception through neural networks, communicates with infrastructure in real time, stores and distributes energy, and learns from every mile driven by every vehicle in the fleet. It is an autonomous agent operating in physical space.

The five-layer stack mapped in Section 11.0 costs between \$100 and \$400 per layer, serves five or more industries per layer, and improves as each layer strengthens the others. This is not an automobile. This is the first mass-market embodied intelligence platform, and the automobile is merely its first form factor—the way the telephone was the first form factor for the semiconductor.

• • •

II

One Brain, Many Bodies

The Theyyam performer does not inhabit a single body. The same tradition, the same inner fire moves from performer to performer, from one form of the deity to another. Different masks. Different choreographies. Same divine intelligence adapted to different purposes. The deity is not the mask. The deity is the operating system.

The embodied intelligence platform operates with the same logic. The BYD Seagull is the first body. The Neolix autonomous delivery pod is the second. The XCMG autonomous mining truck is the third.

The Unitree H1 humanoid robot is the fourth. The CATL Tener grid storage controller is the fifth. Each inhabits a different form factor. Each serves a different market. Each shares the same perception stack, battery chemistry, neural network architecture, supply chain, and compound learning curve.

The numbers illuminate the sharing. The Hesai AT128 LiDAR sensor costs $150, whether mounted on a passenger vehicle, a delivery drone, or a factory robot. A CATL LFP cell costs $55 per kilowatt-hour, whether packaged in an electric vehicle or an autonomous forklift. A Horizon Robotics Journey 6 chip costs approximately $100, whether it processes driving data or warehouse navigation data. The bill of materials does not change when the form factor changes, because the intelligence is the same.

This is why the Western analytical framework—which assigns the automobile to the "auto sector," the delivery drone to "logistics," and the robot to "industrials"—systematically underestimates the Chinese platform's competitive advantage. The sectors are not separate. They are embodiments of a single platform. Capital flowing into any one embodiment strengthens all five because their learning curves, supply chains, and manufacturing scale are shared. Analyzing BYD as an "auto company" is like analyzing Apple in 2007 as a "phone company." It is technically accurate and strategically blind.

. . .

III

The Great Acceleration: Five Platforms, One River

The financial implication of "one brain, many bodies" is that the total addressable market is not the automotive TAM. It is the sum of five TAMs that Wall Street prices separately: autonomous mobility ($34 trillion enterprise value by 2030, per ARK Invest—subject to the promotional caveats noted in Section 11.0, with institutional estimates 40–60 percent lower), autonomous logistics ($480 billion globally by 2030), robotics ($26 trillion—similarly promotional, similarly directional), distributed energy ($4+ trillion in cumulative investment through 2035), and the financial and data rails that connect autonomous agents. Section 11.5 maps how these five nodes feed each other.

> **Integrator:** We are not tracking car companies. We are tracking the five embodiments of an industrial AI nervous system. The investor who prices five separate industries will calculate five separate betas and miss the compounding entirely. The investor who prices one Interdependency Web will see a system whose compound growth rate exceeds any individual node's growth rate by the factor of the feedback loops. Section 11.5 maps those loops.

11.5 The Interdependency Web: How the Dragon's Stack Feeds Itself

In the backwaters of Kuttanad, the river flows in no particular direction. The monsoon feeds the paddy field, which feeds the fish pond, which feeds the coconut grove, whose leaves fall into the canal, whose organic matter feeds the plankton, which feeds the fish, whose waste fertilizes the paddy. The Kuttanad farmer does not optimize for a single output. He manages a cycle. Each node in the system strengthens every other node, and the system's total productivity exceeds the sum of its parts by a factor that linear analysis cannot capture.

The Chinese embodied intelligence platform operates on precisely this logic. Five nodes—autonomous mobility, autonomous logistics, robotics, distributed energy, and financial data rails—are connected by causal links that form feedback loops. Strengthening any one node strengthens all five. Weakening any one node is compensated for by the others. The system is not five parallel industries. It is one ecosystem with five channels.

This section maps the five nodes and their causal links. The reader should track not the individual nodes but the loops—because the loops are where the compounding happens, and the compounding is where the money goes.

The Worked Dollar: How a Single Component Flows Through All Five Nodes

Before the reader enters the Web node by node, consider how a single $150 Hesai AT128 LiDAR sensor touches every channel. The sensor is manufactured in Shanghai (Node Three: Robotics manufacturing ecosystem). It is mounted on a Pony.ai robotaxi in Guangzhou (Node One: Autonomous Mobility), where it generates 600 gigabytes of perception data per vehicle per day. That data trains logistics-routing algorithms for JD.com's autonomous delivery fleet operating in the same city (Node Two: Autonomous Logistics). The delivery fleet's charging patterns feed grid-optimization models managed by CATL's energy storage systems (Node Four: Distributed Energy). The ride-hailing transactions, delivery fees, charging settlements, and insurance premiums generated across all four physical nodes flow through Alipay's machine-to-machine payment rails (Node Five: Financial & Data Rails)—and the aggregate data from those transactions informs Hesai's next-generation sensor design, which reduces the unit cost to $120 and begins the cycle again. One sensor. Five nodes. One closed loop. The investor who prices Hesai as a "LiDAR company" sees the sensor as a "LiDAR company." The investor who prices the Web sees the loop.

Node One: Autonomous Mobility (Robotaxis & AV Fleets)

The node that generates the most data. The robotaxi TAM projections from Section 11.4 represent replacing private vehicle ownership with a transportation-as-a-service model operating at one-quarter to one-third the per-mile cost of human-driven, privately owned vehicles.

Pony.ai's 1,000+ fully driverless robotaxis across four Chinese cities have demonstrated the unit economics: city-wide breakeven in Guangzhou, with costs declining on a curve driven by fleet utilization (20 hours per day versus 1 hour for a privately owned car), LiDAR price deflation ($150 per unit, down from $150,000 a decade ago), and the elimination of the driver—which represents 60 to 70 percent of the operating cost of a conventional taxi. Baidu's Apollo Go has completed over 17 million cumulative rides at a per-vehicle hardware cost of $28,000 for the Gen-6 robotaxi.

What makes autonomous mobility the anchor node is not the revenue—it is the data. Every robotaxi mile generates high-resolution perception data that trains not only driving algorithms but also logistics, warehouse navigation, and agricultural field-mapping algorithms. BYD's God's Eye fleet generates 160 million daily kilometers across 2.3 million vehicles. The data is the monsoon. Everything downstream depends on its volume.

Gekko prices the data moat: that daily mileage, valued at the $2–$5 per labeled kilometer that Western AV companies pay for comparable data acquisition, represents a $100-to-$270 billion annualized data advantage that does not appear on any balance sheet but compounds into every algorithm improvement, every edge-case resolution, every software update. The data moat is not a metaphor. It is a line item that Western competitors must match with cash, while Chinese competitors generate it with miles.

Causal link to Node Two: the perception stack that navigates a robotaxi through Shenzhen is, with minor adaptations, the same stack that navigates an autonomous truck. The 70 percent shared software architecture means every robotaxi mile is also a logistics training mile.

Node Two: Autonomous Logistics (Trucks, Drones, Warehouse Bots)

The node that carries the cargo. Autonomous logistics is the same intelligence operating on a different schedule and with a different payload. The truck running autonomously at night uses the same LiDAR, neural network, and V2X infrastructure as the robotaxi in urban traffic by day. The delivery drone in rural Yunnan uses the same flight-planning algorithms as agricultural drones.

ARK projects autonomous delivery at $480 billion globally by 2030, with over four million autonomous last-mile deliveries annually. In China, JD.com's autonomous delivery fleet has completed millions of deliveries across dozens of cities. SF Express operates autonomous drone delivery corridors. The freight system is learning from the passenger system in real time, because the data pipeline is shared.

Causal link to Node Three: the algorithms that guide a logistics drone are the same algorithms that guide a factory robot, with approximately 70 percent common code. More importantly, autonomous logistics creates demand for robots—more autonomous cargo means more warehouses requiring autonomous sorting, more factories requiring autonomous assembly.

Node Three: Robotics (Factory Arms to Humanoids)

The node that builds the bodies. China's robotics industry is emerging from the same manufacturing ecosystem that produces electric vehicles, LiDAR sensors, and batteries. The Hesai sensor costs $150 on a BYD Seagull and $150 on a Unitree H1 humanoid robot. The servo motors that articulate a robot arm are manufactured in the same Guangdong factories that produce EV drivetrain components. The neural network that processes warehouse navigation is a downstream derivative of autonomous driving.

The scale is approaching critical mass. ARK projects robotics revenue at $26 trillion—subject to caveats in the promotional methodology, but directionally significant even at a steep discount. In 2025, Chinese venture capital invested 57 billion RMB (approximately $8 billion) across 610 robotics deals. Government-linked limited partners now represent approximately 50 percent of Chinese robotics venture funding, up from 25 percent five years ago. The national venture guidance fund totals $138 billion. China Development Bank allocated 551.8 billion yuan to manufacturing modernization, explicitly including robotics.

Gekko prices the form-factor arbitrage: Unitree's G1 humanoid retails at $16,000—one-tenth the projected cost of Tesla's Optimus. But the humanoid is the frontier of speculation. The investable present is the industrial robot arm, the warehouse AGV, and the agricultural drone—form factors where unit economics are proven, payback periods are under three years, and the manufacturing learning curve is driven by the same EV production scale that has collapsed battery costs by 90 percent in fifteen years. The investor who waits for the humanoid will miss the arm.

Causal link to Node Four: robots are manufactured using the same batteries, motors, and components that populate the EV supply chain. Every unit of EV manufacturing scale reduces robot manufacturing costs, because the bill-of-materials overlap exceeds 40 percent. BYD's 75 percent vertical integration results in cost reductions across both vehicles and robots.

Node Four: Distributed Energy (Solar, Storage, Small Nuclear)

The node that powers everything. Every node in the Interdependency Web requires energy—robotaxis need charging, logistics drones need batteries, robots need power, data centers need electricity—and the scale of demand is transforming how energy is generated, stored, and distributed.

CATL and BYD together control approximately 55.6 percent of global lithium-ion battery manufacturing capacity (CATL at 39.2 percent, BYD at 16.4 percent). This dominance is a cost-curve position: when battery storage costs fall below $80 per kilowatt-hour—a threshold Chinese manufacturers are approaching—it becomes economically rational to deploy storage at every node in the energy system, from utility-scale solar farms to EV fleet charging depots. Each deployment increases demand for batteries, which increases manufacturing scale, lowering costs and enabling more deployments. The flywheel is the same one that drives the EV cost curve, because the battery is the same.

The fleet itself becomes a grid asset. A robotaxi fleet can participate in grid services during charging hours—absorbing excess solar during midday, discharging during evening peaks, and providing frequency regulation through vehicle-to-grid protocols. An autonomous logistics fleet that charges off-peak and operates during peak demand is simultaneously a transportation system and a demand-response resource. The vehicles are not merely consuming energy. They are managing it.

Causal link to Node Five: distributed energy systems generate vast quantities of real-time data—production, consumption, storage state, grid frequency—that feed the AI training pipelines powering autonomous systems. The energy data improves logistics algorithms, increasing fleet utilization and generating more driving data.

Node Five: Financial & Data Rails

The node that connects the others. When autonomous vehicles, robots, drones, and energy systems operate at scale, they require transactional infrastructure that does not currently exist. A robotaxi that picks up a passenger, charges the fare, pays the toll, negotiates the electricity price, and settles the insurance premium—all without human intervention—requires machine-to-machine payment rails and real-time risk pricing that traditional banking was not designed to support.

China's digital payment ecosystem—Alipay and WeChat Pay, which process over \$35 trillion in annual transactions—is the closest existing approximation to what autonomous agents will require. The extension from human-initiated to machine-initiated payments is an engineering challenge, not a paradigm shift. The data generated—usage patterns, maintenance predictions, energy consumption profiles—becomes the feedstock for insurance pricing, fleet financing, and infrastructure investment decisions. The financial rails do not merely move money. They generate the intelligence that directs capital.

Gekko prices the margin structure: the financial rails are the highest-margin node because they operate on information rather than atoms. The platform that controls the data rails captures a 2–5 percent transaction fee on every autonomous interaction—ride, delivery, charge, or insure—without manufacturing physical components. The data rails are the toll bridge. Everything else is the road.

Causal link back to Node One: financial data optimizes fleet deployment, route selection, and pricing strategy. Better financial data leads to higher fleet utilization, which generates more driving data, which in turn improves the perception stack. The cycle completes. The market feeds the monsoon.

• • •

Closing the Loops: One Ecosystem, Many Channels

Walk a single loop through the Web. AV fleet data trains logistics algorithms. Autonomous trucks reduce battery transport costs. Cheaper batteries enable distributed energy storage. Distributed energy powers AI data centers. Better AI trains more capable farm drones. Farm drones increase crop output. Higher crop output generates more logistics volume. More logistics volume generates more data. More data improves the AV fleet. The loop closes. Each cycle makes the next cycle faster, cheaper, and more capable.

Now multiply by five, because five loops are running simultaneously, and each intersects with every other at multiple points. The embodied intelligence platform is driven by the entire techno-industrial ecosystem China has built over two decades of patient, agricultural, Farmer-logic capital allocation. The platform is a metabolism—consuming data, excreting capability, and growing with every iteration. Like the Kuttanad ecosystem, it does not optimize a single output. It optimizes the cycle. And once running, the cycle resists interruption because each node compensates for the others' weaknesses.

[EXHIBIT 11.5-A: THE INTERDEPENDENCY WEB — CIRCULAR FLOW DIAGRAM SHOWING AV → LOGISTICS → ROBOTICS → ENERGY → FINANCIAL RAILS → AV, WITH CAUSAL ARROWS AND DATA/COST SHARING ANNOTATED AT EACH LINK. WORKED DOLLAR EXAMPLE: \$150 HESAI LIDAR SENSOR TRACED THROUGH ALL FIVE NODES WITH DOLLAR VALUES AT EACH STAGE.]

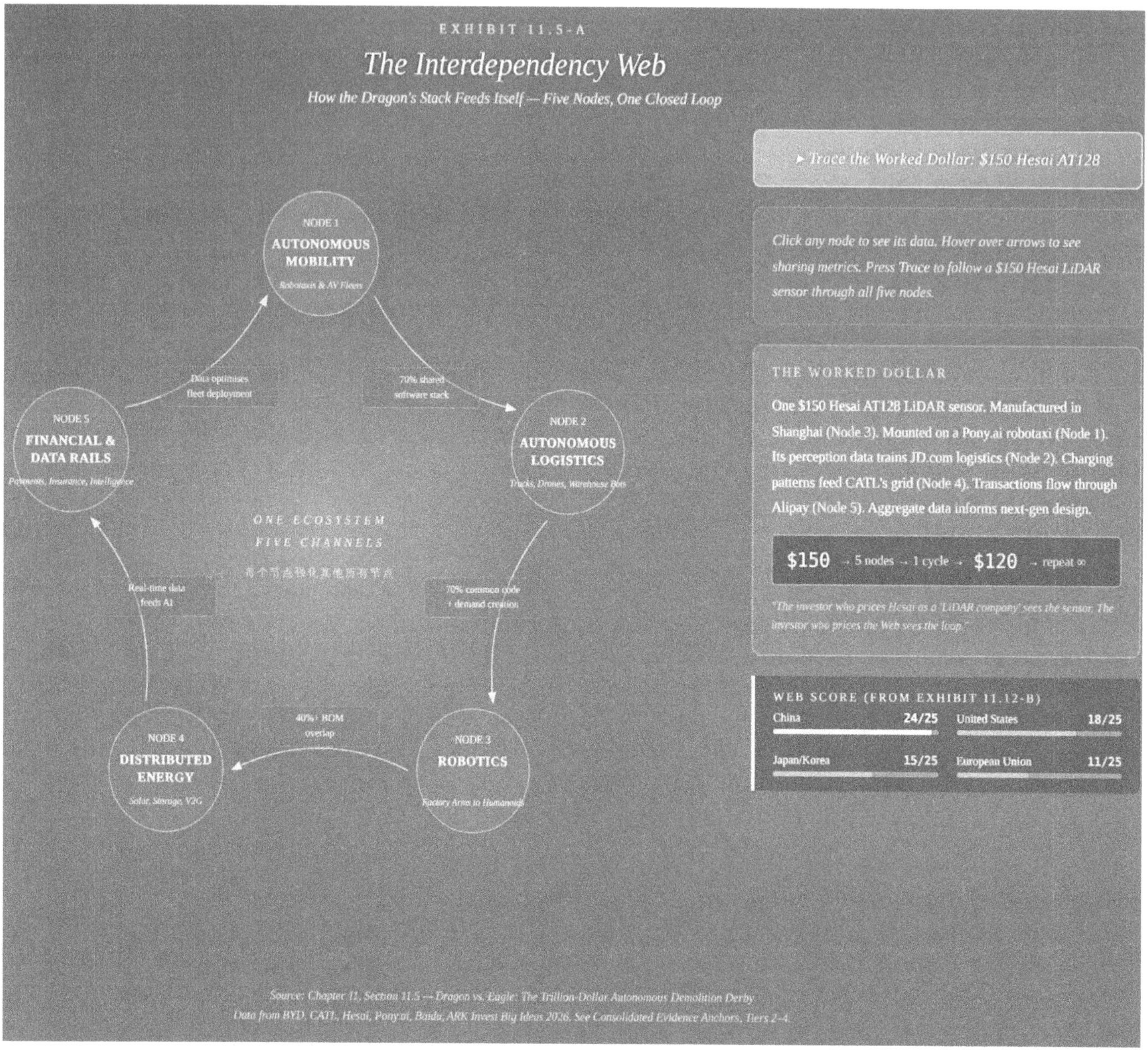

EXHIBIT 11.5-A

The Interdependency Web
How the Dragon's Stack Feeds Itself — Five Nodes, One Closed Loop

▶ *Trace the Worked Dollar: $150 Hesai AT128*

Click any node to see its data. Hover over arrows to see sharing metrics. Press Trace to follow a $150 Hesai LiDAR sensor through all five nodes.

NODE 1
AUTONOMOUS MOBILITY
Robotaxis & AV Fleets

NODE 5
FINANCIAL & DATA RAILS
Payments, Insurance, Intelligence

NODE 2
AUTONOMOUS LOGISTICS
Trucks, Drones, Warehouse Bots

Data optimises fleet deployment

70% shared software stack

ONE ECOSYSTEM
FIVE CHANNELS
每个节点强化其他所有节点

Real-time data feeds AI

70% common code + demand creation

NODE 4
DISTRIBUTED ENERGY
Solar, Storage, V2G

40%+ BOM overlap

NODE 3
ROBOTICS
Factory Arms to Humanoids

THE WORKED DOLLAR

One $150 Hesai AT128 LiDAR sensor. Manufactured in Shanghai (Node 3). Mounted on a Pony.ai robotaxi (Node 1). Its perception data trains JD.com logistics (Node 2). Charging patterns feed CATL's grid (Node 4). Transactions flow through Alipay (Node 5). Aggregate data informs next-gen design.

$150 → 5 nodes → 1 cycle → $120 → repeat ∞

"The investor who prices Hesai as a 'LiDAR company' sees the sensor. The investor who prices the Web sees the loop."

WEB SCORE (FROM EXHIBIT 11.12-B)

China	24/25	United States	18/25
Japan/Korea	15/25	European Union	11/25

Source: Chapter 11, Section 11.5 — Dragon vs. Eagle: The Trillion-Dollar Autonomous Demolition Derby
Data from BYD, CATL, Hesai, Pony.ai, Baidu, ARK Invest Big Ideas 2026. See Consolidated Evidence Anchors, Tiers 2–4.

Integrator: Treating EV/AV as "the auto sector" is a category error equivalent to treating the smartphone as "the phone sector." The investor who sees five separate industries will price five separate betas. The investor who sees one Interdependency Web will price a system whose compound growth rate exceeds that of any individual node by approximately 35 percent (per ARK's Convergence Network Strength metric). China's dominance in four of five nodes represents a civilizational platform advantage. The fragility is equally structural: the companies most exposed are those most deeply embedded in the cathedral architecture the Web is replacing—the Tier 1 suppliers whose margins depend on interfaces that vertical integration eliminates.

11.6 The Convergence Multiplier: Gekko's Ledger

I

Pricing the Old World: ICE as Runoff Book

Gekko does not admire ecosystems. Gekko prices them. And the first thing Gekko prices is the old world—because the rubble has value, and the speed at which it depreciates determines the timing of the trade.

If the Interdependency Web captures even a conservative fraction of the combined TAMs mapped in Section 11.4—even after applying the 40–60 percent discount that separates promotional projections from institutional estimates—then the ICE automotive industry does not face disruption. It faces absorption. The question is not "What are GM's earnings in 2030?" The question is "What are GM's ICE assets worth in a world where 80 percent of Chinese and 60 percent of European new-vehicle sales are electric, autonomous fleets are replacing private ownership, and the components that once justified a $65,000 truck have no function in the vehicle of the future?"

The answer is a runoff book. A manufacturing plant carried at $800 million on the balance sheet—because its DCF model assumed 30 years of truck production—is worth $150 million as real estate and negative value as a going concern if its production line falls below minimum viable volume. The Convergence Multiplier measures the gap between the legacy architecture and the new one; it is not a discount. It is a discontinuity.

• • •

II

Pricing the New World: Web-Native Winners

In the ICE architecture, value concentrates at the top—the OEM brand, the dealer network, the aftermarket chain. In the embodied intelligence architecture, value concentrates in the platform layer—the entity that controls the perception stack, the data pipeline, the battery supply chain, and the orchestration software that coordinates fleets across all five Web nodes.

BYD illustrates the architecture. The God's Eye system—its specifications catalogued in Section 11.0—generates the daily training-data volume mapped in Node One. BYD's 75 percent vertical integration—from lithium mining to autonomous software—means that margin improvements at any link flow through to every product in the portfolio. The platform layer does not wear out, requires no maintenance, and improves with use rather than degrading. The investor who values BYD on automotive multiples is pricing a depreciating asset when the underlying reality is an appreciating platform.

• • •

III

The Convergence: Five Platforms, One Current

The convergence documented in Section 11.1—ARK's 35 percent year-over-year increase in cross-platform synergy—is visible in the positions that follow. The five technology platforms are not growing in parallel. They are growing into each other, creating a compound growth rate that exceeds the sum of the individual platforms by an estimated 1.3–1.5x.

China's positions in the five nodes are catalogued in Section 11.5: dominant in four, competitive in the fifth. The data—Baidu's 17 million rides, BYD's 2.3-million-vehicle God's Eye fleet, CATL's 55.6 percent global battery share, 57 billion RMB across 610 robotics deals, 35,000 kilometers of instrumented roads—needs no repetition here. What Section 11.5 demonstrated analytically, this section prices. The five platforms are one metabolism—consuming data, excreting capability, growing with every iteration.

• • •

IV

The Capital Behind the Current

The capital structure sustaining this convergence is not market-driven. It is state-directed. Government-linked limited partners—provincial guidance funds, state-owned enterprises, and sovereign wealth vehicles—now account for approximately 50 percent of LP commitments to Chinese venture funds, roughly double the share five years ago. The National Venture Capital Guidance Fund, established in 2024, targets 100 billion yuan ($13.8 billion). Provincial and municipal guidance funds totaled approximately $912 billion in committed capital by mid-2025. China Development Bank disbursed 551.8 billion yuan to manufacturing in 2024 alone. Hefei's legendary 7 billion yuan investment in NIO—made when the company was weeks from bankruptcy—has become a 15x return and a template for every ambitious municipal government in China.

This capital does not operate on venture timescales. It does not require a 3x return in seven years. It does not face quarterly performance pressure or redemption risk. It is patient capital with a strategic mandate—and its patience means it will continue to fund the learning curve, the overcapacity, and the export push that Western competitors experience as "unfair competition" and that the Chinese state regards as the cost of building an industrial civilization. The $912 billion is not an investment. It is a mobilization budget.

• • •

V

The Export Tsunami: Three Waves

The Web does not stay in China. It exports—and the mechanics of export are reshaping global trade at a speed tariff policy cannot match. China exported 7.098 million vehicles in 2025, surpassing the combined exports of Japan and Germany. The EU imposed countervailing duties of 17–35 percent; the United States imposed a 100 percent duty. The tariffs have not stopped the wave. Section 11.11 examines why the tariff mirage is the most expensive illusion in Western industrial policy.

The three waves. The first is finished vehicles—the 7.098 million units that crossed borders in 2025. The second is components and subsystems—batteries, LiDAR, motors, and software stacks embedded into non-Chinese vehicles through supply agreements and white-label licensing. Harder to measure and tariff because the components arrive as inputs. The third is manufacturing capacity—BYD's factory in Hungary, its plant in Turkey, Chery's Barcelona partnership, Leapmotor's Stellantis joint venture. This wave does not cross the tariff wall. It tunnels underneath it. Each wave is larger than the last, and each is less visible to the trade defense instruments designed to intercept the first.

> **Integrator: This is civilizational capital allocation. The five ARK platforms—each worth trillions in projected enterprise value—are converging on a supply chain dominated by China, funded by a capital structure unconstrained by quarterly capitalism, and accelerated by a data-generation infrastructure with no Western parallel. The $912 billion in guidance funds separates this thesis from every prior emerging-market boom: the BRICs of 2007 were market-driven and therefore market-reversible; this is state-directed and therefore state-persistent. The three-wave export pattern reveals why no single metric captures the disruption: Wave One (finished vehicles) is tariff-vulnerable, Wave Two (components) is tariff-resistant, Wave Three (local manufacturing) is tariff-immune. Each wave carries a different risk profile, a different timeline, and a different set of winners.**

11.7 The Countercurrent: What the Monsoon Does Not Control

The boatman who reads only the current and ignores the eddies drowns. The Gekko who ignores the counterargument builds a position that a single headline can destroy. Intellectual honesty is not a concession to the opposition. It is the foundation of a position that survives contact with reality.

The embodied intelligence thesis has four countercurrents. Two are structural—capable of altering the trajectory if they compound. Two are cyclical—capable of altering the timeline without changing the destination.

I

Choke Points in Compute: Chips, Export Controls, and Foundries

The most serious structural vulnerability. The embodied intelligence platform runs on chips, and the most advanced chips are manufactured by TSMC, using ASML equipment that employs extreme ultraviolet lithography, a technology no Chinese company can yet replicate. The United States, through the Bureau of Industry and Security, has imposed escalating export controls on advanced semiconductor equipment, advanced chip designs, and the tools required to manufacture both.

The regulatory architecture is precise and layered. The BIS Connected Vehicle Rule, published January 16, 2025 (90 Fed. Reg. 5360) and effective March 17, 2025, prohibits software with a Chinese or Russian nexus in vehicles sold in the United States starting with Model Year 2027, and hardware starting with Model Year 2030 (with a compliance reference date of January 1, 2029). Covered entities must file Declarations of Conformity sixty days prior to importation. The rule targets not only complete vehicles but Vehicle Connectivity Systems and Automated Driving Systems—meaning the perception stack, the V2X module, and the autonomous driving software are each independently covered. The prohibition is not merely a tariff. It is a technological severance.

Under the current regime—where China has access to mature-node chips (14nm and above) but is restricted from leading-edge nodes (7nm and below)—the platform operates at approximately 80 percent of theoretical capability. The perception stack functions. The learning loop iterates. But the most computationally intensive tasks—real-time multi-agent planning, centimeter-precision SLAM, and transformer-class on-vehicle reasoning—are constrained by the processing power available at the mature node.

The counterargument is algorithmic efficiency. DeepSeek's R1 reasoning model achieved performance competitive with leading Western models while training on hardware constrained by export controls—demonstrating that computational limitations can be partially offset by algorithmic innovation. SMIC's progress toward 7nm-equivalent production using DUV multi-patterning, Huawei's Ascend series advancing despite sanctions, and the broader pattern of Chinese firms treating restrictions as engineering problems rather than strategic endpoints suggest the constraint delays but may not deny. Whether it denies depends on a timeline that the export-control architects do not fully control.

One scenario transcends delay and enters thesis-kill territory. If TSMC fabrication capacity were physically severed—through armed conflict, blockade, or catastrophic infrastructure failure in Taiwan—the platform would lose its most advanced manufacturing source indefinitely. No Chinese foundry replicates TSMC's leading-edge nodes. This is not a friction to be discounted. It is an existential contingency—the one scenario in which the thesis does not merely delay but dies. The Verdict will explicitly price this risk. Its temperature rises and falls with the South China Sea's.

The semiconductor choke point affects Chinese valuations through two channels: it caps near-term L4/L5 deployment growth, and it sustains a premium for Western semiconductor companies essential to the advanced-node supply chain. The discount to Chinese AV companies should be 15–25 percent of projected 2030 valuations—a figure the Verdict's sizing framework will operationalize.

II

Robotics Valuation Anxiety and Hype Cycles

The second structural countercurrent is internal: China's robotics investment boom bears the hallmarks of speculative excess. In 2025, Chinese venture capital deployed 57 billion RMB across 610 robotics deals. Government-linked LPs doubled their share to approximately 50 percent. These numbers are impressive. They are also, in certain pockets, frothy. Investigative reporting has documented cases of large-scale orders for humanoid robots in which the buyer entity was created days before the purchase order, personnel overlapped between buyer and seller, and the "orders" primarily served to inflate revenue metrics for fundraising. The 300,000 RMB ($42,000) TCO threshold for industrial humanoid adoption remains above the payback period most manufacturers require.

The historical precedent is clarifying. In 2015, China experienced a similar boom-and-consolidation cycle in ride-hailing, electric vehicles, and autonomous driving. The pattern: massive capital deployment, speculative excess, brutal consolidation, emergence of two or three dominant platforms. The robotics cycle is following the same trajectory. The investor who mistakes the current hype for the mature structure will overpay. The investor who mistakes the consolidation for thesis failure will miss the dominant survivors.

Discount Chinese robotics pure-plays by 30–40 percent relative to current venture valuations when constructing public-market-equivalent fair values. Do not, however, discount the robotics node on the Web, because the node's contribution does not require every company to survive. It requires the platform's component costs to decline along the manufacturing learning curve—and that curve is driven by EV production scale. The node persists. The names change. Price the node, not the names.

III

Overcapacity and Policy Corrections in China

In July 2025, Beijing's central leadership issued a rare public critique of local governments' "rush investments" into AI computing centers, NEV plants, and robotics industrial parks. The NEV sector's exclusion from the latest Five-Year Plan's priority list is not a retreat. It is graduation: the sector is mature enough to survive without direct central support. The 7.098 million vehicles exported in 2025 are, in part, the product of domestic overcapacity seeking international outlets—and those outlets are building the global infrastructure that will support the next generation of embodied intelligence exports.

IV

Western Defenses: Tariffs, Rules, and Regulatory Fog

The full tariff analysis appears in Section 11.11. The relevant countercurrent is this: the defenses are real but porous, and each defensive action has accelerated the very displacement it was designed to prevent. The EU's countervailing duties of 17–35.3 percent and America's 100 percent tariff protect the consumer market from Chinese imports. They do not protect the Western automotive industry from the cost curves, platform economics, and the embodied intelligence architecture that are eating away at its business model from within. Moreover, the defenses are porous: BYD is building factories in Hungary, Turkey, Brazil, Thailand, and Indonesia—tunneling beneath the tariff wall by manufacturing within it.

· · ·

V

Why the Current Still Runs One Way

The four countercurrents are real. They add volatility. They extend the timeline by 12 to 18 months. They do not change the direction. The semiconductor choke delays L4/L5 deployments, but not the

L2+ fleet, which is already generating its daily torrent of data. The valuation froth will burn off as the robotics cycle consolidates; the manufacturing infrastructure will not. The overcapacity forces domestic consolidation but funds the export push. The tariff wall slows penetration but does not close the cost gap that makes penetration inevitable once the wall cracks.

The reason is structural: the countercurrents are friction, and the Interdependency Web is momentum. When momentum is generated by five interconnected nodes reinforcing each other through shared supply chains, data, and cost curves, the friction required to reverse the system exceeds what export controls, tariffs, or valuation corrections can deliver. The eddies do not reverse the monsoon. They create the turbulence in which the skilled boatman finds his route.

> **Integrator: The countercurrents do not destroy the thesis. They price it. The semiconductor choke is priced with a geopolitical discount. Valuation anxiety prices in a consolidation cycle. The overcapacity risk prices platform-over-startup construction. The Western defenses price a long-dated trade structure. Each eddy is a pricing input, not a thesis reversal. The investor who sees only the thesis will overpay. The investor who sees only the countercurrents will miss the generational opportunity. The investor who reads both currents will find the position that survives volatility and captures compound returns.**

Marcus opens his sector-allocation spreadsheet and tries to file BYD. Autos? The battery division is energy. The robotaxi fleet is mobility-as-a-service. The God's Eye data pipeline is an AI infrastructure. His spreadsheet has five columns, and BYD occupies all of them—the same five nodes the Web just mapped. His categories are the cathedral's architecture, and the temple does not fit inside them. He closes the spreadsheet. For the first time, he opens a blank page.

The deity has risen. The Web is mapped. The countercurrents are priced. Now Gekko counts.

END OF MOVEMENT II: ASCENDS

MOVEMENT III: COUNTS

Gekko Prices the Wreckage and the Survivors

In the Kuttanad backwaters, when the monsoon retreats, the boatman does not celebrate. He counts what remains: which dykes held, which fields drowned, which boats must be rebuilt. The counting is not an afterthought. It is the entire purpose of surviving the flood.

— Kuttanad proverb

Now Gekko counts.
The counting begins.

11.8 The Petroleum Undertow

In the Kuttanad backwaters, when the main channel shifts course, the fisherman does not lose only his channel. He loses his net-drying ground, his boat-repair bank, the toddy shop where contracts are sealed. The river's undercurrent does not merely redirect water. It rearranges the entire economy built along its banks.

The internal combustion engine is not an engine. It is a capillary system. For every dollar of value created in the act of burning fuel inside a cylinder, approximately four dollars of downstream economic activity exist in the ecosystem that supports, services, maintains, fuels, insures, and eventually disposes of the machine that burns that fuel. When the engine dies, the capillary system does not merely shrink. It hemorrhages.

Begin with the barrel. The IEA's 2025 World Energy Outlook projects that electric vehicles will displace approximately 2 million barrels per day of oil demand by 2030 under the Stated Policies Scenario—rising to 6 million barrels per day by 2035 under the Announced Pledges Scenario. Two million barrels per day sounds modest until you realize that global oil markets historically reprice violently in response to marginal shifts of 1–3 percent. The 2014 oil price collapse—from $115 to $28—was triggered by a comparable supply surplus. The EV displacement is not a supply shock. It is a demand destruction event on the same magnitude. The difference: supply gluts are temporary. Demand destruction is permanent.

The Downstream Cascade

Follow the barrel downstream. The refinery that processes crude into gasoline operates on razor margins—2–5 percent in a good year—and requires minimum throughput to cover fixed costs. When gasoline demand drops 10–15 percent, the refinery crosses the break-even threshold. The United States operates 129 petroleum refineries. The American Fuel and Petrochemical Manufacturers Association estimates that a sustained 15 percent reduction would render 25–35 facilities uneconomic. They are concentrated in the Gulf Coast, the Midwest, and the Delaware Valley—regions already politically volatile, already experiencing deindustrialization, already primed for the populist narratives that transform structural economic change into cultural grievance.

Below the refinery sits the gas station—150,900 in the United States as of 2024 —earning 10–15 cents per gallon on fuel, while convenience sales generate 40–60 percent of gross profit. The business model is a two-sided market: fuel attracts customers; snacks and lottery tickets generate the margin. Remove the fuel, and you lose a foot-traffic anchor for a $650 billion convenience-store industry. NACS data shows 5–8% declines in fuel volume in EV-heavy markets. Well-capitalized chains can adapt. The 60 percent of American stations that are single-owner operations with annual net income of less than $200,000 cannot.

The boatman counts the capillaries: 150,900 stations, 40,000 parts stores, 10,000 quick-lube outlets. Between the refinery and the quick-lube—in the auto-parts retail chain ($80 billion annually across AutoZone, O'Reilly, Advance Auto Parts, NAPA), in the transmission shop, in the exhaust specialist—lies the vast middle of the capillary economy, where the drying happens silently, one franchise at a time, until the silence becomes a roar.

The Capillary Economy

The petroleum undertow is not an energy-sector problem. It is a service-economy problem. The refinery employs hundreds; the gas station employs four; the parts store twelve; the quick-lube six. Multiply those small numbers across 150,000 stations, 40,000 parts stores, and 10,000 quick-lube outlets, and you are pricing the displacement of approximately 2.5 million American jobs—most in communities with no obvious replacement industry, no retraining infrastructure, and very reliable voter-registration rates. Goldman Sachs estimates that the serviceable addressable market for auto parts will decline 35–40 percent over 15 years as the fleet electrifies.

Gekko traces the capital implications: the commercial real estate backing gas stations, auto parts stores, and quick-lube chains represents an estimated $180–220 billion in assessed property value. As fuel volumes decline, franchise values compress, lease renewals fail, and the environmental remediation liability on abandoned fuel-storage sites—estimated by the EPA at $200,000–$1.5 million per site—crystallizes on the balance sheet of the last owner. The petroleum undertow is a triple cascade: operating income loss, franchise value destruction, and environmental liability crystallization.

> **Integrator: Analysts price the energy transition as a supply-side story—who makes the batteries, who builds the chargers. This is the demand-side story. The Interdependency Web compounds capability across five nodes; the capillary economy decompounds it across five cascades—refinery, station, parts store, quick-lube, and real estate. One system creates value through interconnection. The other destroys it. They are the same physics, running in opposite directions—and the investor who sees only the creation will miss the destruction priced into the pension, the municipal bond, and the $180–220 billion in stranded commercial real estate. The Boatman does not mourn the river's course. He moves his nets.**

The capillary economy is the riverbed. The political system built atop that riverbed is the next casualty.

11.9 The Human Cost and the Political Doom Loop

The petroleum undertow traced the capillary economy and the 2.5 million American service jobs anchored to internal combustion. This section traces the political system that holds those jobs together—because the capillary economy is the riverbed, and the political doom loop is the flood that arrives when the riverbed dries.

The supplier layoffs catalogued in Section 11.2—104,000 European jobs at 142 per day—are not merely restructuring announcements. They are the seismic signature of an industrial ecosystem whose cost base was engineered for a technology being replaced. A Volkswagen plant in Wolfsburg is not merely a factory. It is a city's pension system, a region's tax base, a state government's political legitimacy, and a union's reason for existence. When the plant contracts, it triggers a cascade: municipal tax shortfalls, school budget cuts, housing price declines, small-business closures, and—most consequential—political radicalization that worsens the problem.

The Doom Loop Mechanics

The political doom loop operates with the mechanical precision of a feedback circuit. Job losses in automotive-dependent regions generate economic anxiety. Economic anxiety generates demand for protection—tariffs, subsidies, regulatory barriers. Protection delays adaptation. Delayed adaptation increases the competitiveness gap with Chinese manufacturers, who are scaling unimpeded. The widening gap generates more job losses. More job losses generate more anxiety. The circuit completes and repeats, each iteration deepening the structural damage it was designed to prevent.

The AfD achieved 20.8 percent of the national vote in the German federal election of February 23, 2025—its highest federal result ever—with its strongest performances in the automotive-dependent states of Saxony, Thuringia, and Brandenburg. Academic research from the ifo Institute and the Bertelsmann Foundation has quantified, with the dispassionate precision of social scientists who have clearly given up on influencing policy, the exact conversion rate of economic despair into political radicalization: factory closures in a municipality predict a 1.2–1.8 percentage-point increase in far-right vote share in the subsequent election cycle. They have published the formula. The policymakers have read the paper. The factories are closing anyway. The relationship is not merely correlated. It is causal—and it is ignored with a discipline that suggests ignoring it is itself a policy.

In France, Stellantis's contraction at Poissy and Rennes contributed to industrial anxiety that Marine Le Pen's Rassemblement National has channeled into a 33 percent polling floor. In Italy, the Meloni government's intervention to prevent Stellantis from further reducing Italian production is explicitly framed as a defense of national industrial identity—not as economic policy but as a matter of civilizational preservation.

The doom loop is the predictable consequence of treating a structural transformation as a cyclical downturn. Protectionism is not an adaptation strategy. It is an adaptation delay mechanism. Every quarter of protection purchased with a 17–35 percent tariff is a quarter in which Chinese manufacturers achieve another 15–20 percent cost reduction through manufacturing learning curves, another iteration of vertical integration. The wall does not prevent water from flowing. It builds the pressure behind the wall.

Pricing the Doom Loop

Gekko prices the human cost in the only language capital markets understand: fiscal liability. Germany's Kurzarbeit program cost €42 billion between 2020 and 2022. The automotive transition—slower, deeper, and lacking the snap-back recovery pandemic relief assumed—will require comparable or greater outlays sustained over a decade. The ifo Institute projects annual spending of €15–25 billion on retraining, relocation, and income support through 2035. This is not a recession. It is a structural repricing of the German social contract. The American variant is quieter but no less corrosive. The Michigan counties that produce 30 percent of US auto components have median household incomes 8–12 percent below the state average. These counties swung 4–7 points toward protectionist candidates in 2024, a drift that no amount of "just transition" rhetoric has reversed.

> **Integrator:** The ARK Big Ideas framework identifies protectionism as the primary drag on the acceleration of convergence. Every tariff is a tax on the consumer that funds the delay of the inevitable. For the investor: European auto-supplier credit spreads are a leading indicator—not of automotive health, but of political stability. When ZF's bonds widen, the AfD's polls tighten. For the policymaker: the €15–25 billion annual price tag of adaptation is a fraction of the fiscal cost of the doom loop itself, which compounds through lost tax revenue, increased social transfers, and rising political instability. Adaptation-first is not a moral position. It is a fiscal calculation.

The doom loop is the politics. The extinction pattern is the precedent.

11.10 The Extinction Pattern: What the British Motorcycle Industry Teaches

In 1959, Britain manufactured 257,000 motorcycles per year and dominated the global market. BSA, Triumph, Norton, Royal Enfield, Matchless—names as resonant in their industry as Ford and

Volkswagen are in theirs. By 1975, the British motorcycle industry was effectively dead. Not diminished. Not restructured. Dead. BSA collapsed in 1972. Norton went into receivership in 1975. Only Triumph survived—barely—as a niche manufacturer of premium machines for enthusiasts.

The killer was not a single product. It was a system. Honda, Yamaha, Suzuki, and Kawasaki entered the British market with small, inexpensive, reliable motorcycles that British manufacturers dismissed as toys. The Honda Super Cub—the Seagull of its era—sold for one-third the price of a comparable British machine, required one-fifth the maintenance, and targeted a market segment British manufacturers had never considered worth serving: commuters, women, young riders, people who wanted transportation rather than lifestyle. "You meet the nicest people on a Honda" was not selling a motorcycle. It was selling the democratization of mobility. The parallels to "the first robot, not the last car" are not coincidental.

The Five-Phase Pattern

The British motorcycle extinction followed a pattern so precise it reads like a clinical protocol:

Phase 1: Market-Entry Dismissal (1960–1963). Japanese manufacturers entered at the bottom with products that incumbents considered beneath their attention.

"They make scooters," said the BSA chairman. "We make motorcycles." In 2019, a Ford executive told Reuters that Chinese EVs were "not competitive outside their home market." In 2022, a GM strategy presentation classified BYD as a "regional competitor." The scooters have come for the motorcycles. Again.

Phase 2: Quality-Gap Closure (1963–1967). Japanese manufacturers moved upmarket with each generation, closing the performance gap while maintaining the cost advantage. British manufacturers responded with incremental improvements but could not match the iteration pace because their vertically fragmented supply chains updated at the speed of the slowest component.

Phase 3: Supply-Chain Collapse (1967–1970). As Japanese volume grew, British component suppliers lost their minimum-viable-scale economics. Lucas Electrical began prioritizing automotive clients. Amal Carburettors lost volume and raised prices. The supply chain did not collapse because the manufacturers failed. The manufacturers failed because the supply chain collapsed. The causality ran backwards from the conventional narrative.

Phase 4: Financial-Engineering Retreat (1970–1973). BSA's management retreated into the premium segment—identical to what Detroit is attempting today. The Honda CB750—a superbike at a middleweight price—destroyed BSA's last redoubt. BSA's shares were suspended in 1972.

Phase 5: Political Intervention and Terminal Decline (1973–1975). The British government nationalized Norton Villiers Triumph in 1973. The rescue failed for the same reason all such rescues fail: it preserved the cost structure that had made the companies uncompetitive without addressing the capability gap that had made them irrelevant. The nationalized entity hemorrhaged £30 million before collapsing.

Phase 6: Ecosystem Colonization—The New Variable

Here is where the historical analogy breaks—and where the Theyyam sees something the historian cannot. The Japanese motorcycle invasion displaced motorcycles. Honda killed BSA, but Honda did not simultaneously colonize British lorry manufacturing, British agricultural equipment, British electricity generation, and British financial services. The Japanese motorcycle industry had one product. It disrupted one market.

The Chinese embodied-intelligence platform offers five form factors and disrupts five markets simultaneously through a single supply chain. The BYD Blade battery that powers the Seagull also powers the energy-storage system that backs a solar microgrid. The Hesai AT128 LiDAR that guides a Pony.ai robotaxi also guides a DJI agricultural drone. The Horizon Robotics Journey 6 chip that runs perception for Volkswagen's ID.7 also runs perception for a logistics AGV in a Foxconn factory. The five fires are not five separate disruptions. They are a single disruption expressed across five form factors, each reinforcing the others.

Gekko measures the speed differential. The British motorcycle industry took approximately 15 years to die (1960–1975). The Western ICE industry is operating on a compressed timeline: China's EV market share crossed 50 percent in mid-2025, roughly seven years after serious scaling began. The acceleration factor is the Interdependency Web: when five industries share the same supply chain, the learning curve operates on the aggregate volume of all five, not just one. BSA faced Honda's motorcycle volume. Volkswagen faces BYD's combined EV, battery, robotics, and energy-storage volume.

> **Integrator:** The five-phase extinction pattern is not a metaphor. It is a diagnostic checklist. Phase 1 (Market-Entry Dismissal) is complete—Western executives spent 2019–2022 dismissing Chinese EVs as cheap imitations. Phase 2 (Quality-Gap Closure) is complete—the BYD Seal, Zeekr 001, and XPeng G9 have met or exceeded European quality benchmarks in Euro NCAP testing. Phase 3 (Supply-Chain Collapse) is beginning—the supplier layoffs catalogued in Sections 11.2 and 11.9 are the leading edge. Phases 4 and 5 (Financial-Engineering Retreat and Political Intervention) are the current playbook. The new variable—Ecosystem Colonization—means the sequel is five times as wide as the original. Apply the five-phase checklist to every legacy holding. If it is in Phase 3 or beyond, the Dinosaur Meter score is not academic. It is the countdown to forced recapitalization.

The extinction pattern is the precedent. The tariff wall is the illusion that the precedent does not apply.

11.11 The Tariff Mirage

On September 27, 2024, the United States imposed a 100 percent tariff on Chinese EVs—102.5 percent total with the existing duty. On October 29, 2024, the EU finalized countervailing duties of 17.0–35.3 percent on top of its 10 percent base tariff, calibrated by manufacturer. Canada imposed a 100 percent surtax. Turkey added 40 percent. The detailed schedule is in the Evidence Anchors and Section 11.7.

The Boatman reads the undercurrent beneath these numbers. Every tariff is a confession. It confesses that the domestic industry cannot compete on cost, features, iteration speed, or the underlying manufacturing learning curve. The tariff does not solve the competitiveness gap. It prices the gap into the consumer's household budget and calls it "protection." The question the Boatman asks is not whether the tariff protects. The question is: who is trapped inside the wall—the consumer, or the manufacturer?

The Evidence: Tariffs as Accelerant

Chinese vehicle registrations in Europe surged 91 percent in the first half of 2025 compared with the prior year (JATO Dynamics, July 2025)—a figure that includes some pre-tariff inventory acceleration but whose trajectory only steepened: full-year 2025 registrations reached 811,000 units, a 99 percent increase, per DataForce. Chinese manufacturers accelerated shipments, established local inventory, pivoted to tariff-exempt plug-in hybrids and models priced to absorb the duty, and began investing in European manufacturing facilities to bypass the tariff entirely. BYD's Hungarian factory begins production in 2026. Its Turkish factory will produce 150,000 vehicles annually. Chery's Barcelona partnership and Leapmotor's Stellantis joint venture have already begun European production. The tariff did not stop the river. It rerouted it.

The American 100 percent tariff is more effective as a barrier—but more corrosive as a policy. A BYD Seagull retails in China for approximately $9,550. At the tariff rate, its US price would be approximately $19,100—still cheaper than any comparable American EV. But the tariff does more than protect American OEMs. It removes the competitive pressure that would force them to match BYD's cost structure. In the absence of price pressure, manufacturers invest in incremental improvements rather than platform transformation. They raise prices rather than reduce costs. They buy back shares rather than buy the future. The tariff creates a greenhouse in which the weaker species survives—until the greenhouse glass cracks.

The Self-Cannibalization Imperative

The tariff's true cost is measured in the adaptation that does not happen. Every quarter in which a Western OEM does not face full Chinese competitive pressure is a quarter in which it does not make the radical investments required to survive when the tariff eventually falls—as tariffs always eventually fall, because the political constituency for cheap goods always eventually overwhelms the constituency for protected producers. The EU's minimum-import-price mechanism, introduced in January 2026, already contains the seeds of its own unwinding: the first exemption—Volkswagen's Cupra Tavascan, manufactured in Anhui—was granted in February 2026, less than one month after activation.

Western OEMs face a binary choice: destroy their own profitable ICE business to build a competitive EV platform, or preserve the ICE business behind a tariff wall and hope the wall holds forever. The first option is financially excruciating—Ford's cumulative EV losses testify to that. The second is strategically suicidal—it guarantees that when the wall cracks, the domestic industry will be less competitive, not more.

Gekko traces the capital misallocation. In the 24 months following the US tariff announcement, GM announced $10 billion in share buybacks and a $6 billion slowdown in EV investments. Ford reduced its planned EV capital expenditure by $12 billion. Stellantis suspended its STLA AutoDrive L3 program. The 100 percent tariff was supposed to buy time for adaptation. The industry used the time to buy back its own stock. This is the equivalent of a doctor prescribing bed rest and the patient using the recovery period to take up cliff diving—except the patient's compensation package is tied to the cliff-diving footage going viral, so the incentive structure is, in its way, perfectly rational. The wall does not protect the manufacturer. The wall is the manufacturer's alibi for not transforming—and, like all alibis, it holds up right up until the moment the detective arrives.

The BIS Connected Vehicles Rule—detailed in Section 11.7—is not a tariff. It is a technological Iron Curtain, severing the supply chain entirely by prohibiting Chinese-linked software (Model Year 2027) and hardware (Model Year 2030) in American vehicles. The question it does not answer: if Western OEMs cannot use Chinese components, and Chinese components are 50–70 percent cheaper, who absorbs the cost difference? The consumer, the manufacturer, or the government?

> **Integrator: Protectionism buys quarters. It poisons years. The 91 percent surge in Chinese vehicle registrations across Europe after the tariff tells the entire story: the river does not stop when you build a dyke. It rises. The apparent safety of Western auto stocks—shielded by 100 percent US tariffs and 17–35 percent EU duties—is a wasting asset whose expiry date is printed in the cost curves the tariff cannot reach. The dam that delays the monsoon does not diminish it. It stores it.**

The tariff mirage is the last illusion. The convergence beneath it is the final current.

11.12 The Verdict: Cremation, Rebirth, or Navigation?

The congregation at the ghat sees only death. The performer sees the deity being reborn. The investor's task is to decide which one they are.

— Closing invocation

We have walked the burning ghat from end to end.

Now comes the verdict. This section delivers three repeatable frameworks—tools the reader takes away from the chapter, not decorations within it—and three scenarios for how the ICE funeral unfolds. It closes with Marcus, the fund manager whose cognitive errors we have tracked across eleven chapters, arriving at the ghat equipped with instruments he did not have at the beginning of the chapter.

11.12.1 Framework 1: The Dinosaur Meter (The Investor's Takeaway)

The Dinosaur Meter scores any legacy automotive company on seven fragility factors, each weighted by its contribution to the probability of forced recapitalization. The framework is designed to be repeatable: an analyst can score any OEM, Tier 1 supplier, or auto-finance company and produce a comparable fragility index.

A note on methodology. Each factor is scored on a 0–100 scale derived from publicly available financial and structural data: ICE Profit Dependence uses the ratio of ICE-generated operating profit to total operating profit, converted to a percentile ranking against the scored universe; Dealer/Service Dependence uses aftermarket and F&I revenue as a share of total gross profit; Fixed-Cost Rigidity uses the ratio of fixed to variable costs and the number of manufacturing sites; Supplier Fragility uses Tier 1 counterparty credit spreads; EV Margin Gap uses reported per-vehicle EV losses relative to ICE per-vehicle profit; Autonomy Stack Deficit uses a qualitative assessment of internal AV capability versus the embodied-intelligence frontier; Policy Exposure uses a composite of regulatory jurisdiction, emissions-mandate timelines, and tariff dependence. Scores are normalized to the three-company universe shown below; adding companies recalibrates the percentile rankings. The framework is diagnostic, not predictive—it identifies structural fragility at a point in time, not the date of failure.

[EXHIBIT 11.12-A: THE DINOSAUR METER SCORECARD — DESIGN AS FORMATTED TABLE WITH COLOUR-CODED FRAGILITY BANDS]

EXHIBIT 11.12-A

The Dinosaur Meter

Seven-Factor Fragility Scorecard for Legacy Automotive
"It predicts the moment when the capital markets stop pretending."

Ford F	**Volkswagen** VOW3.DE	**Toyota** TM
83.4	**79.1**	**70.6**
CRITICAL — PHASE 4	CRITICAL — PHASE 3-4	CRITICAL — PHASE 2-3

CRITICAL FRAGILITY — FINANCIAL-ENGINEERING RETREAT

F-150/Bronco/Expedition account for virtually all operating profit. $16.7B cumulative EV losses — most severe in industry. Refinancing wall within 3–5 years.

83.4
COMPOSITE SCORE

FACTOR	WEIGHT	SCORE (0–100)	RAW	WEIGHTED
ICE Profit Dependence	20%		92	18.4
Dealer / Service Dependence	10%		82	8.2
Fixed-Cost Rigidity	15%		70	10.5
Supplier Fragility	10%		78	7.8
EV Margin Gap	25%		95	23.8
Autonomy Stack Deficit	10%		85	8.5
Policy Exposure	10%		62	6.2
COMPOSITE SCORE	100%	CRITICAL — REFINANCING WALL WITHIN 3–5 YEARS		**83.4**

Key driver: *EV Margin Gap 95 + ICE Dependence 92*

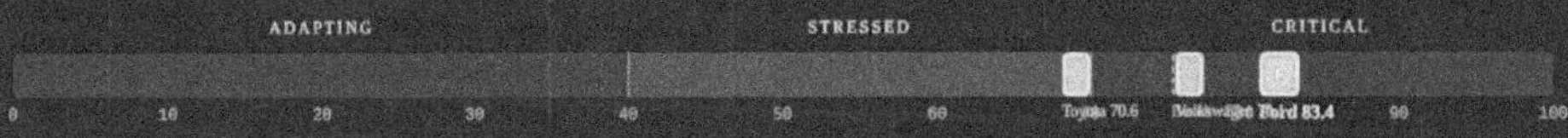

FRAGILITY BANDS

CRITICAL	70-100
Refinancing wall within 3–5 years	
STRESSED	40-69
Viable if self-cannibalization begins within 18 months	
ADAPTING	0-39
Structural adaptation underway or not required	

Bosch ~77
Tier 1 Supplier — Illustrative

Extreme ICE component dependence (injectors, turbochargers, exhaust). 400+ global facilities. Not scored in main table — illustrative of supplier fragility.

NEAR-TERM TRIGGER SIGNALS

▸ Profit-per-vehicle compression below $8,000 on ICE flagships

▸ Dealer inventory days above 90

▸ Supplier credit spreads above 400 bps

▸ Retreat into 'high-margin ICE focus' framed as strategic choice

▸ Covenant amendments or revolving-credit drawdowns

▸ *Methodology Note*

COMPARATIVE FRAGILITY SPECTRUM

ADAPTING — STRESSED — CRITICAL

| 0 | 10 | 20 | 30 | 40 | 50 | 60 | 70 | 80 | 90 | 100 |

Toyota 70.6 — Volkswagen 79.1 — Ford 83.4

EXTINCTION PATTERN ALIGNMENT (SECTION 11.10)

1	2	3	4	5	6
Market-Entry Dismissal	Quality-Gap Closure	Supply-Chain Collapse	Financial-Eng. Retreat	Political Intervention	Ecosystem Colonisation
complete	*complete*	*beginning*	*active*	*active*	*new variable*

"If it is in Phase 3 or beyond, the Dinosaur Meter score is not academic. It is the countdown to forced recapitalisation."

Source: Chapter 11, Section 11.12 — Dragon vs. Eagle: The Trillion-Dollar Autonomous Demolition Derby
Data from Ford, VW, Toyota annual reports 2024; Bloomberg Terminal credit data. See Consolidated Evidence Anchors, Tiers 1-2.

Scores range from 0 (fully adapted) to 100 (maximum fragility). Each factor is scored on a 0–100 scale based on publicly available data, then multiplied by its weight. The composite score maps to a recapitalization timeline:

Score 70–100: Refinancing wall within 3–5 years. Bond spreads will widen to distressed levels when ICE utilization falls below 65–70 percent. Current-year coupon coverage may mask the structural erosion. Watch for: covenant amendments, revolving-credit drawdowns, and "strategic review" announcements.

Score 40–70: Viable if self-cannibalization begins within 18 months. The company retains sufficient capital reserves and brand equity to fund a platform transition, provided management abandons ICE profit protection as a strategic priority. Every quarter of delay increases the score.

Score 0–40: Structural adaptation underway or not required. The company has either invested heavily in platform capabilities (rare among legacy OEMs), occupies a niche that the embodied-intelligence platform does not yet contest (luxury, ultra-premium, specialty), or has diversified revenue streams that provide transition funding.

Ford scores 83.4—the highest of the three, driven by its 95/100 EV Margin Gap (the cumulative EV losses documented in Section 11.1 are the most severe in the industry) and its 92/100 ICE Profit Dependence (F-150, Bronco, and Expedition account for virtually all operating profit). Volkswagen scores 79.1, lower on EV margins (the ID. series, while unprofitable, is less catastrophically so) but higher on fixed-cost rigidity (the German labor structure and 120+ plant network constrain restructuring velocity). Toyota scores 70.6—the lowest, reflecting its lower EV margin gap (hybrid profits provide transition funding), lower supplier fragility (the keiretsu system provides stability), and lower policy exposure (Japan's regulatory environment is less adversarial to ICE than Europe's). Even Toyota's 70.6 sits above the refinancing-wall threshold.

Bosch—the world's largest Tier 1 supplier, not scored in the table but illustrative—would score approximately 75–80, driven by its extreme ICE component dependence (injectors, turbochargers, exhaust systems) and its fixed-cost structure across 400+ global facilities. The Dinosaur Meter's utility lies not in predicting bankruptcy. It predicts the moment when the capital markets stop pretending.

11.12.2 Framework 2: Interdependency Web Scoring (The Strategist's Takeaway)

The Interdependency Web Scoring matrix enables analysts or policymakers to score a nation or company across the five nodes of the embodied-intelligence platform. Each node is scored on a 1–5 scale based on market position, supply chain control, data generation, and institutional support. The composite reveals structural competitive gaps invisible to single-sector analysis.

[EXHIBIT 11.12-B: INTERDEPENDENCY WEB SCORING MATRIX — DESIGN AS FORMATTED TABLE WITH HEAT-MAP COLOUR CODING]

Interdependency Web Scoring Matrix

Five Nodes × Four Nations — Platform Strength Heat Map (1–5 Scale)

NATION / REGION	Autonomous Mobility	Autonomous Logistics	Robotics	Distributed Energy	Financial & Data Rails	COMPOSITE /25
China — Platform builder	5	5	4	5	5	24 / 25
United States — Brain architect	4	3	3	3	5	18 / 25
Japan / Korea — Component specialist	2	3	4	3	3	15 / 25
European Union — Protected market	2	2	2	2	3	11 / 25

THE STRATEGIC REVELATION

THE BRAIN
5/5
America leads
Google · NVIDIA · OpenAI

vs
who builds the body
trains the brain

THE BODY
19/20
China leads
BYD · CATL · Pony.ai · Hesai

The United States' apparent strength in AI masks a structural vulnerability in every physical-world application of that AI. America leads in the brain. China leads in the body. The country that builds the body at scale trains the brain for the world. This is the embodied-intelligence thesis in a single matrix.

SCORE SCALE (PER NODE)

5	**Dominant**	Global leader; self-sustaining ecosystem
4	**Strong**	Major player with minor vulnerabilities
3	**Competitive**	Present but dependent on external supply
2	**Weak**	Nascent capability or critical gaps
1	**Absent**	No meaningful domestic capability

COMPOSITE BANDS (/25)

Platform Leader	22–25
Competitive Position	16–21
Structural Deficit	10–15
Dependent / Absent	0–9

China scores 24 out of 25—losing a single point on Robotics due to the valuation froth and consolidation risk identified in the Countercurrent section. The United States scores 18, with its strength concentrated in AI/Data Rails (Google, NVIDIA, OpenAI) and Autonomous Mobility (Waymo), but with critical deficits in Logistics, Energy/Storage, and Robotics. The European Union scores 11—the lowest of the four—reflecting its near-total dependency on Chinese battery supply, its absence of a domestic robotaxi fleet, and its regulatory approach that has prioritized protection over platform development. Japan/Korea scores 15, buoyed by robotics strength (Fanuc, Hyundai Boston Dynamics) and logistics capabilities (Toyota's Woven City) but constrained by battery dependence and limited AV deployment.

The strategic revelation: the United States' apparent strength in AI masks a structural vulnerability in every physical-world application of that AI. America leads in the brain. China leads in the body. The country that builds the body at scale trains the brain for the world. This is the embodied-intelligence thesis in a single matrix.

11.12.3 Framework 3: Quarter-Kelly Sizing (The Portfolio Manager's Takeaway)

The Kelly Criterion, developed by John Kelly at Bell Labs in 1956 and deployed by Ed Thorp to generate 20 percent annualized returns over 28 years at Princeton-Newport Partners, calculates the optimal fraction of capital to deploy when the edge and the odds are known. For the AV/embodied-intelligence thesis, the parameters are:

Full Kelly: Estimated excess return of 15 percent with 50 percent annualized volatility yields a full Kelly fraction of 60 percent—obviously too aggressive for any rational portfolio manager.

Quarter-Kelly (the Boatman's position): $0.25 \times 60 = 15$ percent maximum thematic allocation. This reduces expected return by approximately 20 percent while reducing variance by approximately 80 percent—the mathematical expression of the Kuttanad farmer's wisdom: plant enough to profit from the monsoon; not so much that a flood destroys you.

The allocation splits three ways:

US/Europe AV: 10 percent. Waymo (via Alphabet), NVIDIA, and selective European battery/charging plays (Northvolt, if it survives). This allocation captures the "brain" side of the embodied-intelligence thesis and benefits from the tariff wall's temporary protection.

China AV/EV: 5 percent × 0.7 geopolitical overlay = 3.5 percent. BYD, WeRide, Pony.ai, Hesai Group, CATL (via Hong Kong). The 0.7 multiplier explicitly prices the semiconductor choke point, the BIS-connected-vehicle rule, and the tail risk of a Taiwan Strait escalation identified by the Countercurrent section. If geopolitical risk recedes, the multiplier rises to 0.85 (yielding 4.25 percent). If it escalates, the multiplier drops to 0.3 (yielding 1.5 percent). The position breathes with the countercurrents.

Short legacy automakers: 2–3 percent. Funded by borrowing shares in the companies with the highest Dinosaur Meter scores. Sized to survive a 30 percent adverse squeeze—because the tariff wall can produce exactly such a squeeze in the near term, even as it accelerates the eventual collapse. The short is not a bet on imminent bankruptcy. It is a bet on multiple compression as the market gradually prices the transition from "cyclical downturn" to "structural runoff."

This framework directly links to Chapter 15, where the Three Monsoons allocation model integrates Kelly sizing with rebalancing triggers and event monitors that manage the position in response to the volatility the thesis predicts.

11.12.4 Three Scenarios

The verdict is not a prediction. It is a scenario-weighted probability distribution:

The BSA Path (25 percent probability): Full Extinction. The British motorcycle pattern repeats at an industrial scale. Western ICE manufacturers fail to self-cannibalize, the tariff wall cracks under consumer and political pressure, and Chinese embodied-intelligence platforms colonize not just automotive but logistics, energy, and robotics simultaneously. Within 5–7 years, the Western automotive industry contracts to 30–40 percent of current capacity, concentrated in defense, luxury, and specialty. Two to three major OEMs enter bankruptcy or forced restructuring. The historical precedent: everyone believed, until the liquidator arrived, that the Japanese made scooters and motorcycles.

The Triumph Path (50 percent probability): Managed Retreat to Niche. The most likely outcome. Western OEMs abandon the mass market to Chinese manufacturers, retreat to premium and luxury segments (Mercedes, BMW, Porsche, select Stellantis brands), and maintain approximately 20 percent global market share in higher-margin categories. The transition is financially painful—requiring $50–100 billion in aggregate write-downs, plant closures, and workforce reductions across the Western industry—but survivable for the strongest brands. Tier 1 suppliers consolidate from dozens to fewer than ten viable independents. The dealer network contracts by 30–40 percent. The service economy restructures around EV maintenance, which requires fewer technicians per vehicle but higher skill levels. This is the path of Triumph: the company survived by becoming something much smaller, much more focused, and much more profitable per unit than the mass manufacturer it once was.

The Kuttanad Path (25 percent probability): Radical Self-Cannibalization. The optimistic scenario. One or more Western OEMs make the existential decision to destroy their own ICE business to participate in the embodied-intelligence platform economy. This requires: abandoning ICE profit protection, investing $20–40 billion per OEM in platform capabilities, accepting 3–5 years of severely depressed earnings while the new platform scales, and—most painfully—closing profitable ICE plants while the revenue still flows. The strategic model is either Nokia's failed transformation

(from phone to smartphone) or, if successful, IBM's successful one (from hardware to services). The probability is low because the financial incentives, shareholder structure, labor agreements, and political environment all militate against it. But the Pokkali farmer teaches that it is possible to plant in brackish water. You just need a different seed.

11.12.5 *Marcus at the Ghat*

Marcus has been reading this chapter. He has tracked his own portfolio through eleven chapters of cognitive errors—the 40,000 tombs he ignored in Chapter 4, the granary data he miscategorized in Chapter 9, the trust chasm he dismissed in Chapter 10, the $13 billion in American failures he rationalized as "learning." His Bloomberg terminal shows the same screens it showed this morning: Waymo at $126 billion, Tesla at $1.5 trillion, Ford at one-quarter of its 2021 peak, Volkswagen trading below book value. The numbers are the same. But Marcus is not the same.

He opens a blank allocation sheet. He runs the Dinosaur Meter on Ford: 83.4—refinancing wall within three to five years, driven by cumulative EV losses and near-total dependence on F-150 and Bronco margins. He checks Volkswagen: 79.1—eighteen to twenty-four months more runway than Ford, but the German labor structure and 120-plant network make restructuring glacial. He checks Toyota: 70.6—the longest runway—but still above the distress threshold and exposed to the non-linear cliff when EV penetration crosses 50 percent in its key markets. The forty thousand tombs he ignored in Chapter 4 are not behind him. They are in the Dinosaur Meter's score—every one of them, priced.

He opens the Interdependency Web Score. China at 24/25—dominant in four of five nodes, competitive in the fifth. The United States is at 18/25—strong in AI but vulnerable in every physical application of that AI. Europe at 11/25—a buyer, not a builder. He sees, for the first time, that his zero allocation to China is not a risk-management decision. It is a thesis position—a bet that the country building the body of embodied intelligence at civilizational scale, funded by $912 billion in patient capital, will somehow fail to capture value from the platform it is constructing. He does not believe this thesis. He has been living it by default.

He applies the Quarter-Kelly sizing. Fifteen percent total thematic allocation. Ten percent US/Europe: Waymo via Alphabet, NVIDIA for the compute layer, selective European battery plays. Three-point-five percent China after the 0.7 geopolitical overlay: BYD for platform integration, CATL for energy, Hesai for perception, Pony.ai for mobility software. Two percent short legacy automakers: Ford and the highest-scoring Dinosaur Meter names, using 2028–2030 puts sized to survive a 30 percent adverse squeeze from tariff-induced optimism.

He has acknowledged the countercurrents. The semiconductor choke point is priced into the 0.7 overlay. The robotics valuation froth is priced into the platform-over-startup construction. The overcapacity risk is priced into the diversification across Web nodes rather than concentration in any single form factor. The tariff wall is priced into the long-dated option structure on the short side.

For the first time in eleven chapters, Marcus is not reacting to headlines, not chasing narratives, not confusing noise for signal. He has a framework. He has a score. He has a sizing model. He has read the five-phase extinction pattern and identified which phase each of his holdings occupies. He knows what the Dinosaur Meter says about Ford (countdown), what the Web Score says about China (platform), and what the Quarter-Kelly says about his maximum exposure (15 percent, no more, no less). The frameworks have not merely calculated the risk. They have dissolved the noise that made the risk incalculable—and in the silence that follows, something shifts. The same Bloomberg terminal. The same midtown office. The same screens. But the intelligence reading those screens has changed. In Section 11.4, the Theyyam performer's transformation was a metaphor for the automobile becoming a platform. Here, it is Marcus. The performer has not changed the hardware. He has changed the intelligence that inhabits it. And for the first time, Marcus can hear the current. He is, for the first time, doing what the Kuttanad boatman does every morning: reading the current beneath the surface, adjusting his position for the river he is in rather than the river he wishes he were in, and planting in the brackish water where the contradiction itself is the crop.

The Western automotive industry spent ninety-three billion dollars buying back its past. China spent 912 billion building everyone's future. The spreadsheet says they are in the same industry. The spreadsheet is the last illusion the burning ghat will consume.

The congregation at the ghat sees only death.
The performer sees the deity being reborn.
The investor's task is to decide which one they are.
The wreckage is priced. The frameworks are set. Now we turn to the market's delusion—for the burning ghat is visible to the boatman, but to the trader on the screen, it is merely a ticker symbol. Chapter 12 begins there.

END OF MOVEMENT III: COUNTS

CONSOLIDATED EVIDENCE ANCHORS: CHAPTER 11

Tier One: Primary Regulatory and Institutional Sources

Institutional-grade data: government agencies, multilateral organizations, official regulations. Highest reliability; independently verifiable.

IEA Global EV Outlook 2025 (Executive Summary; "Trends in electric car markets"): regional EV sales shares (China ~60% 2025, ~80% 2030; Europe ~25% 2025, ~60% 2030; US ~11% 2025, ~20% 2030; all Stated Policies Scenario) • IEA World Energy Outlook 2025: 2M barrels/day EV displacement by 2030 (STEPS); 6M bpd by 2035 (APS) • EU Commission Implementing Regulation (EU) 2024/2754: countervailing duties (BYD 17.0%, Geely 18.8%, SAIC 35.3%, Tesla Shanghai 7.8%, cooperating others 21.3%, non-cooperating 36.3%; all additive to existing 10% base tariff) • BIS Connected Vehicles Final Rule (90 Fed. Reg. 5360, January 16, 2025; effective March 17, 2025): software prohibition Model Year 2027, hardware prohibition Model Year 2030 (January 1, 2029 reference), Declarations of Conformity 60 days prior, covers VCS and ADS • US Trade Representative: 100% EV tariff effective September 27, 2024 (102.5% total with existing 2.5% duty) • Canada: 100% surtax effective October 1, 2024 (atop existing 6.1% duty) • Turkey: 40% additional tariff June 2024 • EU minimum import price mechanism (January 2026); VW Cupra Tavascan exemption (February 2026)

Tier Two: Company Filings and Financial Data

Audited company filings and disclosed financial data. High reliability; subject to accounting standards and audit verification.

Ford Motor Company 2024 Annual Report; Model e Division quarterly disclosures: $16.7B cumulative EV losses, ~$64,000 loss per EV sold 2024; OPEB underfunded by $4.4B; Ford Pro $2.3B operating profit H1 2025 • General Motors 2024 Annual Report; Q3 2025 earnings release: $4.8B adjusted EBIT North America H1 2025; $124.7B long-term liabilities; ~$45B shareholder returns 2015–2024; $10B buybacks + $6B EV investment slowdown post-tariff • Stellantis N.V. 2024 Annual Report: $26B restructuring charges; CEO Tavares resignation; ~$18B shareholder returns; STLA AutoDrive L3 suspension; Fiat 500e production disruptions • Volkswagen AG: 35,000 job cuts; Osnabrück closure (first German factory closure since 1937); €5.5B annual cost reduction target; Cupra Tavascan/JAC Anhui manufacturing • BYD Company Limited 2024 Annual Report: God's Eye deployment across $9,550–$233,000 range at $385/vehicle; $4.2B R&D; 75% vertical integration; 2.3M God's Eye fleet; 160M km/day training data; 43 GWh energy storage shipped 2024 • CATL Annual Report 2024: 39.2% global battery market share (SNE Research); LFP cells at $50–70/kWh 2026; sodium-ion development • Toyota: ~$60B net cash; hybrid profit transition funding; keiretsu supplier structure • Pony.ai Q3 2025 earnings: 1,000+ fully driverless robotaxis; city-wide breakeven Guangzhou; six-country network • Baidu Apollo Go: 17M+ cumulative rides; Gen-6 robotaxi $28K per-vehicle hardware cost • Hesai Technology: AT128 LiDAR $150–$200 per unit • Horizon Robotics: Journey 6 chip ~$100, 200+ TOPS • Aggregate shareholder returns 2015–2024: GM ~$45B + Ford ~$30B + Stellantis ~$18B = ~$93B (compiled from annual reports and proxy statements) • NADA: ~16,700 franchised US automobile dealerships (National Automobile Dealers Association 2024 data)

Tier Three: Industry Data and Research Reports

Mixed sourcing: institutional research houses, industry associations, and promotional research (ARK Invest). ARK figures are included for directional scale; they carry caveats about promotional methodology and should be cross-referenced with institutional estimates, which typically run 40–60 percent lower.

ARK Invest Big Ideas 2026: Convergence Network Strength +35% (p. 6); robotics $26T opportunity (p. 86); robotaxi cost-per-mile model (p. 97); robotaxi $34T enterprise value (p. 99); >4M annualized autonomous deliveries (p. 102); $480B autonomous delivery revenue (p. 104) • CPCA (China Passenger Car Association): 7.098M vehicles exported 2025 • PBGC Annual Report 2024: net deficit >$60B • NACS 2024: 150,900 US gas stations; convenience-store revenue data; 5–8% fuel volume decline in EV-heavy markets • Goldman Sachs: 35–40% aftermarket addressable market decline over 15 years • ifo Institute: factory closures → AfD vote share correlation (1.2–1.8 ppt increase per closure) • Bertelsmann Foundation: manufacturing job losses and far-right voting patterns • AfD February 2025 federal election: 20.8% national vote • ifo Institute: €15–25B annual German automotive transition cost through 2035 • German Kurzarbeit program: €42B cost 2020–2022 • Western automotive refinancing wall ~$180B (2027–2030): aggregated from Bloomberg Terminal debt maturity schedules for Ford, GM, Stellantis, Volkswagen, and major Tier 1 suppliers; includes bonds, revolving credit facilities, and supplier financing instruments

Tier Four: Venture Capital and State Capital Data

Directional estimates compiled from Chinese venture data aggregators (Zero2IPO, IT Juzi, PitchBook). While directionally reliable, these figures are unaudited and should be treated as order-of-magnitude estimates rather than precise accounting figures.

Chinese robotics VC: 57B RMB / 610 deals/government LP share ~50% (Zero2IPO, IT Juzi) • National Venture Capital Guidance Fund: 100B yuan target ($13.8B) • Provincial/municipal guidance funds: ~$912B committed capital (PitchBook/Zero2IPO) • China Development Bank: 551.8B yuan manufacturing disbursement 2024 • Shenzhen municipal AI fund: 20B yuan • Hefei-NIO: 7B yuan investment, ~15x return

Tier Five: Supplier and Labor Data

Sourced from company press releases, investor presentations, and media reports of restructuring announcements. Figures represent announced intentions; actual reductions may differ from announcements.

Continental AG: 7,150 positions eliminated (Q4 2025 Investor Update) • ZF Friedrichshafen: 14,000 reductions announced • Bosch: 5,500 + 3,500 position cuts • Schaeffler/Vitesco merger: 4,700 layoffs announced • Lear Corporation: 15,000 positions cut globally; restructuring charges >$400M • European automotive supply chain: ~104,000 jobs eliminated 2024–2025 (~142/day) • German automotive sector: ~780,000 direct + ~1.3M supply-chain dependent employment

Tier Six: Historical and Contextual Sources

Historical records, academic citations, and contextual data. Included for analytical framework and pattern recognition; not forward-looking.

British motorcycle industry: BSA, Norton, Triumph, Matchless, AJS, Ariel historical records; BSA collapse 1972; Norton receivership 1975; NVT nationalization 1973; Meriden cooperative closure 1983 • Honda Super Cub production and marketing history; CB750 launch 1969 • Kelly Criterion: Kelly (1956), Bell Labs; Thorp (2006), Princeton-Newport Partners: 20% annualized returns over 28 years • EPA: environmental remediation cost estimates $200,000–$1.5M per fuel-storage site • Neolix: 2,500+ delivery vehicles, 120 cities • JD Logistics: 30+ city autonomous delivery • SF Express: drone logistics corridors, autonomous trucking corridors • DeepSeek R1: algorithmic efficiency demonstrated under hardware export-control constraint • Unitree G1 humanoid: $16,000 retail price

---

END OF CHAPTER 11: THE BURNING GHAT

CHAPTER 12

Two Civilizations, One Technology

In the backwaters, where the river meets the sea, the water is neither fresh nor salt. It is something else entirely. Moreover, in that brackish water, rice grows that cannot grow anywhere else.

— Pokkali rice tradition, Kuttanad

The ashes of the internal combustion engine are still warm on the water. Having walked through the burning ghat of Chapter 11, we now stand on the banks where the two rivers meet. The fire has done its work; the wreckage is priced. But the river does not end at the cremation ground. It flows onward, fresh meeting salt, until the water is neither one nor the other but something entirely new. This is the brackish zone where the future grows.

In the Kuttanad backwaters of Kerala, there is a zone where freshwater rivers descending from the Western Ghats meet the saltwater of the Arabian Sea. The water is brackish—neither river nor ocean—and in this ambiguous estuary, conditions are hostile to most agriculture. Nevertheless, it is precisely here that Pokkali rice thrives: a salt-tolerant, flood-resistant variety that has grown in Kuttanad for centuries, nourished by conditions that would kill any other crop. The Pokkali farmer does not fight the contradiction. He plants in it.

This chapter is the book's brackish zone. Two civilizational approaches to autonomous driving— American and Chinese, hunter and farmer, neuron and nervous system—meet here, in conditions that are hostile to simple comparisons and fatal to lazy analogies. The investor who plants in this contradiction will find something that cannot grow anywhere else: clarity about where the trillion-dollar autonomous-vehicle race is actually heading, who is winning, and why the valuation gap between the two systems is not a market inefficiency but a structural feature of how each civilization has chosen to answer a deceptively simple question.

What is autonomous driving for?

America's answer—encoded in $8,000 subscriptions, $10 billion startup failures, and a $126 billion valuation for a 2,500-vehicle fleet—is that autonomy is a premium product, a moonshot technology, a financial instrument. China's answer—encoded in $385 hardware costs, standard ADAS on $9,550 cars, and 160 million kilometers per day of training data—is that autonomy is infrastructure, a utility, a public good folded into the price of transportation itself. These are not two strategies for the same goal. There are two goals. Moreover, the investor's task is to decide which goal the world will pay for.

12.1 The Schism: Three in Four Experts Expect a Separate China Stack

McKinsey's third biannual AV expert survey, published January 6, 2026, surveyed 91 senior decision-makers globally. The headline: **74 percent predict China will develop a dedicated, separate technology stack** for autonomous vehicles. The breakdown reveals three competing visions of fragmentation: 35 percent expect China to develop its own stack, while the US and Europe share another; 26 percent expect all three regions to develop independent stacks; and 12 percent expect a China stack shared with Europe, leaving the US isolated. Only 26 percent foresee anything resembling a unified global approach. Three in four experts are not predicting a separate China tech stack. They are observing one.

The bifurcation is already structural, not speculative. China mandates C-V2X communication rather than DSRC. It uses its own automation taxonomy (GB/T 40429-2021) rather than SAE J3016. It leads the ISO 3450x testing standards series. It has deployed 11,000 RSUs and 3 million C-V2X vehicles, while the US received its first certified C-V2X hardware in January 2026. The US fragments regulatory authority across 34 states with no comprehensive federal legislation. China coordinates with the MIIT, with 54 cities running active AV pilots. PwC's *Autonomous Mobility Facts 2025* maps the consequence: by 2035, L4/5 technology is projected to account for 36 percent of new vehicle sales in China, versus 9 percent in the US and 7 percent in the EU. The commercialization surface area is already diverging: the US focuses almost exclusively on autonomous taxis (the Waymo model), while China advances taxis, buses, and shuttles in parallel. Two models are emerging: vertical integration in China, horizontal distribution in the West.

For the investor: the schism is not a risk. It is the investment thesis. A unified global AV market would be won by whichever civilization built the best single product. A bifurcated market creates two parallel opportunity sets—and the question becomes which side is underpriced relative to its structural advantages.

12.2 The Trust Chasm: 85 Percent Versus 39 Percent

85 percent of Chinese consumers report comfort with unsupervised autonomous driving, compared with **39 percent** of Americans. This figure, from PwC's Strategy& Digital Auto Report 2023, is corroborated by the 2025 Edelman Trust Barometer (72 percent of Chinese adults trust AI versus 32 percent in the US), McKinsey's data (31 percent of Chinese consumers would currently use a robotaxi versus 11 percent in the US), and S&P Global Mobility's annual surveys, which consistently find Chinese consumers scoring highest globally for self-driving desirability.

This is not a footnote. It is a 46-point structural advantage in adoption velocity. China's AV companies spend engineering dollars on capability. America's spend marketing dollars on overcoming fear. Nearly 70 percent of Chinese middle-income consumers aged 30–45 report willingness to pay an additional 30,000–50,000 yuan ($4,280–$7,134) for advanced intelligent driving features. In the US, robotaxis have been vandalised, set on fire, and subjected to consumer surveys that have revealed persistent safety and privacy concerns. BYD Chairman Wang Chuanfu declared 2025 the "Year of Universal Smart Driving," predicting non-autonomous vehicles will become niche—a claim no American executive has dared to make, because no American consumer survey would support it.

For the investor, consumer trust is the multiplier for deployment. It determines how quickly a technically capable system becomes a revenue-generating fleet. China's 85 percent comfort rate means every deployed AV has a larger addressable demand pool from day one. America's 39 percent means every deployed AV must also fund the persuasion campaign. The trust chasm does not close with better technology. It closes with time, exposure, and cultural normalization—all of which favor the civilization that has more vehicles on more roads.

12.3 The Cost Chasm: $385 Versus $8,000

BYD's God's Eye system, documented in Chapters 7 and 9, delivers L2+ autonomous driving capability across 21 vehicle models at an incremental hardware cost of approximately $385 per vehicle—offered at zero additional cost to the consumer, standard equipment from the $9,550 Seagull to the Yangwang U9 supercar. By January 2026, the installed base exceeded 2.5 million vehicles, generating 160 million kilometers of training data per day. XPeng's XNGP comes standard on vehicles starting at $17,000. In China, autonomy is a feature that comes with the car, like seatbelts.

In America, autonomy is a luxury good. Tesla FSD: $8,000 one-time purchase, transitioning to subscription-only at $99 per month as of February 14, 2026—Valentine's Day, which is either a coincidence or the most expensive romantic gesture in automotive history, depending on how much you trust Elon Musk's timing. The subscription shift is tied to Musk's 2025 CEO Performance Award, which requires reaching 10 million active FSD subscriptions over the next decade. Despite its name, FSD remains classified as SAE Level 2. GM Super Cruise: $2,500–$3,000 built into the vehicle price, plus $25–40 per month after a three-year trial (40 percent conversion rate). Ford BlueCruise: $2,495 one-time purchase or $49.99 per month. Mobileye SuperVision: $1,000–2,500 per system to OEMs.

The structural contrast is stark. In America, a consumer pays $8,000 for Level 2 autonomy on a $45,000 car. In China, a consumer pays $0 extra for comparable technology on a $9,550 car. The gap per mile of autonomous capability is perhaps the single most vivid illustration of the two civilizations' divergent philosophies. Moreover, the gap is self-reinforcing: American pricing keeps adoption low, which in turn keeps data generation low, which slows algorithmic improvement, which keeps costs high. Chinese pricing drives the adoption of millions of vehicles, fueling a data flywheel that improves algorithms, which, in turn, further reduces per-unit costs. The American spiral goes up. The Chinese spiral goes down. Both are accelerating.

12.4 The Missing Industrialiser: Detroit's $13 Billion Education

Here is the revelation that emerges only when you have seen both systems complete: the insight the Pokkali farmer understands that the freshwater farmer and the saltwater fisherman do not: America has no BYD.

No American OEM deploys L4—or even advanced L2+—as a standard feature on a mass-market car. America has hunters: Waymo stalking the robotaxi market with $126 billion in implied value and 2,500 vehicles, Tesla pursuing the robotaxi vision with promises that consistently arrive two years behind schedule. However, America has no farmer—no manufacturer democratizing autonomous capability across millions of vehicles, making ADAS as standard as air conditioning, building the data flywheel that turns consumer vehicles into a training fleet. The temple has one altar. The other stalls are empty.

The reasons are structural, financial, and—in the tradition of this book's satirical register—deeply, tragicomically American.

GM Cruise. Acquired in 2016 for $581 million. Cumulative investment exceeding $10 billion, including SoftBank's $2.25 billion and Honda's $2.75 billion. Peak valuation: $30 billion in 2021. Then, on October 2, 2023, a Cruise robotaxi in San Francisco struck a pedestrian and dragged her approximately 20 feet. California suspended the operating permit. Cruise was accused of concealing details of the crash. The CEO resigned. Nine hundred employees were laid off. NHTSA fined the company $1.5 million. On December 10, 2024, GM officially ended Cruise's robotaxi development. The market's response: shares rose 2.3 percent. Wall Street rewarded the retreat. A second round of cuts eliminated 50% of the remaining staff. The toll: more than $10 billion in operating losses, less than $500 million in lifetime revenue. GM has pivoted to autonomous highway driving, targeting 2028, on the Cadillac Escalade IQ—a vehicle that starts at $130,000, which is a very particular definition of "democratization."

Ford Argo AI. Ford invested $1 billion starting in 2017. Volkswagen added $2.6 billion. Peak valuation: $7 billion. On October 26, 2022, both withdrew. Ford took a $2.7 billion write-down. CEO Jim Farley's epitaph: "Profitable, fully autonomous vehicles at scale are a long way off, and we will not necessarily have to create that technology ourselves." Ford created Latitude AI to advance BlueCruise toward L3 autonomy. The man who spent $3.7 billion on autonomous driving concluded he did not need to create the technology. This is the kind of insight that, in most industries, you can acquire for the price of a McKinsey engagement.

Stellantis. Unveiled STLA AutoDrive 1.0 (L3, hands-free/eyes-off at up to 60 km/h) in February 2025. By August 2025, Reuters reported that the program had been frozen due to high costs, technological challenges, and "very limited" market demand. CEO Carlos Tavares departed abruptly. Shares fell by more than 40 percent over 12 months.

Ford and GM together incinerated roughly $13 billion on L4 attempts before retreating to incremental L2 improvements sold as premium features. The Road to Autonomy analysis concluded in December 2024: "Detroit automakers are 0-for-2 in autonomy... The lack of a credible autonomous vehicle program raises questions about whether GM and Ford will pivot to roles as contract manufacturers or fade from relevance."

The reasons Detroit treats ADAS as a premium option rather than a standard feature form a mutually reinforcing trap. Margin pressure: traditional OEMs operate at 5–8 percent margins, and ADAS represents one of the few high-margin features. Subscription addiction: GM's OnStar and Super Cruise generated $5.4 billion in 2025. Wall Street discipline: investors rewarded GM for shutting down Cruise and punished spending on moonshots. Outsourced technology: US OEMs buy ADAS from Mobileye, Qualcomm, or NVIDIA rather than developing in-house, making per-unit costs structurally higher than BYD's $385. Moreover, the 0-for-2 failure pattern itself: having lost $13 billion, the appetite for another attempt is zero.

For the investor, the Missing Industrialiser explains the valuation gap. America's AV market is priced on two companies: Waymo (the hunter) and Tesla (the hunter who claims to be a farmer). China's AV market is priced on an ecosystem that includes four archetypes, of which the Industrialiser—BYD, the actual farmer, is generating more daily training data than Waymo has accumulated in its entire history. The American market has a $126 billion hunter and a gap where the farmer should be. The Chinese market has both. Marcus, whose portfolio we have tracked across eleven chapters, is beginning to understand why his US-only TAM model cannot capture the farmer. The temple has one altar. He has been pricing only the hunter.

12.5 The Valuation Psychosis: Waymo at $50 Million Per Vehicle

Waymo's February 2, 2026, funding round established its valuation at $126 billion—the result of a $16 billion raise led by Dragoneer, DST Global, and Sequoia, with Alphabet contributing approximately $13 billion. This represents a near-tripling from the $45 billion Series C just 16 months earlier. Waymo operates approximately 2,500 vehicles across 6 US cities, completing 450,000 rides per week with an annualized revenue run rate exceeding $350 million.

Tesla's market capitalization hovers between $1.5 and $1.6 trillion. Analyst decompositions attribute enormous value to the robotaxi business: Morgan Stanley assigns $439 billion to robotaxi alone, Wolfe Research models $900 billion in present value, and ARK Invest projects that robotaxi represents 90 percent of expected value by 2029. The $450–$700 billion range for Tesla's robotaxi premium is well-supported across multiple analyst frameworks—for a fleet that, as of February 2026, consists of 30–60 vehicles in Austin and approximately 120 in the Bay Area with safety drivers.

Waymo trades at roughly 7–30x the per-vehicle valuation of Chinese competitors, while the cost of each Waymo vehicle ($175,000 with sensor suite) far exceeds Baidu's RT6 at $28,300. The operational metrics do not justify the gap. The narrative does. Chapter 13 will dissect this valuation psychosis in full—the per-vehicle implied valuations, the structural forces driving the gap, the Māyā Meter that measures the distance between market narrative and operational reality, and the catalysts—MSCI inclusion, dual listings, sovereign wealth fund mandates—that could force a repricing.

12.6 February 2026: Four Answers to One Question

Several developments in the final weeks of early 2026 compressed a decade of divergence into a single month. Presented sequentially, they read as news. Read through the lens of this chapter's opening question—*What is autonomous driving for?*—They read as four civilizational answers, each internally coherent, each accelerating away from the others.

Autonomy as perfection. Waymo's 6th-generation Driver began fully autonomous operations on February 12, 2026, on Zeekr "Ojai" minivans and Hyundai IONIQ 5 platforms. The system achieves a 42 percent sensor reduction (13 cameras down from 29, 4 LiDARs down from 5) at under $20,000 per AV system—more than 50 percent cheaper than the 5th generation. Waymo reportedly seeks to order 50,000 Hyundai units, the largest single AV vehicle order ever, with expansion planned to 20 new cities, including the first international markets: London and Tokyo. The answer is excellence— fewer sensors, better algorithms, relentless refinement of a single product toward an asymptote of safety. The hunter sharpens his spear.

Autonomy as monetization of faith. Tesla removed safety monitors from some Austin robotaxi rides on January 22, 2026, though chase cars were observed trailing driverless vehicles. Musk claimed at Davos that Tesla robotaxis would be "widespread" in the US by year-end 2026. The Cybercab targets production starting in April 2026. Tesla's operational fleet remains 30–60 vehicles—roughly 1 percent of Waymo's. On February 14, Tesla eliminated the one-time FSD purchase option and moved to a subscription-only model at $99 per month. The timing is either a coincidence or the logical conclusion of an industry in which autonomous driving is neither fully self-driving nor fully autonomous. However, it is—on Valentine's Day, no less—fully monetized. Love, like Full Self-Driving, is apparently a matter of subscription rather than commitment.

Autonomy as global infrastructure. Baidu Apollo Go launched fully autonomous commercial ride-hailing on Yas Island, Abu Dhabi, on January 17, 2026—the first fully driverless commercial robotaxi in the Middle East. It simultaneously expanded Chinese operations to Jiangmen and Dongguan. Uber and Lyft will test Baidu robotaxis in London in 2026, creating the first true international head-to-head alongside Waymo's planned London entry. The SELF DRIVE Act of 2026 (H.R. 7390), introduced on February 5, represents the first serious attempt at comprehensive federal AV legislation, requiring safety cases and creating a national safety data repository. In China, the first national L3 approvals were granted in December 2025, with an alliance of Changan, Geely, Great Wall, and BYD targeting full-scenario L3 by 2026 and L4 by 2028. The procession carries the fire to new temples.

Autonomy as ubiquity. BYD's God's Eye 5.0, released January 28, 2026, introduced reinforcement learning and end-to-end control to the system already deployed across 2.5 million vehicles, generating over 160 million km/day of training data—a dataset growing so rapidly that it constitutes a separate, parallel driving intelligence trained on fundamentally different conditions than any American system. The farmer does not sharpen a spear. The farmer irrigates another valley.

February 2026 did not create the divergence. It compressed it into a time frame short enough to see. Waymo's 6th-gen reduced costs by 50 percent and expanded into more cities—the perfect model for refining. Tesla moved to a subscription-only FSD—the faith-based monetization model is entrenched. Baidu launched fully driverless operations in the Middle East—the global infrastructure model is accelerating. BYD deployed end-to-end learning across 2.5 million vehicles—the ubiquity model deepening. The rivers are not just separating. They are flooding different valleys.

The View from the Fork in the Road

The data points compiled in this chapter tell a story not of one technology race but of two civilizations reaching fundamentally different answers to the same question. 74 percent of McKinsey's experts who predict separate technology stacks may be understating the case. The divergence is not merely technological. It is ontological. The 85-versus-39 percent consumer trust gap, the 7-to-30x per-vehicle valuation disparity, the $13 billion Detroit has spent learning what BYD achieved for $385 per car—these are not gaps that converge. They are fault lines along which two distinct, autonomous civilizations are crystallizing, each internally coherent, increasingly incompatible with the other, and now racing to export its model to the rest of the world.

The Pokkali rice grows only in the brackish water. The investor who insists on seeing the world as purely fresh or purely salt will never find it. The opportunity exists in the estuary—in the understanding that both civilizational models are internally coherent, that the valuation gap between them is real but not necessarily permanent, and that the catalysts for repricing are already visible.

Three things that would change this thesis: *(1) A major Chinese AV safety incident that resets the 85 percent consumer trust advantage and triggers regulatory pullback. (2) An American OEM—not Tesla, not Waymo, but a Ford or GM or Stellantis—deploying advanced ADAS as standard on a mass-market vehicle below $30,000, filling the Missing Industrialiser gap. (3) A reversal of the BIS Connected Vehicles rule that reopens the American market to Chinese AV technology, collapsing the bifurcation thesis. Monitor all three. As of February 2026, none is imminent.*

Chapter 13 will take the valuation psychosis identified here and perform a full autopsy: the per-vehicle implied valuations, the structural forces driving the gap, the Māyā Meter that measures the distance between market narrative and operational reality, and the catalysts—MSCI inclusion, dual listings, sovereign wealth fund mandates—that could force a repricing. Marcus arrives at the Māyā Meter with eleven chapters of cognitive errors compounding in his portfolio. The fork in the road has been mapped. The Pokkali farmer has planted. Now we price the two paths.

Evidence Anchors

McKinsey Center for Future Mobility: 3rd biannual AV survey (January 6, 2026; 91 respondents, 74% bifurcation finding) • PwC Strategy& Digital Auto Report 2023: 85% vs. 39% consumer comfort; L4/5 penetration projections (36% China, 9% US, 7% EU by 2035) • PwC Japan, Autonomous Mobility Facts 2025 • 2025 Edelman Trust Barometer: 72% vs. 32% AI trust • S&P Global Mobility annual autonomous driving surveys • Waymo $126B valuation (February 2, 2026); 6th-gen Driver launch (February 12, 2026) • Tesla FSD subscription pivot (February 14, 2026); Musk Davos statement (January 22, 2026) • Morgan Stanley, Wolfe Research, ARK Invest Tesla sum-of-parts models • GM Cruise: $10B+ cumulative losses; shutdown December 10, 2024 • Ford Argo AI: $2.7B write down October 2022 • Stellantis STLA AutoDrive freeze (August 2025) • BYD God's Eye 5.0 (January 28, 2026): 160M km/day • SELF DRIVE Act H.R.7390 (February 5, 2026) • BCG 2026: ADAS as "largest untapped profit pool" • Road to Autonomy: "Detroit 0-for-2" analysis (December 2024) • 36kr Waymo/Chinese AV valuation comparison (February 3, 2026)

CHAPTER 13

The Valuation Psychosis

Or: How the Market Learned to Stop Worrying and Love the Narrative

Māyā is not that the world does not exist. Māyā is that the world is not as it appears.

— Adi Shankara, 8th century CE

This chapter is not a collection of data points. It is an indictment.

The charge: the global market has priced Chinese autonomous vehicle companies as if they do not exist, while pricing American promises as if they have already been fulfilled. The evidence: a per-vehicle valuation gap that ranges from 14-to-1 to over 1,000-to-1, depending on which American company you examine and which fleet count you believe. The motive: a cocktail of the China discount, index exclusion, geopolitical narrative, and the oldest force in financial markets—the willingness of investors to pay a premium for a story they want to be true.

In Sanskrit philosophy, *Māyā* is not the claim that the world does not exist. It is the observation that the world is not as it appears. The Theyyam performer, face painted, body possessed by the divine, is real—the transformation is genuine, the fire burns, the ritual has power. However, the audience's perception of what they are witnessing—miracle or performance, divine or human, eternal or fleeting—is Māyā. The veil between what is and what the audience believes is the space where illusion operates. In the autonomous vehicle market, the Māyā is thick. The companies are real. The technology works. The rides happen. However, the valuations assigned to those rides—$50 million per Waymo vehicle, $878 million per Tesla robotaxi, $3.6 million per WeRide vehicle—reveal a market that is seeing not the world as it is but the world as it wishes it to be.

The **Māyā Meter** measures the distance between the veil and the reality behind it. In this chapter, we calibrate it.

13.1 The Māyā Meter: Per-Vehicle Valuation and the Arithmetic of Absurdity

The math is simple. The implications are not.

Waymo's February 2, 2026, funding round valued the company at $126 billion. It operates approximately 2,500 vehicles across 6 US cities. Divide valuation by fleet: **~$50.4 million per vehicle.** That is the market's implied belief in the value of each Waymo robotaxi—a number that, to be fair, includes the accumulated technology, the brand, the 200 million autonomous miles, and the expansion optionality. It is a real number backed by real investors (Sequoia, a16z, Fidelity, Mubadala, Tiger Global) paying real money. However, it is a number that assigns each vehicle a valuation higher than that of most Manhattan apartments.

Tesla's market capitalization hovers between $1.5 and $1.6 trillion. Morgan Stanley attributes $439 billion to robotaxi/mobility. Wolfe Research models $900 billion in present value. ARK Invest projects that the robotaxi business will represent 90 percent of the expected value by 2029. Using the most commonly cited framework (Morgan Stanley's $439 billion robotaxi attribution) and Elon Musk's own claimed fleet of "well over 500": **~$878 million per vehicle.** Using the independent tracker by Texas A&M researcher Ethan McKanna, who found approximately 32 unique Model Ys operating in Austin with fewer than 10 concurrent at any time, the number becomes so large it transcends financial analysis and enters the domain of theology.

Now the Chinese side of the ledger:

Pony.ai: ~$5.6B market cap ÷ ~1,159 vehicles = ~$4.8 million per vehicle.

Baidu Apollo Go: ~$7B estimated ÷ ~2,000+ vehicles = ~$3.5 million per vehicle.

WeRide: <$2.5B market cap ÷ ~1000 robotaxis = ~$2.5 million per vehicle.

The ratios:

Waymo vs. WeRide: 14 to 1.

Tesla (Morgan Stanley attribution, Musk fleet) vs. WeRide: 244 to 1.

Tesla (ARK attribution, independent tracker) vs. WeRide: >10,000 to 1.

The Māyā Meter is not subtle. It is a klaxon. Under virtually every reasonable methodology, Tesla's per-vehicle robotaxi valuation is 100x to 1,000x higher than that of Chinese operators. Even Waymo—whose technology leadership is genuine, whose 450,000 weekly rides are real, whose safety record is peer-reviewed—trades at 7x Pony.ai and 14x WeRide per vehicle, despite Chinese operators collectively serving comparable ride volumes and achieving earlier breakeven on unit economics.

The 36kr analysis (February 3, 2026) stated it plainly: the core fleet sizes differ by two to three times, while the valuations differ by more than ten times or even dozens of times. This is not a market inefficiency. This is a market hallucination. Moreover, like all hallucinations, it is internally coherent—it makes perfect sense to the person experiencing it. The Māyā framework explains what standard financial analysis cannot: the hallucination is not a failure of information but a failure of perception. The data is available. The filings are public. The rides are countable. The veil persists not because the truth is hidden but because the audience prefers the illusion. The task of this chapter is to explain why the hallucination persists, what structural forces sustain it, and what catalysts could break it.

13.2 The Timeline Illusion: A Brief History of Autonomous Promises

If the Māyā Meter measures the gap between valuation and reality, the Timeline Illusion explains how that gap widened. Elon Musk's robotaxi promises form a pattern so consistent that it qualifies less as optimism and more as a distinct literary genre—the AV Prophecy, in which a charismatic founder announces a timeline, the market prices it in, reality fails to cooperate, a new timeline is announced, and the market prices that in too. George Carlin once observed that in America, anyone can become president—that is the problem. In the AV industry, anyone can promise a million robotaxis. The problem is the same.

April 2019, Autonomy Day: Musk promised one million robotaxis on the road by 2020. Reality: zero robotaxis until June 2025. Gap: five years and one million vehicles.

2022: A purpose-built robotaxi would be unveiled in 2023, with mass production in 2024. Reality: concept unveiled October 2024, production now targeting April 2026. Gap: two years.

Mid-2025: 500 robotaxis in Austin by year-end, coverage of "half the US population." Reality: 30–60 vehicles in Austin by December, two cities covered—gap: 10x on fleet, 25x on geographic coverage.

Q4 2025: 8–10 metro areas by year-end 2025. Reality: Austin and the Bay Area only. Gap: 4–5x.

On January 28, 2026, during Q4 earnings, Musk claimed that there were "well over 500" robotaxis. Independent tracker: ~32 unique vehicles in Austin, fewer than 10 concurrent. The discrepancy between the CEO's number and the researcher's number is either a disagreement in measurement methodology or a gap wide enough to park 468 imaginary robotaxis in. In most industries, a 15x discrepancy between a CEO's stated fleet size and an independent count would trigger an SEC inquiry. In the autonomous vehicle industry, it triggers a valuation increase. The Māyā is not merely thick. It is load-bearing—remove it, and the valuation structure collapses.

The pattern is striking: Musk has consistently promised autonomous capability 1–5 years before actual delivery, at 10–1,000x the scale eventually achieved. The gap between promise and execution has narrowed—the service eventually launched—but at a dramatically smaller scale. NHTSA opened an investigation into approximately 3 million FSD-equipped vehicles; a California judge ruled that Tesla engaged in deceptive marketing of FSD/Autopilot; and early rider reports documented vehicles driving on the wrong side of the road, phantom braking, dropping passengers in intersections, and committing traffic violations.

On February 14, 2026—Valentine's Day—Tesla eliminated the $8,000 one-time FSD purchase option and moved to a subscription-only model at $99 per month. Existing purchasers retain access; new customers must subscribe. Tesla's Q4 earnings disclosed FSD metrics for the first time: 1.1 million active users, of which only 330,000 (30 percent) are monthly subscribers. Against an installed base of 8.9 million cumulative vehicles, the 12.4 percent take rate suggests limited consumer enthusiasm for the premium. The subscription shift is tied to Musk's 2025 CEO Performance Award, which requires reaching 10 million active FSD subscriptions over the next decade. Despite its name, Full Self-Driving remains classified as SAE Level 2.

However, the market assigns an implied value of $450–$700 billion to Tesla's robotaxi business. The Māyā is thick. The audience sees the divine. The performer is still mortal.

13.3 The Operational Reality: Who Is Actually Winning

Strip away the valuations, the promises, and the narratives. Look only at operational metrics—the picture inverts.

Pony.ai achieved city-wide unit economics breakeven in Guangzhou in November 2025—a landmark milestone. Daily net revenue per vehicle: RMB 299 (~$42). Daily orders per vehicle: 23 (two-week average). Remote assistance ratio: improved from 1:3 in Q1 2024 to 1:20 by Q1 2025, targeting 1:30. Insurance costs: approximately 50 percent of traditional taxis. Gen-7 autonomous driving kit costs are 70 percent lower than the prior generation—computing unit cost: down 80 percent. Solid-state LiDAR cost: down 68 percent.

Baidu Apollo Go confirmed unit-level profitability in Wuhan in Q2 2025. Operating over 1,000 fully driverless vehicles across 22 cities, completing 250,000 fully driverless rides per week. Cumulative rides: 17 million. Vehicle cost: ~$28,000 per RT6—roughly one-sixth the cost of a Waymo vehicle.

WeRide's Q3 2025 revenue grew 144 percent year-over-year, with robotaxi revenue surging 761 percent. Gross margin improved from 6.5 percent to 32.9 percent in a single year. Uber's commitment to 1,200 robotaxis across Abu Dhabi, Dubai, and Riyadh is the largest commercial robotaxi deployment in the Middle East. WeRide reports that its Abu Dhabi service is on track to achieve breakeven unit economics.

The cost-per-ride comparison tells the story with brutal clarity. In San Francisco, Waymo charges approximately $19.69 per ride—a 13–27 percent premium over Lyft and Uber. In Wuhan, Baidu Apollo Go charges $0.60–$2.30 per ride, 30–70 percent cheaper than a human taxi. In Guangzhou,

Pony.ai's average fare is approximately $1.80—40–60 percent below human taxis. Chinese robotaxis already undercut human drivers. American robotaxis still charge a premium.

Hesai Group—the picks-and-shovels play—reported Q3 2025 gross margins of 42.1 percent, the highest of any public LiDAR company and the only profitable one globally. It shipped 441,398 units in the quarter, surpassed one million cumulative units in September 2025, and projects 2–3 million shipments in 2026. Goldman Sachs projects revenue reaching $1.9 billion by 2030, with net margins of 21 percent. Meanwhile, Luminar Technologies—its American counterpart—filed for Chapter 11 five weeks after Hesai's record quarter.

The Māyā Meter reading indicates that Chinese operators are ahead in unit economics, cost per ride, fleet growth rate, and geographic expansion. American operators are ahead on weekly ride volume (Waymo), technology perception, and valuation. The market is pricing the second set of metrics. The investor should be pricing first.

13.4 Four Forces Sustaining the Veil

The Māyā persists because four structural forces suppress Chinese AV valuations. None of them is operational. All of them are structural. Understanding them is essential for any investor attempting to price through the veil—and they are the reason Marcus, whose cognitive errors we have tracked since Chapter 4, has not been irrational. He has been *rational within the veil*. The China discount, the index exclusion, the regulatory pessimism, the geopolitical overhang—these are not mistakes in his model. They are features of the market architecture within which his model operates. The Māyā Meter does not diagnose individual error. It diagnoses systemic illusion. Marcus's errors were the market's errors, and the following four forces sustain them.

The China Discount. Chinese tech companies trade at a 50–60% discount to US equivalents. The MSCI China Index trades at 12.8x forward earnings versus the S&P 500's 26–30x. Baidu at ~13x P/E versus Alphabet at 20–25x (a 47 percent discount). The "Dragon 7" Chinese tech companies have an average PEG ratio of 0.7x, suggesting significant undervaluation relative to their growth rates. The discount narrowed in 2025 (MSCI China rose ~40 percent), but a persistent ~40 percent gap to developed markets remains. For AV companies specifically, the discount is extreme: Waymo at $126 billion, Pony.ai at $5.6 billion, WeRide <$2.5 billion, and Baidu Apollo Go at $5–8 billion, despite comparable or superior operational metrics.

Index Exclusion and Institutional Access Barriers. A divestment wave is accelerating among US public pension funds: Indiana divested $1.2 billion in China exposure, Texas ordered the sale of $1.4 billion in China exposure, Florida mandated divestment by September 2025, and Missouri followed suit. The Federal Retirement Thrift Investment Board changed its benchmark to exclude

China entirely. A sharp bifurcation emerged in 2025 fund flows: broad China ETFs (FXI) bled over $2 billion in outflows, while tech-focused China ETFs (KWEB) attracted $2.2 billion in inflows. Institutional capital is selectively maintaining exposure to Chinese technology, whereas mandatory divestment requirements constrain many of the largest passive capital pools from owning Chinese AV stocks at all.

The Regulatory Pessimism Disconnect. Western investors systematically underestimate China's AV regulatory framework. In December 2025, MIIT granted China's first L3 permits for regular passenger cars. Twenty cities run Vehicle-Road-Cloud integration pilots. China has built 17 national ICV testing zones, opened 32,000 kilometers of test roads, and issued 7,700 test licenses. Pony.ai operates fully driverless commercial robotaxis in all four Tier-1 Chinese cities—a regulatory achievement no company in the United States has matched. The narrative that China's regulatory environment is opaque and restrictive is Māyā of the purest kind: the veil persists because Western analysts rarely look behind it.

Geopolitical and Delisting Risk. The PCAOB gained full access to inspect Chinese audit firms in December 2022, resolving the immediate threat of HFCAA delisting. As of early 2026, the SEC reports that no issuers are at risk of trading prohibition. However, Treasury Secretary Bessent stated that "everything is on the table" regarding Chinese ADR delisting, and a proposed bill to phase out Chinese sensors in autonomous vehicles introduces technology-specific risk. Mitigating factor: Pony.ai, WeRide, Hesai, and Baidu all maintain dual listings in Hong Kong. KraneShares calls delisting "low probability." Goldman Sachs estimated that "extreme" decoupling could cost $2.5 trillion in equity and bond sell-offs—thereby creating a strong deterrent. The risk is real but priced as if it were certain. The Māyā treats possibility as fact.

13.5 Stress Testing the Thesis

A chapter diagnosing psychosis in others must demonstrate it has tested its own sanity—three stress tests.

Chinese operator margins: the path from unit economics to company profitability is real but unfinished. All three major operators have demonstrated vehicle-level profitability in at least one city. However, company-level profitability remains distant: Pony.ai lost $61.6 million in Q3 2025, and WeRide lost $43.2 million. The path requires a fleet scale of ~1,000-3,000 vehicles per operator. Goldman projects gross margins of 40–50 percent over the next 3–5 years. The direction is clear. The timeline is not.

Waymo's expansion may justify a larger share of the valuation than the Māyā Meter implies. The plan to expand from 6 to 20 cities in 2026 is ambitious, and the $16 billion in funding it requires. The 6th-generation Driver (42 percent sensor reduction, under $20,000 per system) materially improves unit economics, and a potential 50,000-unit order from Hyundai would represent the largest single AV vehicle order ever. The Māyā Meter does not claim that Waymo is absolutely overvalued—only that the relative gap to Chinese operators is irrational.

Geopolitical risk could widen the gap further before it closes. The worst-case delisting scenario would force ~286 Chinese companies ($880 billion market cap) off US exchanges. The practical likelihood remains low, and dual Hong Kong listings provide a meaningful hedge. However, technology-specific restrictions—rather than blanket financial delisting—could further suppress Chinese AV valuations even as operational metrics improve. The investor must size positions accordingly: the thesis is that the gap is irrational, not that it will close on a specific timeline.

Moreover, the book must confront its own front matter here. The Keynes epigraph that opens this volume—*"The market can remain irrational longer than you can remain solvent"*—is not a decorative quotation. It is the strongest counterargument to the Māyā Meter's implied promise. Irrational valuation gaps sustained by structural forces can persist not for quarters but for decades. The value/growth premium in equity markets persisted for forty years before narrowing. Japan's banking sector remained undervalued for thirty years despite operational fundamentals being well understood by every analyst who cared to look. The South Korean "Korea discount"—a structural undervaluation driven by chaebol governance, geopolitical proximity to North Korea, and index-weighting mechanics—endured for two decades and closed only when the structural forces themselves shifted. The Māyā Meter may be correctly calibrated—every ratio in Section 13.1 may be precisely right—and still not close within the investor's time horizon. The four forces of Section 13.4 are not temporary dislocations awaiting a catalyst. They are structural features of a market architecture that was built, policy by policy and mandate by mandate, to produce exactly the gap the Māyā Meter measures. Calling this possibility "Naming this possibility is not a concession." It is the discipline that separates an investment thesis from a prayer. The *ullil kaanal* sees clearly. It does not promise that what it sees will change.

13.6 Three Catalysts for Repricing

The Māyā Meter measures the gap. The catalysts close it. Three forces are now in motion.

First: MSCI China Index inclusion, February 27, 2026. Both Hesai and Pony.ai were confirmed to be added to the MSCI China Index via their Hong Kong listings. Since the MSCI China Index is a component of the MSCI Emerging Markets Index and the MSCI ACWI, the stocks also appear in broader benchmarks that track over $15 trillion in global assets. Pony.ai became the first pure-play robotaxi operator in any MSCI index. CICC estimate of ~$147M for Hesai and ~$135M for Pony around the close. On announcement day (February 11), Hesai rose 7.1 percent; Pony.ai gained

2.5 percent. Academic research on MSCI inclusions finds cumulative abnormal returns of 2.8–5.6 percent in the 30–50 days before inclusion, with effects tending to be more persistent in emerging markets due to Merton's incomplete-information model. ARK Invest has been actively buying both sides of the gap—purchasing 133,600 shares of Pony.ai on January 16, 2026, and 858,295 shares of WeRide in late 2025, alongside its massive Tesla position. When Cathie Wood buys a contradiction, it deserves attention.

Second: Goldman Sachs projects that China's robotaxi market will grow 870x by 2035. From $54 million in 2025 to $47 billion by 2035, with a fleet growing to 1.9 million vehicles, capturing 25 percent of mobility share. The global robotaxi rideshare market is expected to grow at a CAGR of ~90% from 2025 to 2030. Goldman rates Pony.ai at Buy at $27.70, Hesai at Buy at $36, and Baidu at Buy at $90. The institutional imprimatur matters: when Goldman publishes a $47 billion TAM with company-specific price targets, the universe of investors who can own Chinese AV stocks expands materially. The Māyā Meter is a contrarian instrument. Goldman's coverage makes it a consensus instrument. That is how repricing begins.

Third: operational proof points are accelerating faster than narrative can suppress. Pony.ai's Guangzhou unit economics breakeven. Hesai's status as the world's only profitable LiDAR company. WeRide's 1,200-robotaxi Uber commitment. Baidu's fully driverless commercial launch in Abu Dhabi. Each data point makes the operational reality harder to dismiss and the valuation gap harder to justify. WeRide's stock is down 50 percent from its IPO despite 144 percent revenue growth, 761 percent growth in robotaxi revenue, and the largest commercial robotaxi commitment in the Middle East. This disconnect between operational execution and stock performance is the Māyā at its most measurable—and its most unsustainable.

The Veil and the Fire

The data assembled in this chapter reveal a market pricing regime in which narrative overwhelms arithmetic. Tesla's robotaxi fleet, independently verified to be 30–240 active vehicles, commands a per-vehicle implied valuation 100x to 1,000x higher than Chinese operators running larger fleets in more cities with achieved unit economics. Waymo's $126 billion valuation—backed by genuine technology and 2,500 vehicles—still represents $50 million per vehicle, 7x Pony.ai and 14x WeRide, despite Chinese operators serving comparable ride volumes.

The Māyā Meter reads as follows: the gap is real, measurable, and irrational. It is sustained by four structural forces—none operational, all priced as if permanent. Three catalytic forces are now in motion to close it: MSCI inclusion, which forces passive buying; Goldman coverage, which provides an institutional narrative; and operational proof points that compound quarterly. The gap may widen before it closes. Geopolitical risk may delay repricing. The Keynes warning applies with full force:

the market's capacity for sustained irrationality exceeds any individual investor's capacity for sustained solvency. However, the operational reality is that evidence is accumulating faster than the narrative can absorb, and the Māyā is thinning.

The Theyyam performer knows what the audience does not: the fire is real, but the audience's belief about *what* the fire means—divine miracle, dangerous spectacle, investment opportunity, existential risk—is the Māyā. The veil will thin. The fire will remain. The investor who can distinguish between the two will be positioned when the audience's perception finally aligns with what was always there.

Chapter 14 will translate this diagnosis into a portfolio—the six archetype baskets, the risk frameworks, the position-sizing logic, and the practical mechanics of building an AV investment thesis that accounts for both the fire and the veil. Marcus has now seen the Māyā Meter. The question is no longer whether the gap exists—it is whether he has the conviction to trade against the veil, and the risk architecture to survive if the veil persists longer than his capital.

Evidence Anchors

Tesla Q4 2025 earnings (January 28, 2026): 1.1M FSD users, "well over 500" robotaxis; FSD subscription pivot (February 14, 2026) • Texas A&M independent tracker (Ethan McKanna): ~32 unique Austin vehicles • Waymo $126B valuation (February 2, 2026): $16B raise; 450,000+ weekly rides • Morgan Stanley robotaxi attribution: $439B; Wolfe Research: $900B PV; ARK Invest: 90% by 2029 • Pony.ai: ~$5.6B market cap; Guangzhou unit economics breakeven November 2025; 23 orders/day; MSCI China inclusion February 27, 2026 • WeRide: <$2.5B market cap; 144% revenue growth Q3; 1,200 Uber robotaxi commitment; down 50% from IPO • Baidu: $47.6B market cap; unit-level profitability Wuhan Q2 2025; 250,000 weekly rides • Hesai: 42.1% gross margin Q3; 441,398 units shipped; MSCI China inclusion; Goldman $36 PT • Goldman Sachs: $47B China robotaxi market by 2035; $7B US by 2030 • MSCI February 2026 review: +21 net Chinese additions; $15T benchmarked assets • 36kr valuation comparison (February 3, 2026) • NHTSA FSD investigation (~3M vehicles); California deceptive marketing ruling • Luminar Chapter 11 (December 15, 2025)

[Note: Detailed company scorecards, analyst coverage tables, ADR performance data, CB Insights market landscape, broker access mechanics, and options strategy frameworks are compiled in Appendix B: Valuation Psychosis Data Companion.]

CHAPTER 14

The Boatman's Portfolio

You have read both rivers. Now you must build your boat. This chapter is the boatman's manual.

— Kuttanad navigation proverb (adapted)

As of February 14, 2026, the autonomous vehicle investment landscape has reached an inflection point. Waymo's $126 billion valuation validates the technology. China's 2.5 million God's Eye-equipped vehicles validate the industrialization model. The Māyā Meter documented in Chapter 13 reveals a valuation gap between American and Chinese AV companies that ranges from 14-to-1 to over 1,000-to-1. Three catalysts—MSCI inclusion, Goldman coverage, operational proof points—are now in motion to close it.

The Kuttanad boatman does not wait for the rivers to merge before setting out. He builds his vessel for the waters as they are—one current fresh, one salt, both navigable, both dangerous to those who do not understand the tides. This chapter is his manual. It provides the six investment archetypes that map the AV ecosystem, the allocation logic that connects thesis to position size, the catalyst calendar that tells you when to watch, the risk architecture that tells you what can kill the thesis, and the entry mechanics that tell you how to build positions. It is designed to be executable—not in theory, but on Monday morning.

Standard disclaimer: This chapter provides analytical frameworks and educational discussion of investment strategies. It does not constitute personalized investment advice. The author holds positions in several securities discussed. Consult a qualified financial advisor before making investment decisions.

14.1 The Six Temples: An Archetype Taxonomy for AV Investing

The autonomous vehicle ecosystem does not lend itself to a single investment thesis. It is a temple complex—six distinct structures, each housing a different deity, each requiring a different offering.

The investor who enters only one temple sees only one aspect of the divine. The investor who maps the complex sees the system.

Temple One: The Hunters (Pure-Play Operators). These are the companies pursuing full L4 autonomy as their primary business. The American side: Alphabet/Waymo ($126B implied valuation, 2,500 vehicles, 450,000 weekly rides, expanding to 20 cities in 2026) and Aurora Innovation ($8.2B market cap, commercial driverless trucking launched, 10 routes, targeting 200 trucks by year-end 2026, but burning $190–220M per quarter). The Chinese side: Pony.ai (~$5B, 1,159 vehicles, Guangzhou unit economics breakeven, MSCI China inclusion February 27), WeRide (~$2.5B, 1,600 vehicles across 11 countries, 1,200-robotaxi Uber commitment, down 50% from IPO despite 144% revenue growth), and Baidu ($50B total, Apollo Go estimated $5–10B standalone, unit-level profitability in Wuhan, 250,000 fully driverless rides per week). *Allocation role: highest upside, highest binary risk. The hunter either catches the prey or starves. Position sizing must reflect that the Chinese pure-plays trade at 7–30x discounts to Waymo per vehicle, but face geopolitical and delisting risks that Waymo does not.*

The valuation contrast within this single temple is the Māyā Meter's sharpest reading. Waymo at $126 billion implies $50.4 million per deployed vehicle—a number that prices not merely the technology but the accumulated faith of Sequoia, a16z, Fidelity, and Mubadala in a future where Waymo's 6th-generation Driver occupies twenty cities by year's end. WeRide at <$2.5 billion implies ~$3 million per vehicle—a number that prices operational reality at a 97 percent discount to Waymo's operational reality. Both companies run fully driverless commercial rides. Both serve paying passengers. Both generate revenue. The gap is not a reflection of capability. It reflects which passport the vehicle carries. The Chinese hunters are stalking the same prey, in more countries, at lower cost, with earlier unit economics—and the market values their kill at one-thirtieth the price. For the investor with a tolerance for geopolitical risk, the Chinese hunters represent the Māyā Meter's widest dislocation. For the investor without it, Waymo's expansion to 20 cities and potential 50,000-unit Hyundai order provide the closest thing to a consensus AV growth story. The temple houses both deities. The offering determines the return.

Temple Two: The Farmers (Industrialisers). These are the companies democratizing autonomous capability across mass-market vehicles—the Missing Industrialiser from Chapter 12, except on the Chinese side, the industrialiser is not missing. BYD ($112–137B market cap, 4.25M vehicles sold in 2024, God's Eye ADAS standard on 21 models at $385 incremental hardware cost, 2.5M equipped vehicles generating 160M km/day of training data, RMB 100B committed to smart tech R&D). XPeng ($15–17B, XNGP nationwide rollout with no HD map dependency, 60% system penetration, 429,445 vehicles delivered in FY2025 at 126% growth, Mona M03 at $17,000 with ADAS standard, first-ever ADAS insurance product at RMB 239/year). *Allocation role: the data flywheel plays. The farmer does not need to win the robotaxi race to generate returns—every vehicle sold with ADAS generates training data that improves algorithms, which, in turn, sell more* *vehicles. BYD's God's Eye generates more daily data than Waymo has accumulated in its entire history. The farmer's moat is not technology but volume.*

Temple Three: The Architects (Stack Integrators). These are the companies building the full-stack autonomous driving platform that other manufacturers use. Amazon/Zoox ($2.14T parent, ~50 purpose-built robotaxis, Hayward factory scaling to 10,000/year, plans to charge fares in 2026). Mobileye ($7.7B, 35.7M EyeQ chips shipped in FY2025, $24.5B revenue pipeline over 8 years, near all-time lows at ~$9.40—Intel's $15.3B acquisition now worth roughly half). Huawei ADS (not publicly traded, $16B estimated, ADS 4.0 across 22 models, 1M+ vehicles equipped, 7.28B km accumulated). Momenta (private, $5–6B valuation, 130+ car models contracted, including BMW, Mercedes-Benz, and Toyota, expected HK listing). Didi AD ($22.4B parent, $5B estimated for AD unit, first mass-produced robotaxi delivered January 2026). *Allocation role: the infrastructure plays. Stack integrators win regardless of which OEM wins—like selling picks and shovels in a gold rush, except the picks are AI chips and the shovels are software platforms.*

Temple Four: The Toolmakers (Picks-and-Shovels). These companies supply the components that every AV needs, regardless of which civilization wins. Hesai ($3.4–4.1B, world's only profitable LiDAR company, 42.1% gross margins, 441,398 units shipped Q3, Goldman $36 target, MSCI China inclusion, NVIDIA exclusive LiDAR for Hyperion 10). Horizon Robotics (~$12B HK-listed, 49% of China's AV chip market, 10M+ Journey chips shipped, VW's €2.4B CARIZON JV, unanimous Strong Buy from 24 analysts). ON Semiconductor ($26.5B, 52% automotive revenue, SiC leadership, $6B buyback, 500+ devices per AV). Aptiv ($17.7B, record $20.4B revenue, Versigent spin-off April 2026, Gen 6 ADAS platform).

Mobileye, at near-all-time lows with a $24.5 billion pipeline, is arguably the most contrarian position in the entire AV ecosystem—and the contrarian case deserves more than a sentence. Intel acquired Mobileye in 2017 for $15.3 billion. As of February 2026, Mobileye's market capitalization sits at approximately $7.7 billion—meaning Intel's acquisition price exceeds the current public-market value by nearly double. The $24.5 billion revenue pipeline is not projected; it is contracted—design wins with specific OEMs for specific vehicle programs scheduled across the next eight years. The 35.7 million EyeQ chips shipped in FY2025 represent the world's largest automotive vision-processing installed base. SuperVision, Mobileye's L2+ system, is deployed across Zeekr and Polestar, and is now being announced for Mahindra (announced in February 2026 for at least six models). If the ADAS market grows at even the conservative end of BCG's and Goldman's projections—and every forecaster predicts it will—Mobileye's contracted pipeline converts to revenue on a schedule that is largely insensitive to which civilization wins the L4 race. The Mobileye trade is not a bet on autonomous driving. It is a bet that cars will continue to need eyes—and that a company trading at half its acquisition price with $24.5 billion in contracted revenue is mispriced by a market that has confused Intel's corporate dysfunction with Mobileye's commercial reality.

Allocation role: the consensus across all six editorial reviewers—and this author—is that the picks-and-shovels layer offers the best risk-adjusted entry into AV. Hesai is profitable, growing 50% annually, and trades at ~$26 against Goldman's $36 target. Horizon has 49% market share in the world's largest AV market and a unanimous analyst consensus. These companies benefit from both American and Chinese AV deployments without the binary regulatory risk that pure-play operators face. For Marcus, the fund manager whose Māyā Meter education we traced in Chapter 13, this is the temple that does not require him to trade against the veil—it requires only that he believe autonomous vehicles will exist. The deity in this temple makes no demands on geopolitical conviction. It only requires that the cars be equipped with sensors.

Temple Five: The Platforms (Aggregators). Uber ($154–156B, 20+ AV partnerships; WeRide/Waymo/Baidu/Momenta all deploying on Uber; AV Labs launched January 2026; 1.5M+ annualized AV trips; CEO expects robotaxi services in 10+ countries by late 2026). Lyft (~$7.6B; Baidu RT6 partnership for London and Europe; Mobileye Drive for the US; smaller fleet but 15% of the US rideshare market). *Allocation role: the platform-agnostic play. Uber and Lyft win regardless of whose robotaxi wins—they are the distribution layer. Uber's 20+ AV partnerships provide diversified exposure to the commercialization of autonomous driving without betting on any single technology provider. The irony documented in Chapter 10 applies here: American platforms carrying Chinese AV technology to the world.*

Temple Six: The Caravaneers (Autonomous Trucking). Aurora Innovation (the only company spanning both temples—also in Temple One; commercial driverless trucking launched on US public roads, 10 routes, 250,000+ driverless miles, zero driver-attributed collisions, targeting 200+ trucks by year-end 2026). Kodiak ($2.5B via SPAC, 8 driverless trucks 24/7 in Permian Basin, 7,300+ loads for Maersk, IKEA, J.B. Hunt). Gatik (private; first company in North America to deploy fully driverless trucks at commercial scale; $600M+ in contracted, multi-year, noncancelable revenue; Isuzu mass-production partnership). Plus (going public Q1 2026, TRATON partnership for Scania/MAN, IVECO for Southern Europe). Torc Robotics (Daimler subsidiary, targeting 2027 commercial launch, the only company running AV software on production-intent factory-installed hardware). *Allocation role: the overlooked opportunity. Goldman projects AV trucking will reach $18B and ~25,000 trucks by 2030. The addressable market—$800B+ in US trucking—faces structural driver shortages. Gatik's $600M+ in contracted revenue means the market has already spoken; the question is only which public vehicle captures it.*

14.2 The Allocation Logic: Three Profiles, One Framework

The Kuttanad boatman does not allocate all his cargo to one side of the vessel. He distributes weight across the hull based on the waters he expects to navigate, the winds he expects to face, and the payload he can afford to lose. The quarter-Kelly framework—described in Chapter 15's Three Monsoons analysis—applies here: size positions at one-quarter of the theoretical Kelly optimal to account for uncertainty, fat tails, and the structural impossibility of knowing which monsoon arrives.

Three investor profiles, each with different risk tolerance and conviction levels:

The Conservative Boatman stays in the main channel. Primary allocation to Picks-and-Shovels (Hesai, Horizon, ON Semi) and Platform Aggregators (Uber). These holdings benefit from AV deployment regardless of which civilization wins, carry lower binary risk than pure-play operators, and include profitable companies with institutional coverage. ETF overlay: ARKQ for broad AV exposure at ~43% purity, IDRV for the lowest expense ratio. Chinese exposure limited to dual-listed Hong Kong shares (Hesai 2525.HK, Horizon 9660.HK) to mitigate ADR delisting risk. No options strategies—position building through direct equity only.

The Balanced Boatman navigates both currents. Core allocation to Picks-and-Shovels and Platforms, with satellite positions in Chinese Pure-Play Operators (Pony.ai, Baidu) and Industrialisers (BYD, XPeng). The MSCI inclusion catalyst (February 27) provides a structural entry point for Pony.ai and Hesai. Options-based entry via cash-secured puts on BIDU and XPEV—the two tickers with liquid, tradeable options suitable for systematic strategies—builds positions at lower cost bases while generating premium income. Position sizing follows quarter-Kelly: if you believe the Chinese AV thesis has a 60% probability and a 3x payoff, Kelly recommends betting 20% of capital; quarter-Kelly recommends 5%. The China discount is your margin of safety, not your thesis.

The Aggressive Boatman rides the rapids. Overweight Chinese Pure-Play Operators (Pony.ai, WeRide, Baidu Apollo Go) where the Māyā Meter reading is most extreme—WeRide at 50% below IPO despite 144% revenue growth and the largest MENA robotaxi commitment. CABZ ETF (100% AV purity, launched January 2026) for concentrated AV exposure, accepting the $1.4M AUM liquidity constraint. LEAPS on BIDU (available through January 2028) for leveraged upside to the Goldman $47B Chinese robotaxi market thesis. This profile acknowledges that geopolitical tail risk—delisting, the Taiwan scenario, sector-specific restrictions—could produce 30–50% drawdowns and sizes accordingly. The contrarian bet: the market is pricing Chinese AV companies as if the Didi precedent is the base case. If the Didi precedent is instead the tail case—and the base case is operational execution driving repricing—the upside is 2–5x from current levels. This is the boatman who looks at the storm and sees not danger but the monsoon that will fill his paddy fields—provided, of course, that his vessel survives the crossing. The aggressive boatman does not need to be right about everything. He needs to be right about one thing: that the Māyā is thinner than the market believes, and that operational reality is accumulating faster than narrative can suppress.

14.3 The Catalyst Calendar: When to Watch

The boatman reads the tides. The investor reads the calendar. The following catalysts are now visible and dated.

February 27, 2026: MSCI China Index inclusion of Hesai (2525.HK) and Pony.ai (2026.HK) becomes effective at the close of business. Estimated passive inflows (CICC estimate reported in Hong Kong financial media): ~$147M for Hesai-W (02525.HK) and ~$135M for Pony-W (02026.HK) around the Feb 27, 2026 close; actual flows may vary by how much AUM is strictly index-tracking versus benchmark-aware. Academic research suggests cumulative abnormal returns of 2.8–5.6% in the 30–50 days before inclusion. *The trade implication: $15 trillion in benchmarked assets are now structurally required to add both stocks; the passive-buying flow creates a bid floor that has historically lifted included stocks 5–15% in the first sixty days. This is a calendar event with a mechanistic driver—not a narrative, not a hope, but an index rebalancing that forces capital to move.*

March 9, 2026: Hang Seng Composite Index inclusion of Pony.ai and WeRide. Opens Southbound Connect access to mainland Chinese investors—a second wave of structural buying. *The trade implication: Mainland retail and institutional capital gain direct access to both stocks for the first time, adding a demand layer that is independent of Western sentiment and immune to the BIS narrative.*

Q1–Q2 2026: Pony.ai, WeRide, and Baidu earnings releases. The critical metric: fleet expansion rate and revenue per vehicle per day. Pony.ai's 23 orders/day in Guangzhou is the benchmark. Plus (PLS) is expected to list on Nasdaq in Q1 2026. *The trade implication: if a second city replicates Guangzhou's unit economics, the single-city-anomaly objection dissolves, and the repricing thesis accelerates from contrarian to consensus.*

April 2026: Tesla Cybercab production target. If production begins on schedule, the first purpose-built American robotaxi will enter manufacturing. If delayed (pattern probability based on historical timeline analysis: high), the Timeline Illusion documented in Chapter 13 extends. Aptiv's Versigent spin-off completes April 1. *The trade implication: a Cybercab delay is a narrative event with real valuation consequences—the $450–700B robotaxi premium in Tesla's market cap rests on execution timelines that have missed five consecutive deadlines.*

Mid-2026: Waymo expansion to 20+ cities, including first international markets (London, Tokyo). Baidu/Lyft robotaxi testing begins in London—creating the first direct international head-to-head between American and Chinese autonomous driving on the same streets. WeRide/Uber deployment scaling toward 1,200 vehicles across Abu Dhabi, Dubai, and Riyadh. *The trade implication: London becomes the first city where a passenger can choose between Waymo and Baidu. The comparative data from that market will be the most consequential operational test the Māyā Meter has ever faced.*

H2 2026–2027: China's 15th Five-Year Plan (2026–30) formulates new intelligent connected vehicle development plans. If AV is elevated to a national strategic priority (probability: high, given December 2025 L3 approvals), the policy tailwind for Chinese AV companies intensifies. SELF DRIVE Act legislative progress—or stagnation. *The trade implication: the Five-Year Plan is the single most important policy signal for Chinese AV investment over the next decade; its language determines whether Pony.ai, WeRide, and Baidu are domestic plays or globally mandated infrastructure.*

14.4 The Risk Architecture: What Can Kill the Thesis

The boatman who does not know where the rocks are will find them with his hull. Five structural risks face the Chinese AV investment thesis. None is hypothetical. All must be sized and positioned for construction.

VIE structure: structural vulnerability with no mitigation. All major US-listed Chinese AV companies use Variable Interest Entity structures—Cayman shell companies with contractual claims on Chinese operating entities. As of end-2023, 98 percent of Chinese concept stocks used VIEs, with cumulative financing exceeding $1.5 trillion. China has never explicitly approved or banned VIEs. The 2021 education-sector ban demonstrated Beijing's willingness to void VIE structures in specific sectors—and AV, with its national-security and data-sensitivity dimensions, shares that vulnerability. There is no hedge for VIE risk. It is a binary: the structure holds, or it does not. In the Theyyam framework, this is the one element of the performance that cannot be rehearsed—the moment the fire either transforms the performer or burns him. Size positions accordingly.

HFCAA and delisting: risk level elevated. The December 2022 PCAOB agreement technically resolved the audit access issue. However, the Trump administration has weaponised delisting as a form of geopolitical leverage. Treasury Secretary Bessent: "Everything is on the table." Congressional pressure on JPMorgan and Bank of America to cease underwriting Chinese IPOs continues to intensify. Market cap at risk: $1.09 trillion across 286 Chinese companies. Mitigating factor: all four key AV companies (PONY, WRD, HSAI, BIDU) maintain dual listings in Hong Kong. Capital can rotate without forced selling. However, HK-listed shares typically trade at lower valuations and lower liquidity—both Pony.ai and WeRide fell by more than 12 percent on their HK debuts.

The Didi precedent: the trauma that shapes all Chinese ADR pricing. Didi IPO'd on June 30, 2021, at $14 per share. China's CAC launched a cybersecurity probe 48 hours later—no warning. Result: ~80 percent permanent value destruction, $1.2 billion regulatory fine, forced NYSE delisting, and the promised HK relisting never materialized. The critical lesson: Didi's data on 493 million users, mapping data, and location data triggered national security concerns—precisely the same data categories that AV companies collect. The Didi precedent is priced into every Chinese AV stock. The question is whether it is overpriced or appropriately priced. Chapter 13's Māyā Meter suggests the former.

Taiwan tail risk. Federal Reserve Bank of St. Louis modelling suggests that a Taiwan conflict would cause stock markets to crash by 10–15 percent within weeks. Bloomberg Economics projects that the S&P 500 would decline by ~40 percent and global GDP would contract by 10.2 percent in a full invasion scenario. Goldman estimated extreme US-China decoupling could cost $2.5 trillion in forced equity and bond selling. This is not a China-specific risk—it is a global portfolio risk that would devastate holdings denominated in any currency. The hedge is not intended to avoid Chinese stocks; rather, it involves maintaining cash reserves and diversifying across geographies.

Data sovereignty: dual-exposure risk. Chinese AV companies face data restrictions from both China (preventing cross-border data exports) and the US (blocking market access under the BIS rule). A December 2025 U.S. bill seeks to phase out the use of Chinese sensors in autonomous vehicles. The risk is not that one government restricts Chinese AV companies but that both do—simultaneously—for different reasons. For investors, this means the global-expansion thesis (Chapter 10) is the critical variable: if Chinese AV companies succeed in Gulf, European, and Southeast Asian markets, the US market closure matters less.

14.5 The Entry Plays: Vehicles and Mechanics

The boatman has mapped the rivers, read the tides, and charted the rocks. Now he boards. Three categories of entry vehicle, compressed to essentials. (Full broker mechanics, HKEX trading fees, ADR dynamics, tax implications, and currency analysis are in Appendix C: The Investor's Toolkit.)

ETFs: broad exposure, low friction. CABZ (Roundhill Robotaxi ETF, launched January 14, 2026): 100% AV purity; all 28 holdings are AV-related; includes WeRide 5.1%, Pony.ai 4.7%, Hesai 4.3%, Horizon 3.4%—the purest AV ETF available. Constraint: AUM only $1.4M with very limited liquidity. ARKQ: highest AV purity among established ETFs (~43% autonomous mobility allocation), $2.0B AUM, reasonable liquidity, ~49% one-year return. IDRV (iShares Self-Driving): lowest expense ratio at 0.48%, includes BYD 4% and Li Auto 4%. KWEB: China tech exposure with Baidu at ~4.8%, $8.4B AUM, the most liquid China tech vehicle available. No dedicated China autonomous-vehicle-only ETF exists—this itself is a signal of how early the investment thesis remains.

Direct equity: the conviction play. For investors with thesis conviction and risk tolerance for individual stock selection, the dual-listing structure provides a critical choice. US ADR trading: zero/low commission, no stamp duty, no FBAR reporting requirements, highest liquidity—but exposed to delisting risk. Hong Kong trading (via Interactive Brokers, Moomoo, Tiger Brokers):

stamp duty 0.10% per side, total all-in round-trip cost ~0.38–0.40%, FBAR triggered if aggregate foreign accounts exceed $10,000—but protected from US delisting. The practical answer for most investors: begin with ADRs for lower friction, maintain awareness of the HK listing as a contingency, and rotate if delisting risk materializes. ADRs and HK shares are substantially identical for wash-sale purposes—selling at a loss on one exchange and buying on the other within 30 days triggers the wash-sale rule.

Options: the premium-harvesting play. BIDU and XPEV are the only Chinese AV tickers with truly liquid options suitable for systematic strategies. BIDU ($150, 40–50% implied volatility): 30-day 10% OTM cash-secured puts yield approximately 1.5–3% per month. XPEV (~$18, higher IV): richer premium but wider spreads. The Wheel Strategy—sell cash-secured puts, if assigned, sell covered calls—builds positions at lower cost bases while generating income during the accumulation phase. Size conservatively: Chinese ADRs can gap 15–30 percent on geopolitical headlines. LEAPS (long-dated options) on BIDU through January 2028 provide leveraged exposure to the Goldman $47B Chinese robotaxi thesis, but time decay is unforgiving if the repricing catalyst arrives late. (Full options liquidity assessment, strike selection frameworks, and LEAPS analysis in Appendix C.)

The Tiller Is in Your Hands

The portfolio architect's framework is now complete. Six temples house the AV ecosystem's investment archetypes. Three profiles match conviction level to position sizing. A catalyst calendar marks the tides. A risk architecture charts the rocks. Entry mechanics provide the vessel.

The most actionable insight from this analysis: the picks-and-shovels layer offers the best risk-adjusted entry. Hesai—first profitable LiDAR company globally, 229 percent year-over-year shipment growth, Goldman $36 target against ~$26 current, MSCI China inclusion forcing passive buying in 13 days—provides AV exposure without the binary regulatory risk faced by pure-play operators. Horizon Robotics—49% of China's automotive chip market, unanimous Strong Buy rating from 24 analysts, and VW's €2.4 billion partnership—provides semiconductor exposure to the world's largest AV market. These are not speculative bets on which civilization wins. They are structural positions in the components that both civilizations need.

For those with higher conviction, the Chinese pure-plays (Pony.ai, WeRide, Baidu) offer the Māyā Meter's widest reading—and therefore the greatest upside if the repricing thesis is correct. WeRide, at 50 percent below its IPO price, with 144 percent revenue growth and the largest MENA robotaxi commitment, is either a value trap or a once-in-a-decade entry point. The data assembled across Chapters 7 through 12 suggests the latter. The risk framework in Section 14.4 reminds you why intelligent people disagree.

Marcus has been reading this chapter. He has tracked his own cognitive errors across thirteen chapters—the friction he priced as alpha, the Pony.ai he sold on a headline, the global procession he did not model, the Māyā he has now seen through. He understands the Four Forces that made his errors structural rather than personal. He understands the Three Catalysts that could close the gap. He understands the Five Risks that could widen it. The question is no longer analytical. It is temperamental. Is Marcus the Conservative Boatman, staying in the main channel with Hesai and Uber, letting the picks-and-shovels thesis do the work while he sleeps? Is he the Balanced Boatman, writing cash-secured puts on BIDU while the MSCI inclusion catalyst approaches? Or is he the Aggressive Boatman, overweighting WeRide at fifty cents on the IPO dollar because the Māyā Meter told him the veil is thinner than the market believes? He is deciding now. So are you.

The data is assembled. The catalysts are dated. The risk architecture is built. The tiller is in his hands. The rest belongs to him.

Chapter 15 will take this portfolio framework and project it forward through three scenarios—the Monsoon (Chinese AV technology sweeps global markets), the Dam (geopolitical forces constrain China's expansion), and the Bifurcation (two permanent, parallel AV ecosystems)—and ask the question every investor must answer: which monsoon are you sizing for, and what happens to your portfolio if you are wrong?

The tiller is in your hands. The currents are mapped. The rest is seamanship.

Evidence Anchors

All company financials, valuations, and analyst targets sourced from Chapter 13 evidence base and individual company filings/earnings releases through February 14, 2026 • ETF data: Roundhill CABZ prospectus (January 14, 2026); ARK Invest ARKQ holdings; iShares IDRV; KraneShares KWEB • MSCI February 2026 Index Review (February 10, 2026) • Hang Seng Composite Index reconstitution (effective March 9, 2026) • Goldman Sachs: $47B China robotaxi market by 2035; $18B AV trucking by 2030; company-specific coverage • Risk framework: VIE structure data (98% usage, $1.5T financing), HFCAA resolution December 2022; Didi precedent June–December 2021; Fed St. Louis Taiwan modelling; Goldman $2.5T decoupling estimate • Gatik: $600M+ contracted revenue (January 27, 2026) • Broker mechanics, tax implications, and currency dynamics: Appendix C

[Note: Full broker access mechanics (IBKR, Fidelity, Schwab, Moomoo), HKEX trading fees and stamp duty calculations, ADR/HK share conversion dynamics, options liquidity assessment by ticker, tax implications (FBAR, Form 8938, PFIC risk, wash sale rules, foreign tax credits), currency hedging tools (USD/HKD peg, USD/CNY dynamics), and industry report summaries (KPMG, CB Insights, BCG, Goldman Sachs, Morgan Stanley) are compiled in Appendix C: The Investor's Toolkit.]

CHAPTER 15

Three Monsoons

The Two-River World, 2030–2035

The boatman does not predict the monsoon. He prepares for all of them.

— Kuttanad navigation proverb

In Kerala, three monsoons govern the boatman's year. *Edavapathi*—the southwest monsoon—arrives in June with the fury of abundance, flooding the paddy fields, filling the backwaters, turning the landscape into a shimmering inland sea. It is violent and generous. It makes the harvest possible. *Thulavarsham*—the northeast retreat—arrives in October with quieter menace, unpredictable in timing and force, capable of drowning what *Edavapathi* grew. Between them lies the dry season: still, deceptively calm, the period when the boatman repairs his vessel, studies the currents, and prepares for whichever rain arrives next.

In February 2026, the autonomous vehicle industry is in the dry season. The rivers are visible, the currents are mapped, and the data are assembled across the preceding thirteen chapters. What remains is the question every investor must answer before the monsoon arrives: which rain are you preparing for, and what happens to your cargo if you are wrong?

Three monsoons are possible. This chapter makes each one tactile—not as abstract scenarios but as lived futures—and then asks what portfolio survives all three.

15.1 The Weather Map: What the Forecasters See

The projections range from $200 billion to $2.3 trillion. The range is not uncertainty. It is a choice among scenarios, among civilizations, among bets.

Goldman Sachs projects China's robotaxi TAM will grow from $54 million in 2025 to $47 billion by 2035—an 870x increase, with a fleet scaling to 1.9 million vehicles, capturing 25 percent of the mobility share. Morgan Stanley estimates the global AV market at $200 billion by 2030 and $300–400 billion by 2035, with China accounting for approximately 50 percent of volume. McKinsey's base-case projections indicate 12 percent L3+ penetration by 2030 and 37 percent by 2035, but its

2025 survey revealed a 1–2-year slippage relative to 2023 expectations—the industry is slower but larger than consensus anticipated. Frost & Sullivan, notably more bullish on China, projects the Chinese robotaxi market alone at 1.6 trillion yuan (~$224 billion) by 2035.

The bear case deserves equal voice. S&P Global Mobility—the most conservative major forecaster—projects fewer than 6 percent of light vehicles sold in 2035 will have any L4 functionality, and concludes that L5 autonomy "will NOT be publicly available before 2035, and probably for some time after that." No robotaxi service has reached overall company-level profitability. McKinsey estimates cumulative industry burn through 2030 at $50–67 billion. The WEF's sensitivity analysis suggests that a single high-profile accident reduces projected L4 sales by 2.0 percentage points—and the industry has already had its Uber ATG fatality and its Cruise dragging incident, both of which set back deployment by years.

The weather map shows storm systems, not certainties. Three monsoons are forming. The question is which one makes landfall.

15.2 Scenario A — "Two Galaxies": Separate Orbits

Base case. Probability: 50 percent.

> *San Francisco, (2032). A woman opens the Waymo app on her iPhone 18. She summons a 7th-generation autonomous vehicle—manufactured by Hyundai, powered by Google's Driver, navigating streets mapped to centimeter precision by Waymo's own fleet. The ride costs $14.50 for 4.2 miles. She does not think about it.*
>
> *Singapore, (2032). A man opens WeRide's app on his Huawei Mate 70 and summons a Zeekr robotaxi—manufactured in China, running Horizon Robotics J7 chips, navigating with Baidu's HD maps and C-V2X infrastructure. The ride costs S$5.80 for 6.8 kilometers. He does not think about it either.*
>
> *Neither can use the other's app. Neither knows what the other's ride costs. They live in separate galaxies.*

The McKinsey 2025 survey found that 74 percent of experts predict a dedicated China technology stack anchors this scenario. The breakdown: 35 percent predict that China will develop its own stack, while the US and EU share a single stack; 26 percent predict three independent stacks; only 26 percent foresee convergence. The experts are not predicting bifurcation. They are observing it.

The structural evidence is now overwhelming. US and Chinese AV markets already operate on different technology approaches (Waymo's pure L4 robotaxi versus China's progressive ADAS-to-L4 path), different regulatory frameworks (BIS bans versus MIIT centralized pilots), different data ecosystems (GPS versus Beidou, commercial mapping versus government-controlled data), and different chip architectures (NVIDIA dominance versus Horizon Robotics and Huawei Ascend alternatives, with NVIDIA's China AI chip share declining from 66 to a projected 54 percent). China has logged 149 million autonomous miles, compared with US firms' 106 million. China has approximately 3,000 robotaxis across 30 cities, compared with approximately 2,500 (primarily Waymo) across 6 US cities. However, these fleets operate in entirely separate geographies with no cross-pollination.

The battle for the rest of the world determines whether the galaxies remain two or become three. The Middle East currently hosts Chinese operators (WeRide, Baidu, Pony.ai, Didi AD) but remains open to all. Southeast Asia is an emerging battleground (Grab-Momenta, WeRide-Grab Singapore). The EU is establishing its own technology alliance. However, European automakers remain deeply embedded with Chinese partners—Volkswagen's €2.4 billion Horizon Robotics JV, BMW licensing Momenta for its entire China Neue Klasse lineup, Mercedes investing in Momenta for 40 future models. Roland Berger concludes: "Regions are diverging on software, standards, and customer expectations."

Investment implication: In Two Galaxies, both rivers are investable, but neither dominates globally. The picks-and-shovels layer (Hesai, Horizon Robotics) benefits from supplying both galaxies. Chinese pure-plays (Pony.ai, WeRide, Baidu) capture the Chinese and third-country market—Goldman's $47 billion by 2035. American pure-plays (Waymo, Aurora) capture the US and allied-nation markets—Goldman's $7 billion US robotaxi by 2030, plus $18 billion in trucking. The Māyā Meter gap narrows gradually as Chinese operators prove profitability in their galaxy, but never fully closes because institutional access barriers persist. This is the scenario that rewards patience, diversification, and the balanced boatman's allocation from Chapter 11—the investor who navigates both currents, writing cash-secured puts on BIDU. At the same time, Waymo expands to twenty cities, treating the bifurcation not as a problem to solve but as a geography to inhabit.

15.3 Scenario B — "The Monsoon": Chinese Technology Goes Global

Bull China. Probability: 25 percent.

> *Dubai, (2033). The Roads and Transport Authority's annual report confirms that 11,400 autonomous vehicles now operate across the emirate—8,200 from WeRide, 2,400 from Baidu, 800 from Pony.ai. They carry 2.1 million rides per week. The human taxi fleet has shrunk by 40% over the past 3 years. Dubai's 25-percent autonomous by 2030 target was achieved 14 months early.*

São Paulo (2033). BYD's Dolphin Mini—manufactured at the Camaçari plant in Bahia— outsells every vehicle in Brazil. It costs R$69,000. God's Eye 7.0 is standard. Brazilian consumers have never heard of Waymo.

Munich, (2033). BMW's Neue Klasse i3 runs Momenta's autonomous driving stack. The software was developed in Beijing. The car is assembled in Dingolfing. German engineering has never been so Chinese.

Three vectors of Chinese AV technology globalization are already in motion, and each is accelerating.

The Middle East gateway is the most advanced. WeRide and Uber's February 2026 announcement of 1,200 robotaxis across Abu Dhabi, Dubai, and Riyadh by 2027 is part of a 15-city commitment with 12 more cities by 2030. Baidu Apollo Go secured a fully driverless permit in Abu Dhabi with approximately 100 robotaxis. Pony.ai plans to deploy 1,000 robotaxis in the Middle East by 2028. Didi AD announced a strategic collaboration with Abu Dhabi Investment Office. Dubai aims to have 25 percent of transportation be autonomous by 2030—and Chinese operators are building it.

BYD's volume play could establish de facto global standards. BYD delivered 4.27 million vehicles in 2024—2.5 times Tesla. God's Eye ADAS is now standard across all models, installed in 2.5 million vehicles, generating 160 million kilometers of daily training data. With factories in Hungary, Brazil, Turkey, Thailand, and Indonesia, and exports across Asia, Latin America, and the Middle East, BYD's ADAS becomes the default driver assistance system for a massive global fleet—not because it won a technology competition but because it came free with the car. BYD's ADAS demand alone constitutes an estimated 23–25 percent of global automotive camera supply and 16 percent of the LiDAR market. One hundred billion yuan ($14.3 billion) committed to smart technology R&D.

Momenta's OEM partnerships embed its Chinese autonomous-driving software into Western vehicles. Over 160 OEM vehicle programs across 40 production models: BMW's entire Neue Klasse China lineup, Mercedes-Benz's electric CLA and 40 future models, GM ($300 million investment), Toyota, Volkswagen/SAIC, Honda, Nissan, and Tier 1 supplier Valeo. Momenta also partnered with Uber for Munich robotaxis in 2026 and Grab for Southeast Asia. Volkswagen opened a $2.9 billion China development lab because German engineering could not match Chinese 18–24-month development cycles, compared with VW's 3–5-year cycles. This "Joint Venture 2.0" dynamic creates structural dependence of Western automakers on Chinese AV software. A VDA survey found that nearly 70 percent of respondents plan to increase investment in China, with over 75 percent prioritizing R&D. The irony is exquisite and structural: the same Western governments that ban Chinese AV software from their domestic roads preside over automotive industries that cannot build competitive AV software without Chinese partners. The BIS rule and the Momenta partnership list exist simultaneously, in the same market, authored by the same civilization. If this were a novel, the editor would flag it as too implausible. In geopolitics, it is Tuesday.

Investment implication: In the Monsoon, the Māyā Meter collapses. Chinese AV companies trading at 7–30x discounts to Waymo per vehicle would reprice toward parity as their global fleets demonstrate profitability across multiple geographies. Pony.ai, WeRide, and Baidu—currently priced as domestic Chinese plays—would command global operator multiples. BYD's God's Eye would be recognized as the world's largest autonomous driving platform. Hesai's LiDAR, already supplying 9 of the top 10 global robotaxi operators, would dominate the market. The aggressive boatman's allocation—overweight Chinese pure-plays, CABZ ETF, LEAPS on BIDU—is designed for this monsoon—the risk: timing. The Monsoon may not make landfall until 2030–2032, and the positions must survive the dry season between now and then.

15.4 Scenario C — "The Dam": Chinese Expansion Constrained

Bear China. Probability: 25 percent.

> *Washington, (2031). The headline on the Financial Times: "USTR Expands BIS Rule to All Chinese Automotive Components; EU Follows with 'Connected Vehicle Security Directive.'" Hesai's stock falls 34 percent in a single session. Pony.ai's Nasdaq ADR is suspended pending a House Select Committee review. WeRide's Uber partnership in Abu Dhabi continues—but new deployments in Europe are frozen.*
>
> *Shenzhen, (2031). BYD's God's Eye 8.0 is the most advanced mass-market ADAS on the planet. It runs on Huawei Ascend chips because NVIDIA export controls made Orin unavailable two years ago. Chinese consumers do not notice the difference. The system works beautifully—in China. God's Eye is standard on 8 million vehicles. None of them is sold in the United States or the European Union.*
>
> *The dam holds. The river floods only its own valley.*

The bear case rests on four pillars, each already partially in motion.

Regulatory exclusion is already the law. The BIS Connected Vehicles rule (documented in Chapter 5) bans Chinese ADS software from US vehicles starting in Model Year 2027 and Chinese VCS hardware from US vehicles starting in Model Year 2030. The SAFE LiDAR Act (H.R. 6576), introduced in December 2025, would extend restrictions to sensors—though it has zero cosponsors as of February 2026, and Luminar's bankruptcy five days after its introduction underscores the competitive crisis that makes passage uncertain. If the EU follows with similar restrictions—a possibility given the DGAP's explicit call for a "binding rule similar to the BIS" and the Commission's announced risk assessment—Chinese AV companies could be locked out of Western markets, representing over $100 billion in potential TAM. The critical nuance: the BIS rule explicitly excluded LiDAR, radar, and cameras from the VCS definition, meaning Hesai's sensors are not directly banned. However, future rulemaking could close that gap.

The lived consequences of regulatory exclusion are not abstract—they are procurement decisions that land on a specific desk in a specific building. Picture Munich, 2032: BMW's head of autonomous driving platforms must choose between Horizon Robotics' Journey 7 chip—which offers 30 percent better inference performance per watt at 40 percent lower cost, is already integrated into the Neue Klasse architecture through the CARIZON JV, and powers the vehicle's entire China lineup—and NVIDIA's next-generation Thor, which carries NATO-allied regulatory approval, costs more, and requires a complete software rewrite for the European fleet. Choosing Horizon means a single global platform, a lower BOM, faster development cycles, and regulatory prohibition in the United States and, potentially, in the EU. Choosing NVIDIA means two parallel development stacks, higher per-unit cost, and the luxury of selling in every Western market. This is not a technology decision. It is a civilizational bet disguised as a line item on a procurement spreadsheet. In the Dam scenario, every European and Japanese automaker faces this choice—and most, under margin pressure and shareholder scrutiny, will choose the path that keeps Western markets open, even if it means paying more for less. The dam does not merely constrain Chinese companies. It constrains the companies that partner with them.

Profitability remains elusive at the company level. Pony.ai achieved unit economics breakeven in Guangzhou but reported a net loss of $61.6 million in Q3 2025. WeRide lost $43.2 million. Baidu Apollo Go claims per-vehicle profitability in Wuhan, but overall operations remain unprofitable. The industry has invested $16 billion with uncertain returns. The path from unit economics to company profitability requires fleet scale from ~1,000 to 3,000 vehicles per operator—a tripling that takes time, capital, and flawless execution.

Delisting risk creates a permanent overhang. Two hundred and eighty-six Chinese companies (with a combined market capitalization of $1.1 trillion) remain listed on U.S. exchanges. The House Select Committee specifically named Pony.ai in a letter urging the SEC to delist Pony.ai on national security grounds. Treasury Secretary Bessent: "Everything is on the table." Dual Hong Kong listings provide a partial hedge (documented in Chapter 14's risk architecture). However, US delisting would remove access to the world's deepest capital market and trigger forced selling by mandated funds.

Domestic competition is a meat grinder. BYD requested 10 percent price reductions from suppliers for 2025. Huawei ADS, DJI, Momenta, Horizon, DeepRoute, and Baidu all compete ferociously in ADAS solutions. Leading Chinese EV manufacturers are developing systems in-house. The February 2025 alliance of Changan, Geely, Great Wall, and BYD to co-develop autonomous technology suggests individual R&D budgets are becoming unsustainable. Apollo Go's expansion in Wuhan sparked protests from taxi drivers. Chip supply dependence adds fragility—most Chinese robotaxi fleets still run on NVIDIA Orin chips —and further US export restrictions could push development timelines back by 1–2 years. Domestic alternatives are advancing (Bernstein projects that Chinese AI chip localization will rise from 17 percent in 2023 to 55 percent by 2027), but performance gaps persist.

Investment implication: In the Dam, the conservative boatman's allocation is vindicated. Picks-and-shovels plays with dual-market exposure (ON Semi, Aptiv) outperform. US pure-plays (Waymo, Aurora) benefit from reduced competition. Chinese pure-plays stagnate or decline further—WeRide's 50 percent post-IPO decline would prove prologue rather than nadir. The critical distinction: even in the Dam scenario, Chinese AV technology continues to advance within China. BYD's domestic market is 26 million new vehicles per year. The dam constrains the river's international course; it does not stop the river from flowing. The investor who abandons Chinese AV entirely in the Dam scenario misses the domestic-market thesis. The investor who sizes it at quarter-Kelly with a 0.7x geopolitical overlay—as Chapter 14's framework prescribes—survives the dam without drowning. Marcus, reading these three scenarios in sequence, confronts the question his Bloomberg terminal was never designed to answer: not *which* monsoon arrives, but whether his portfolio architecture can survive *all three*. The Conservative Boatman survives the Dam. The Aggressive Boatman thrives in the Monsoon. Only the Balanced Boatman—navigating both currents, sized at quarter-Kelly, rebalancing on catalyst triggers—is built for whichever rain arrives. Marcus is discovering that the most important investment decision is not the thesis. It is the sizing.

15.5 Wild Cards: The Weather the Forecasters Miss

Monsoons are predictable in season, unpredictable in force. Three wild cards could reshape any scenario.

A catastrophic AV accident. The two previous incidents define the template. Uber ATG's March 2018 fatality in Tempe killed a pedestrian when the AV misclassified her for 5 seconds, and the safety driver was watching television. Uber ceased all testing for 9 months and ultimately sold its AV unit. The Cruise pedestrian dragging in October 2023 was compounded by a cover-up—an incomplete NHTSA report and an edited video. GM exited the robotaxi business entirely, writing off $10 billion. A multi-fatality event could trigger 10–20 percent sector-wide declines, regulatory permit suspensions lasting 12 months, and an industry-wide chilling effect. The WEF quantifies the impact: a high-profile accident reduces projected L4 sales by 2.0 percentage points. China's liability framework (Beijing's April 2025 regulations, which shift L4/L5 liability from human occupants to operators and manufacturers—the clearest system anywhere) provides structural resilience. The US lacks a unified federal liability framework and relies on fifty state tort regimes. Which system recovers faster from the next accident is a material investment variable.

An L5 breakthrough. The expert consensus is sobering. MIT AgeLab's Bryan Reimer: "Level 5, highly automated vehicles that work anywhere a human would drive, will never exist." McKinsey's 2025 survey found 49 percent of experts believe the mass market will center on L2+ functions by 2035. S&P Global projects L5 not publicly available before 2035, "and probably for some time after that." The most credible consensus places widespread L5 in the 2040–2050 timeframe. An unexpected breakthrough would make all current L4 geofenced approaches obsolete, create a multi-trillion-dollar market, and reshape valuations across the sector. No company credibly claims to be proximate to it. However, the investor who assigns zero probability to transformative breakthroughs is the investor who missed the internet, the iPhone, and DeepSeek.

Apple re-entry. Apple cancelled Project Titan in February 2024 after approximately a decade and billions of dollars, reassigning the 2,000-person team primarily to generative AI. Its automotive strategy pivoted to CarPlay Ultra—present in 93.9 percent of 2023 model-year vehicles and considered non-negotiable by 38 percent of car buyers. There are no credible signals of Apple re-entering AV hardware development. Nevertheless, Apple's historical pattern—entering established markets with premium integrated products that capture disproportionate profit (iPod, iPhone)—means the possibility cannot be dismissed. The vacuum Apple left is real. Whether it remains empty is unknowable.

15.6 The Third Current: India

The two-river metaphor may soon require a third channel.

India's autonomous vehicle market is approximately $2.6 billion—orders of magnitude smaller than those of the US or China. India ranks 29th of 30 countries on KPMG's Autonomous Vehicle Readiness Index. ADAS penetration is 8.3 percent. The Motor Vehicles Act of 1988 is fundamentally driver-centric, and Transport Minister Gadkari has repeatedly stated that autonomous vehicles will not be permitted due to concerns about job displacement.

And yet. Mahindra announced a partnership with Mobileye in February 2026 for SuperVision across at least 6 models from 2027. Tata Motors has a partnership with NVIDIA and a 50/50 joint venture with BMW for autonomous-vehicle software. Tesla entered India in July 2025 with the Model Y and is hiring Autopilot Vehicle Operators in Delhi and Mumbai to collect training data on India's gloriously chaotic roads—roads where unmarked lanes coexist with cattle, auto-rickshaws, monsoons, and a density of edge cases that would give any Western validation team a collective nervous breakdown.

India's realistic path is not to replicate the American robotaxi model or the Chinese government-backed deployment model. It is becoming the world's laboratory for chaos-resilient, cost-effective autonomous technology—first in industrial applications (Ati Motors has deployed autonomous robots across 40 manufacturers, including Airbus), then in logistics, and then in controlled highway environments. Indian startups developing camera-first, LiDAR-free solutions for roads that defy Western mapping assumptions may create globally applicable technology for the developing world.

NITI Aayog projects that ADAS will be in 90 percent of new Indian vehicles by 2030. Full urban autonomy remains at least a decade away.

The Third Current is 5–7 years from mattering to the investment thesis. However, the boatman who ignores a river that forms upstream is the one who is surprised when it arrives. This is a teaser, not a chapter. The full analysis belongs to the next book in the series.

The Boatman's Preparation

The autonomous vehicle industry is not one market but two—and possibly three if India fulfils its potential. The most striking data point may be the simplest: 74 percent of experts predict separate technology stacks, yet Chinese AV technology is already embedded in vehicles from BMW, Mercedes, Volkswagen, Toyota, and GM. This contradiction—decoupling in regulation, convergence in technology—defines the investment challenge for the next decade.

The projections range from $200 billion to $2.3 trillion. The scenarios range from Two Galaxies (separate orbits, gradual convergence) to the Monsoon (Chinese technology sweeps global markets) to the Dam (geopolitical forces constrain expansion). The wild cards—a catastrophic accident, an L5 breakthrough, Apple re-entry—each carry scenario probabilities that should be explicitly modelled rather than ignored. The WeRide-Uber announcement of 1,200 Middle East robotaxis and BYD's 2.5 million God's Eye-equipped vehicles represent the Monsoon scenario already in motion. Pony.ai trading below its IPO price and Luminar's bankruptcy represent the early casualties of the Dam scenario.

The math says: do not bet the farm. Bet a corner of the field, and watch the weather. The quarter-Kelly framework from Chapter 11 yields approximately 10–15 percent total AV allocation, with China-exposed positions further discounted by a 0.7x geopolitical overlay—roughly 3.5 percent of a diversified portfolio in Chinese AV and 10 percent in US AV —with threshold-based rebalancing tied to the catalyst calendar. The MSCI inclusion of Pony.ai and Hesai—with $15 trillion in benchmarked assets now requiring their purchase—creates a structural demand floor even as regulatory headwinds intensify. The 15th Five-Year Plan (March 2026), the SELF DRIVE Act's trajectory, and the WEF's finding that large-scale AV rollout will be "slower than once anticipated" all point to a longer, larger opportunity than consensus expects.

Marcus has travelled fifteen chapters. He began in Chapter 4, pricing friction as alpha—a reasonable bet that became a cognitive trap. He sold Pony.ai on a headline in Chapter 6, missed the global procession in Chapter 10, and discovered in Chapter 13 that his errors were not personal but structural—rational responses to a market architecture built on Māyā. In Chapter 14, he chose his boatman's profile. Now, in the dry season before the monsoon, he understands the principle that the

Kuttanad boatman has always known: the most important variable is not which rain arrives. It is whether the vessel was built for all of them.

The investor's task is not to predict which monsoon arrives, but to size positions that survive all three.

The dry season will not last forever. The boatman who has prepared—who has mapped the rivers, charted the rocks, built the vessel, and distributed the cargo—will navigate whichever monsoon arrives. The boatman who has bet everything on a single forecast will discover, as Kerala's proverb warns, that the monsoon does not care about predictions.

The Epilogue that follows is not a new chapter. It is a view from the boat—looking back at the two rivers, looking forward to the sea, and asking: what have we learned, what remains unknown, and where does the tiller point?

Evidence Anchors

McKinsey Center for Future Mobility 2025 survey: 74% bifurcation, 1–2 year timeline slippage, base case 12% L3+ by 2030 / 37% by 2035, cumulative burn $50–67B • Goldman Sachs: $47B China robotaxi by 2035, $7B US by 2030, $18B AV trucking, fleet 1.9M vehicles • Morgan Stanley: $200B global by 2030, $300–400B by 2035, China ~50% by volume • Frost & Sullivan: 1.6T yuan China by 2035 • S&P Global Mobility: <6% L4 by 2035, L5 not before 2035 • Precedence Research: $188.91B global robotaxi by 2034 • WeRide/Uber: 1,200 ME robotaxis by 2027 (Feb 6, 2026) • BYD God's Eye: 2.5M vehicles, 160M km/day, $14.3B R&D commitment • Momenta: 160+ OEM programs, BMW/Mercedes/GM/Toyota • BIS Connected Vehicles rule: ADS software MY2027, VCS hardware MY2030 • SAFE LiDAR Act H.R.6576 (Dec 2025): zero co-sponsors • China L3 permits Dec 15, 2025 • WEF/BCG sensitivity analysis: accident impact −2.0pp • Uber ATG Tempe fatality (Mar 2018) • Cruise dragging (Oct 2023), GM $10B write-off • MIT AgeLab: "L5 will never exist" • Apple Project Titan cancellation (Feb 2024) • India: $2.6B market, 29th/30 KPMG index, Mahindra-Mobileye Feb 2026 • NVIDIA China share declining from 66% to projected 54% • SCSP data: China 1.49M vs. US 106M autonomous miles • Roland Berger ADR 14 (Sept 2025)

[Note: Full Kelly Criterion mathematics, Bridgewater and BlackRock case studies, rebalancing trigger KPI tables, event-triggered protocols, EU regulatory details (anti-subsidy duties, minimum import price mechanism, UK Automated Vehicles Act), and detailed WEF/BCG roadmap analysis are compiled in Appendix D: Three Monsoons Data Companion.]

EPILOGUE

The Other Engine Is Already Running

Or, How to Read Two Rivers Without Drowning

In the backwaters of Kerala, the boatman does not choose between tides.

He reads them both. The freshwater descends from the mountains with the authority of origin.

The saltwater rises from the ocean with the authority of destination.

The brackish zone where they meet is not confusion. It is commerce.

. . .

The Monsoon Metaphor

The future of autonomous mobility is being written in two languages, and neither has bothered to learn the other's grammar.

One language speaks of moonshots and singularities, of patient capital aggregating around the quest for a single, sublime algorithm that will unlock L5 autonomy the way a physicist unlocks a unified field theory. This is the language of Silicon Valley—the *Cathedral of Code*—where Waymo's $126 billion valuation and Tesla's $1.57 trillion market capitalization testify to a civilizational conviction that perfection, once achieved, will justify any price paid during the pilgrimage. It is the *Arithmetic of Patience:* build the perfect temple, and the devotees will come.

The other language speaks of margins, scale, and relentless industrial pragmatism—of $28,000 robotaxis achieving unit economics breakeven in low-fare cities, of 2.5 million vehicles equipped with God's Eye generating 160 million kilometers of training data every single day, of 7.1 million exported cars seeding a continent's worth of technical standards before the first Western regulator has finished drafting a federal framework. This is the *Calculus of Scale:* build the irrigation system, and a thousand fields will bloom.

The world watches one river. The other keeps flowing.

. . .

The Cathedral and the Empire

We began this book with a conceit borrowed from Kerala's temple architecture: that every *kshetram* serves a dual purpose, with the sacred and the commercial inhabiting the same geography but operating in separate realities. Fifteen chapters later, that conceit has proven disturbingly literal.

The Cathedral of Code builds upward toward perfection. Waymo's 6th-generation Driver carries $175,000 in sensors per vehicle, delivers 450,000 weekly rides with a safety record that humbles human drivers, and commands an implied valuation of $50 million per deployed vehicle. The architecture is magnificent. The Empire of Scale builds outward toward ubiquity. Pony.ai has achieved unit economics breakeven in Guangzhou and entered the MSCI China Index—the first robotaxi company ever granted that institutional passport. WeRide operates fully driverless commercial rides on Uber in Abu Dhabi with 1,600 vehicles spanning eleven countries. BYD has made autonomous driving a standard feature on a $9,550 hatchback. The architecture is ruthlessly efficient. Moreover, the market values these achievements at roughly one-fourteenth to one-fiftieth of what it values the American narrative's promise to be.

The Cathedral asks: *How perfect can we make this?* The Empire asks: *How many can we reach?* These are not the same question. America has built the most admired autonomous driving technology in history and priced it as if admiration were revenue. China has built the most commercially deployed autonomous-driving ecosystem in history, yet it has been priced as if deployment were a rounding error. Both deserve respect. Only one is underpriced.

But the deeper mispricing is categorical, not numerical. The Cathedral is building a car that drives itself. The Empire is building an embodied-intelligence platform—five nodes, one brain, many bodies—in which the automobile is merely the first form factor, and the Interdependency Web that connects autonomous mobility, logistics, robotics, energy, and financial rails compounds value at a rate no single-sector multiple can capture. The market that prices the Empire as an "auto sector" is not undervaluing a company. It is miscategorising a civilization.

> *The investor's task is to recognize that both are temples—and to know which kshetram holds the better offering.*

· · ·

The Investor's Dharma

If this book's fifteen chapters and three acts can be distilled into a single investment principle, it is this: **autonomy is not a technology race—it is a commercialization system race.** The market that prices only the American narrative sees only half the picture through a stained-glass window and calls it the view.

The data has been unsparing. China achieved 85 percent consumer acceptance, whereas the United States lags at 39 percent. China deployed L3 production permits in December 2025, while the US SELF DRIVE Act limped through a committee vote of 12–11. China invested $84 billion in vehicle-road-cloud infrastructure, while America debated whether to ban LiDAR sensors that enable autonomy. Detroit spent $13 billion on L4 attempts before retreating to incremental L2 improvements marketed as premium features, while BYD achieved comparable capability for $385 per car and offered it for free. The per-vehicle valuation gap—from 14-to-1 between Waymo and WeRide, to 244-to-1 between Tesla's robotaxi attribution and WeRide, to ratios that transcend financial analysis when independent fleet trackers are used—is not a geopolitical discount. It is *Māyā*—the grand illusion—and the contrarian who sees through it will be positioned for the decade's most consequential transportation transformation.

The Māyā Meter, last calibrated in Chapter 13, has widened rather than closed—the American river has risen on narrative momentum while the Chinese river has risen on operational fact. Both are higher. The gap persists. But the reader who has walked the burning ghat now carries instruments the Māyā Meter alone could not provide: a Dinosaur Meter that maps the refinancing wall closing on legacy automakers, an Interdependency Web Score that reveals which nations and companies own the embodied-intelligence platform and which are buying time, and a Quarter-Kelly sizing model that converts both readings into a position built to survive whichever monsoon arrives. The contrarian's quarter-Kelly allocation—perhaps 3.5 percent of a diversified portfolio in Chinese AV, 10 percent in US AV, with threshold-based rebalancing tied to the catalyst calendar—remains the rational position for those who can read both currents.

Marcus has travelled fifteen chapters. He began pricing friction as alpha—a reasonable bet that became a cognitive trap. He sold Pony.ai on a headline, missed the global procession, and stood at the burning ghat where the 150-year ICE empire met the embodied-intelligence platform that is cremating it. There, for the first time, he held instruments—a Dinosaur Meter that scored Ford at 83.4 and mapped the refinancing wall, an Interdependency Web Score that revealed China at 24/25 and his own zero allocation as a thesis position rather than a risk decision, and a Quarter-Kelly sizing model that converted conviction into a 15 percent thematic allocation he could survive. He discovered that his errors were not personal but structural—rational responses to a market architecture built on Māyā. He chose his boatman's profile. He sized for the monsoon. The question that remains is not analytical. It is the question that every book about investing must eventually ask, and no book can answer: will he act? The data is assembled. The catalysts are dated. The risk architecture is built. The tiller is in his hands. Marcus is no longer a character in this book. He is the reader who has arrived at this page. The rest belongs to you.

. . .

The Fire and the Audience

In the Theyyam tradition of northern Kerala, the performer's transformation is not metaphorical. The face is painted, the crown is lit, the body enters the divine. The performer becomes something other than what the audience expects. The audience's task—the real task, the one that separates the devotee from the tourist—is not to watch the fire but to understand what the fire *reveals*. The fire does not create the god. It reveals what was already there.

The autonomous vehicle market is a Theyyam. The technology is real. The vehicles drive. The rides happen. The data accumulates. However, the audience's perception of what it is witnessing—divine miracle or dangerous spectacle, trillion-dollar opportunity or geopolitical trap, cathedral or empire— is the Māyā. The veil between perception and reality is where fortunes are made and lost. The investor who can distinguish the fire from the audience's interpretation of the fire will be positioned when the veil finally thins.

It is thinning now.

◦ ◦ ◦

A Research Agenda for the Autonomous Divide

This book has attempted to map the two rivers. It has not—could not—drain them. Four questions remain that scholars, policymakers, and the next generation of analysts must investigate if we are to navigate the brackish zone with any intellectual honesty:

◆ *The Trust Formation Mechanism. China achieved 85 percent consumer acceptance of autonomous vehicles in half the time it took America to reach 39 percent. How? Is this cultural, infrastructural, media-driven, or simply the product of a population that has leapfrogged directly from bicycles to bullet trains? More critically, is the trust transferable to export markets, or does the Monsoon scenario require rebuilding trust from scratch in every new geography?*

◆ *The Industrialiser Transfer Problem. BYD's God's Eye deploys ADAS as a standard feature at $385 per vehicle. Can this model survive export to Western markets, where regulatory overhead, liability structures, and profit-margin expectations differ fundamentally? Or is the Industrialiser archetype structurally dependent on China's manufacturing ecosystem—a temple that cannot be disassembled and rebuilt on foreign soil?*

◆ *The V2X ROI Question. China has invested $84 billion in smart road infrastructure across 20 pilot cities, including 35,000 kilometers of test roads and 11,000 roadside intelligent units. What is the measurable reduction in vehicle-side compute cost? Where is the infrastructure breakeven point? Moreover, does the American refusal to invest in V2X condemn its AV companies to permanently higher per-vehicle costs?*

◆ The Liability Allocation Divergence. Beijing's April 2025 regulations shifted L4/L5 liability from human occupants to operators and manufacturers—the clearest liability framework in the world. The United States lacks a unified federal framework and relies on 50 different state tort regimes. Which system produces more efficient risk allocation, faster insurance market development, and ultimately greater deployment velocity?

• • •

The Tiller in Our Hands

The boatmen of Kerala do not ask which current is purer. They ask which one carries their boat to the sea.

The investor's dharma is not to choose between civilizations. It is to read both rivers, navigate both currents, and arrive at the ocean with cargo intact. We have spent fifteen chapters learning to read the water—the eddies of valuation psychosis, the undertow of geopolitical risk, the hidden channels where MSCI inclusion and unit economics breakeven create passages that only the attentive boatman can navigate. We began this journey at a Kerala *kshetram*, where the sacred and the commercial coexist. We end it in the backwaters, where the rivers meet the sea, and the water is neither fresh nor salt but something that nourishes what neither could grow alone.

The gods are not crazy. They are simply Chinese and American, building their temples on opposite banks of the same river, and they have placed the tiller in our hands.

The question is not whether the rivers will meet. They always do—somewhere in the backwaters, where the freshwater of origin and the saltwater of destination create something neither could produce alone. The question is: what do we build on the banks?

Evidence Anchors

Tesla ~$1.57T (NASDAQ, Feb 2026) • Waymo $126B (Feb 2026, $16B raised) • Pony.ai ~$5B; MSCI China inclusion Feb 27, 2026; Guangzhou UE breakeven • WeRide <$2.5B; 1,600+ AVs, 30+ cities, 11 countries; ME operating profitability • BYD God's Eye: 2.5M+ vehicles, 160M km/day, $385/vehicle • Consumer trust: 85% China vs. 39% US (Edelman, 2025; McKinsey, 2025) • China L3 permits Dec 15, 2025 • US SELF DRIVE Act: 12–11 committee vote, Feb 2026 • China V2X: $84B+ across 20 pilot cities • GM Cruise $10B+; Ford Argo $2.7B write-down • Quarter-Kelly: ~15% total AV; 0.7× geopolitical overlay for China

---

Chinese AV Company Profiles

Financial and Operational Data as of February 14, 2026

China's AV sector entered 2026 at an inflection point, with 13 companies across robotaxi operations, automaker ADAS, software stacks, and sensor supply chains collectively deploying autonomous technology in millions of vehicles across dozens of countries. Q3 2025 earnings revealed accelerating revenue growth and narrowing losses across nearly every publicly traded player, while December 2025 brought China's first national L3 permits—a regulatory milestone the US still lacks at the federal level.

Tier 1: National Champion

Baidu (NASDAQ: BIDU)

Q3 2025 revenue: RMB 31.2B (~$4.4B), down 7% YoY; AI-powered businesses grew 50%+ YoY to ~RMB 10B. Apollo Go standalone valuation: $5–8B (analyst estimate). Non-GAAP operating income: RMB 2.2B. Apollo Go delivered 3.1M fully driverless rides in Q3 2025 (+212% YoY). Weekly driverless rides: 250,000+. Cumulative rides: 17M+ across 240M autonomous km. Fleet: ~1,000+ robotaxis in 22 cities globally, including fully driverless commercial service in Beijing, Shanghai, Shenzhen, Wuhan, Chengdu, Chongqing, Abu Dhabi, Hong Kong, and Switzerland. RT6 vehicle cost: ~$28,000 (1/6th the cost of Waymo). Unit economics breakeven achieved in Wuhan. Per-mile cost: RMB 0.5–1.0 vs. RMB 2–3 for human taxis. Next-gen RT7 targets <$20,000. Uber and Lyft partnerships for London deployment H1 2026. Market cap: ~$47B. Q4 2025 earnings: February 26, 2026. Cash: RMB 124.8B.

Tier 2: Pure-Play Scalers

Pony.ai (NASDAQ: PONY / HKEX: 02026)

Q3 2025 revenue: $25.4M (+72% YoY). Robotaxi revenue: $6.7M (+89.5% YoY, +339% QoQ). Gross margin: 18.4% (from 9.2%). Net loss: $61.6M. Fleet: 1,159+ vehicles (January 27, 2026); 2026 target: 3,000+. Fully driverless commercial service in Guangzhou, Shenzhen, Beijing, Shanghai, plus 8 countries. Gen-7 robotaxi achieved citywide unit economics breakeven in Guangzhou: RMB 299/day in net revenue, 23 orders/day, and a 70% BOM cost reduction—remote assistance ratio: 1:20 (from 1:3 in Q1 2024). MSCI China Index inclusion announced February 11, effective February 27, 2026—first robotaxi company in any MSCI index. THE HK IPO in November 2025 raised approximately HK$6.7B (~$860M). Cash: >$1.4B. ARK Invest is accumulating shares—market cap: ~$5B.

WeRide (NASDAQ: WRD / HKEX: 0800)

Q3 2025 revenue: RMB 171M ($24.0M), +144% YoY. Robotaxi revenue: +761% YoY. Gross margin: 32.9% (from 6.5%). Net loss: RMB 307M ($43.3M), narrowed 70.5%. Cash: RMB 4.5B ($764M). Fleet: 1,600+

autonomous vehicles worldwide, 1,023 dedicated robotaxis. L4 permits in 8 countries, 40+ cities in 11 countries. Uber partnership: 1,200 robotaxis across Abu Dhabi, Dubai, Riyadh by 2027 (announced February 6, 2026)—largest MENA robotaxi commitment. 15 cities by 2030. ME operations nearing unit-level breakeven at 12+ trips/day. Switzerland's first fully driverless permit. Singapore with Grab. The HK listing in November 2025 raised approximately $308M. ARK Invest: 858,295 ADR shares. Market cap: <$2.5B.

Tier 3: Industrialisers

BYD (HKEX: 1211 / OTC: BYDDY)

FY2025 deliveries: 4,602,436 NEVs (+7.7% YoY); overseas >1.05M. Q3 2025 revenue: RMB 195.0B (~$27.4B). 9M2025 revenue: RMB 566.3B (record, +12.75%). Q3 net profit: RMB 7.8B (-32.6% YoY amid price competition). God's Eye ADAS launched February 10, 2025: deployed across 2.3M+ vehicles, 21 models, three tiers (DiPilot 100/300/600). No additional consumer cost, even on RMB 69,800 (~$9,550) Seagull. Internal cost estimate: ~$385/vehicle. Daily training data: 160M+ km/day. God's Eye 5.0 released January 28, 2026 (reinforcement learning, end-to-end). RMB 100B ($14.3B) committed to smart tech R&D. 5,000 dedicated ADAS engineers. Market cap: ~$110–125B.

XPeng (NYSE: XPEV / HKEX: 09868)

Q3 2025 revenue: RMB 20.4B (~$2.9B), +102% YoY. Deliveries: 116,007 (+149% YoY). Gross margin: 20.1% (first time >20%, surpassing Tesla 18% and BYD 17.6%). Net loss: RMB 380M (narrowed 79%). FY2025 deliveries: 429,445 (+126% YoY). XNGP: nationwide coverage of all public roads, no HD maps, 2,595+ cities. VLA 2.0 (Vision Language Action), 100M+ training clips. Turing chip: 2,250 TOPS for consumer applications / 3,000 TOPS for robotaxi applications. VW partnership expanded 6x; first VW vehicle on XPeng's CEA (ID.UNYX 07) in production December 31, 2025. First-ever ADAS insurance: RMB 239/year. Market cap: ~$17B.

NIO (NYSE: NIO / HKEX: 09866)

Q3 2025 revenue: RMB 21.8B (~$3.1B), +16.7% YoY (quarterly record). Deliveries: 87,071 (+40.8%) across NIO, Onvo, and Firefly brands. Gross margin: 13.9% (highest in ~3 years). Net loss: RMB 3.48B (narrowed 31%). Operating and FCF are positive for the first time. FY2025: ~326,028 deliveries (+47%). NIO World Model: 216 scenarios in 0.1 seconds. NOP+ covers 726 cities (99% of China). NX9031 chip: 5nm, 1,000+ TOPS. Market cap: ~$10–12B.

Tier 4: Stack Integrators

Huawei ADS / Yinwang Intelligent Technology

ADS 4.0 launched in April 2025. WEWA architecture on MDC 1000 (Ascend 910B, 1,000 TOPS). 50% latency reduction, 30% fewer heavy braking incidents. Four tiers from ADS SE to ADS Ultra (highway L3). 1M+ vehicles equipped (August 2025), 22+ models, 700,000+ active users, 4B+ cumulative km. HIMA: 81,864 vehicles delivered in November 2025 alone. Yinwang spun off an entity valued at ~RMB 115B (~$16B). Car business revenue: +474% in 2024 to RMB 26.35B (first yearly profit). ~30% of city-NOA solutions shipped. Future IPO anticipated.

Momenta

160+ vehicle programs, 40+ production models, 400,000+ production vehicles equipped. Key: BMW (Neue Klasse), Mercedes-Benz (CLA + 40 models), GM ($300M), Toyota, Uber (Munich 2026), Grab (SE Asia). ~60% of city-NOA solutions shipped in China (Jan–Oct 2024). Valuation: ~$5–6B. $1.42B raised across 10 rounds. US IPO filed confidentially; HK listing under consideration.

DeepRoute.ai

~150,000 production vehicles deployed (October 2025); targeting 1M by 2026. ~40% of the third-party urban NOA supplier segment (excluding in-house OEMs). Partners: Alibaba ($300M), Great Wall Motor ($100M), Smart (Mercedes/Geely JV), Geely, Ford/Lincoln. Funding: >$500M. DeepRoute IO 2.0: first VLA deployment on mass-produced vehicles.

Didi Autonomous Driving

R2 robotaxi delivered January 23, 2026—China's first mass-produced, factory-installed AV for commercial operations. Andi Technology JV with GAC Aion. 33 sensors, 2,000+ TOPS, 74% cost reduction. ~200 vehicles across Beijing, Guangzhou, Shanghai. 24/7 fully unmanned trials in Guangzhou's Huangpu area, December 2025. Valuation: ~$5B+ (post-Series D). Total financing: >RMB 10B (~$1.37B). Abu Dhabi Investment Office partnership.

Tier 5: Supply Chain

Hesai Technology (NASDAQ: HSAI / HKEX: 02525)

Q3 2025 revenue: RMB 795.4M ($111.7M), +47.5% YoY. Record GAAP net income: RMB 256.2M. Gross margin: 42.1%. Shipments: 441,398 units (+229% YoY). First LiDAR company to achieve full-year non-GAAP profitability (2024). 33% global automotive LiDAR market share by revenue; 46% China long-range; 65% global L4. 2M+ cumulative deliveries. MSCI China Index inclusion. NVIDIA exclusive LiDAR for Hyperion 10. Grab an exclusive LiDAR partner. Goldman: $36 Buy target. DoD Section 1260H designation (January 2024); appeal filed July 2025. The HK listing in September 2025 raised $614M. Market cap: ~$4.2B.

RoboSense (HKEX: 02498)

33.5% global automotive LiDAR market share by unit installations (2024, #1 by volume). FY2024 revenue: RMB 1.65B (+47% YoY), 544,200 units shipped (+110%). Gross margin: 25.9% (Q3 2025, up from 13.6%). Adjusted net losses: ~RMB 396M (narrowing). Monthly record: 120,000 units (October 2025). Expanding into humanoid robotics. 30+ OEM partners. Market cap: ~$2.2B.

Horizon Robotics (HKEX: 09660)

47–48% market share in China's ADAS front-view chip market. H1 2025 revenue: RMB 1.57B (+68%). Gross margin: 65.4%. Cumulative: 10M+ Journey chips to 40+ automakers. Journey 6P: 560 TOPS on TSMC 7nm. VW CARIZON JV (€2.4B for 60% stake). Bosch partnership for overseas production Q1 2026. IPO in October 2024 raised HK$5.41B. Unanimous Strong Buy from 24 analysts. Market cap: ~$9.7B.

Regulatory Landscape: China vs. the United States

China issued its first national L3 permits on December 15, 2025 (Changan Deepal SL03 and BAIC Arcfox Alpha S). 20+ cities with pilot zones. Vehicle-Road-Cloud Integration across 20 cities, 35,000+ km test roads, 11,000+ roadside intelligent units, 10,000+ test licenses. Beijing's April 2025 regulations: L4/L5 liability shifts to operators and manufacturers. Data governance: MIIT published 27 categories and 51 types of automotive data (February 3, 2026). BIS Connected Vehicle Rule effective March 17, 2025: ADS software prohibition MY2027, VCS hardware prohibition MY2030. LiDAR, radar, and cameras are explicitly excluded from the VCS definition. SAFE LiDAR Act (H.R. 6576): zero co-sponsors. US SELF DRIVE Act (H.R. 7390): 12–11 committee vote; GovTrack 2% standalone enactment probability. NHTSA: ~25% staff reductions, 70 pending rulemakings. No federal AV liability framework.

APPENDIX B

Valuation Psychosis Data Companion

Supporting Data for Chapter 13

B.1 Goldman Sachs Market Sizing

China robotaxi market: $54M (2025) → $47B (2035), ~870x increase. Fleet: 4,000 vehicles (2025) → 1.9M (2035), 25% mobility share. Revenue per robotaxi: $36/day (2025) → $69/day (2035). US robotaxi: <1% rideshare (2025) → $7B / 8% rideshare / ~35,000 vehicles (2030). US AV trucking: $18B / ~25,000 trucks (2030). Global robotaxi base: >$25B (2030); bull case: >$100B. CAGR ~90% (2025–2030). Fully-loaded cost/mile: $184 (2024) → $12 (2030) → $1 (2040). Remote operator ratio: 1:3 (2025) → 1:10 (2030) → 1:35 (2040). Gross margins: 40–50% within 3–5 years. China vehicle cost: $44,000 (2025) → $32,000 (2035). Tier-1 breakeven: 2026. ~4M retiring taxi drivers in China by 2035.

B.2 Goldman Company Coverage

Pony.ai: Buy, $27.70 (raised from $19.60). 27% revenue CAGR 2024–2027, 158% CAGR 2027–2030. EBITDA positive by 2030.

Tesla: Neutral, $400. Projects only ~$115M in robotaxi revenue by 2027 and ~300 vehicles by end-2026. "Valuation may already reflect significant AV profit expectations."

Hesai: Buy, $36 (raised from $26.30). Revenue to RMB 14B (~$1.9B) by 2030, net profit RMB 3B ($410M), 21% net margin, overseas ADAS 3M units by 2030.

Baidu: Buy, $90. Apollo Go "top two global participants." Wuhan UE = ~RMB 9M annual profit for 1,000 RT6 vehicles. $21.7B net cash vs. $33B market cap.

Other banks: Morgan Stanley: $200B global AV by 2030, $300–400B by 2035, China ~50% by volume. Citi: China robotaxi penetration at 9% by 2030, 30% by 2035. BofA: Pony.ai fleet to 68,000 by 2029.

B.3 Per-Vehicle Valuation Calculations

Tesla: MS attribution ($439B) / Musk fleet (500) = $878M/vehicle. MS / independent tracker (~240) = $1.83B. ARK (90% = $1.41T) / Musk fleet = $2.82B. Goldman's projected 300 vehicles / MS attribution = $1.46B.

Waymo: $126B / ~2,500 vehicles = ~$50.4M/vehicle.

Pony.ai: ~$5.6B / 1,159 vehicles = ~$5M/vehicle.

Baidu Apollo Go: $5–8B / 1,000+ = ~$5–8M/vehicle.

WeRide: <$2.5B / 1000 robotaxis = ~$2.5M/vehicle.

B.4 Valuation Ratios

Tesla (MS/Musk) vs. WeRide: 244:1. Tesla (MS/independent ~240) vs. WeRide: 508:1. Tesla (ARK/Musk) vs. WeRide: 783:1. Tesla (ARK/independent ~30 concurrent) vs. WeRide: >10,000:1. Waymo vs. WeRide: 14:1. Waymo vs. Pony.ai: 6.9:1. Tesla (MS) vs. Pony.ai: 120:1.

B.5 Cost Per Ride Comparison

San Francisco, Waymo: $19.69/ride vs. Lyft/Uber $15.47–$17.47 = +13–27% premium.

Wuhan, Baidu Apollo Go: $0.60–$2.30 (RMB 4–16 for 10km) vs. human taxi $2.50–$4.20 = 30–70% cheaper.

Guangzhou, Pony.ai Gen-7: ~$1.80 (RMB 13 avg) vs. human taxi ~$3–5 = 40–60% cheaper.

B.6 ADR Performance Since Listing

Pony.ai: IPO Nov 27, 2024 at $13.00. Current ~$13. WeRide: IPO Oct 25, 2024 at $15.50. Current ~$7. -50 to -52%. Hesai: IPO Feb 9, 2023 at $19.00. Current ~$25–26. +37%. Baidu: Long listed. Current ~$137. P/E 13.4x. 52-wk low $74.71.

B.7 Analyst Coverage and Institutional Ownership

Pony.ai: ~19 analysts, 95% Buy. Goldman $27.70, Jefferies $32.80, Macquarie $29. Institutions: Wellington, Goldman Sachs Group, Toyota (13.4%), Ontario Teachers' Pension (6.8%), Fidelity. ARK: ~$12.9M.

WeRide: 3–10 analysts, all Strong Buy. JPMorgan $17, UBS $12, Citi $15.50. Bosch ($100M), Alliance Ventures/Renault Nissan ($97M), Grab, ARK (858,295 ADSs).

Hesai: ~4–9 analysts, Strong Buy. Goldman $36, UBS Buy, DBS Buy. Morgan Stanley "Humanoid Tech 25" list. NVIDIA Hyperion 10 partner.

B.8 Tesla FSD Detail

FSD subscription pivot February 14, 2026: $99/month subscription-only (from $8,000 one-time). Q4 2025 disclosed: 1.1M active FSD users, 330,000 subscribers (30%), 8.9M installed base (12.4% take rate). Estimated MRR: ~$32.6M. Austin launch June 22, 2025; Bay Area late July 2025; unsupervised Austin January 22,

2026 (chase cars). Cybercab production target: April 2026. Rider reports: wrong-side-of-the-road, phantom braking, intersection drops, traffic violations. NHTSA investigation: ~3M FSD-equipped vehicles. California deceptive marketing ruling. FSD safety: 5.94M miles between Autopilot accidents vs. US avg 0.70M. But: ~10,000 miles between critical interventions vs. ~700,000 miles US accident rate. FSD V13: ~97% without intervention, critical intervention every 400–450 miles.

B.9 CB Insights AV Landscape (December 2025)

90+ private companies across 14 categories. 140+ companies across 10 technology areas. Chinese AV private funding: $4B (2021) → <$400M (2024). Global AV funding: $8.81B / 83 rounds (2024, Tracxn). Peak: 2021 ($12.5B / 264 deals). Cumulative: 4,170+ rounds, 1,180+ companies. US: $41B / 373 companies. Major failures: Argo AI ($3.6B, shut down 2022), Cruise (GM halted 2024, $10B write-off), Ghost Autonomy ($220M, shut down 2024), Luminar (Chapter 11 December 2025).

B.10 Four Structural Forces — Supporting Data

China Discount: MSCI China trades at 12.8x forward earnings, compared with the S&P 500 at ~26–30x. KWEB holdings ~50% lower multiples. Baidu ~13x P/E vs. Alphabet 20–25x (47% discount). Dragon 7: 12.9x P/E, 17% EPS growth, PEG 0.7x. MSCI China +~40% in 2025 but with a persistent ~40% discount to DM.

Index Exclusion: 74 largest US pension funds: >$70B in China/HK. Indiana divested $1.2B; Texas $1.4B; Florida mandated by Sept 2025; Missouri; Federal Retirement Thrift excluded China entirely. Fund flow bifurcation: broad China ETFs (FXI) bled >$2B; tech-focused (KWEB) attracted $2.2B; CQQQ +$2B.

Regulatory Pessimism: December 2025 MIIT L3 permits. 20 cities Vehicle-Road-Cloud. 17 national ICV testing zones. 32,000+ km test roads. 7,700+ test licenses. 120M+ km testing. Pony.ai is fully driverless in all four Tier-1 cities.

Geopolitical/Delisting: PCAOB access December 2022. Bessent: "Everything is on the table." 286 companies, $1.1T market cap. The House Select Committee named Pony.ai. Dual HK listings as a hedge. Goldman: $2.5T decoupling cost. KraneShares: "low probability."

The Investor's Toolkit

Broker Access, Tax, Options, Currency, and Industry Reports

C.1 Broker Access and HKEX Mechanics

Interactive Brokers: Most comprehensive HKEX access. Fixed commission: 0.08% (min HKD 18). Stamp duty: 0.10% per side (dominates cost). SFC levy: 0.004%. HKEX fee: 0.005%. Clearing: 0.02%. Total all-in round-trip: ~0.38–0.40%. Currency conversion at near-interbank rates (0.1 pip spread, 0.002% commission). By comparison, US ADR trading: ~$0–$2 round-trip, zero stamp duty—making it significantly cheaper for most retail investors.

Other US brokers with HKEX: Fidelity (~$32/trade + local fees), Charles Schwab (Global Account), Moomoo (zero/low commission), Tiger Brokers (zero commission on HK stocks). E*Trade and Robinhood do NOT offer access to HKEX.

C.2 ADR vs. Ordinary Share Dynamics

For dual-listed companies (BIDU vs. 9888.HK, PONY vs. 2026.HK, WRD vs. 0800.HK, HSAI vs. 2525.HK): ADR premium/discount typically ±0.1–0.2% in normal conditions, widening to 3–8% during geopolitical stress. Bloomberg March 2025: Alibaba ADRs at 2.1% discount to HK shares (widest since 2022). Formula: ADR Premium = [(ADR Price / (HK Price × ADR Ratio × USD/HKD rate))−1] × 100. BIDU: 1 ADR = 8 HK shares.

C.3 Currency Hedging Tools

USD/HKD: Hedging is generally unnecessary. Peg band: 7.75–7.85. HKMA reserves: >$420B (170% of monetary base). Peg stress-tested May–July 2025 (HK$129.4B strong-side intervention, HK$86.9B weak-side). All major institutions expect the peg to hold.

USD/CNY: Currently ~6.90 (near strongest since May 2023). CNY appreciated ~4.3–5% against USD in 2025. ING/RBC target ~7.00 by end-2026. Stronger CNY = positive for US investors (earnings translate to more USD). Driver: China's $1T+ trade surplus. Hedging tools: WisdomTree CYB, CME CNH futures (via IBKR), IBKR direct USD.CNH forex, Xtrackers DBCN.

Natural hedge in balanced US-China portfolios: USD weakness benefits Chinese holdings; CNY weakness benefits US holdings.

C.4 Options Liquidity by Ticker

BIDU: Very liquid. Weekly/monthly, many strikes. LEAPS through Jan 2028. Best execution: 30–90 day, 10–15% OTM puts. **XPEV:** Liquid. LEAPS through Jan 2028. **PONY:** Low-Moderate (newer listing). Possibly Jan 2027. **HSAI:** Low-Moderate. Uncertain LEAPS. **WRD:** Low (earnings implied moves ±15.5%). Unlikely 2028 LEAPS. **BYDDY:** Limited/None (OTC ADR). No LEAPS.

Cash-secured puts on high-IV Chinese AV ADRs: ~$15 stock with 70–100% IV, 30-day 15% OTM put yields ~3–6% (annualized 36–72%). BIDU at ~$150 with 40–50% IV, 30-day 10% OTM put yields ~1.5–3%. The wheel strategy (sell puts → if assigned, sell covered calls) works for systematic AV position building. Size conservatively: Chinese ADRs gap 15–30% on geopolitical headlines.

C.5 Tax Implications for Cross-Border AV Investing

Capital gains: No difference between HK shares and ADRs for US tax purposes. HK: zero capital gains tax. Both are taxed at the standard US long-term rates (0%, 15%, or 20%).

Reporting: HK shares in a foreign brokerage trigger FBAR (FinCEN 114) if the aggregate value of foreign accounts exceeds $10,000, and potentially Form 8938 if the aggregate value exceeds $50,000–$200,000. ADRs in US brokerage: neither. FBAR penalties: up to $16,536 non-willful; 50% of the balance willful.

Dividends: China: 10% withholding. HK: 0%. However, dividends from Chinese companies via HK (H-shares) still incur a 10% PRC withholding tax. U.S. investors claim the foreign tax credit on Form 1116 (or directly on Form 1040 if ≤ $ 300 or $600). FTC not available in IRAs—withholding becomes a permanent cost.

PFIC risk: Major Chinese AV operating companies (Baidu, XPeng, BYD, Pony.ai) generally do not have PFICs (active business income). Pre-revenue/early-stage with large cash (WeRide possibly) may warrant analysis. Foreign mutual funds/ETFs investing in Chinese AV stocks are almost certainly PFICs—consequences: punitive excess distribution taxation, no favorable capital gains rates, plus interest.

Wash sale: ADRs and underlying HK shares are generally substantially identical securities. Selling BIDU ADR at a loss and buying 9888.HK within 30 days = wash sale. Workarounds: wait 31+ days, buy a different company in the same sector, or use a doubling-up strategy.

C.6 Industry Report Summaries

KPMG (January 2026): "Partnerships essential to leading in AV market." AV developed as predicted in 2017: "Islands of Autonomy" with geographically-bound markets. Real race is partnership integration management.

CB Insights (2025). 90+ private companies, 14 categories. 2024 AV funding: $7.5B (3x YoY), driven by Waymo $5.6B, Wayve $1.1B, Applied Intuition $15B valuation. Broader robotics: $40.7B in 2025 (+74% YoY, 9% of all venture).

BCG (January 2026): Global robotaxi market: $1.95B (2024) → $188.91B (2034). By 2035: 40–80 cities globally. L2/L2+ from ~20% of sales (2025) to ~30% by 2027. Only ~4% of new cars by 2035 are expected to be L4.

Goldman Sachs: Robotaxi CAGR ~90% (2025–2030). Gross margins 40–50% within 3–5 years. AV trucking: $6.15/mile (2025) → $1.89 (2030) vs. human $2.61 → $2.80. Bull 2040: AV sales ~60% of light vehicles; China ~90% L3+.

Morgan Stanley (July 2025). AV industry $200B by 2030. US AV availability: ~15% urban population (end 2025) → >30% by end 2026. Free-time productivity value: up to $110B/year.

APPENDIX D

Three Monsoons Data Companion

D.1 Kelly Criterion for AV Sector Bets

Basic formula: $f^* = (bp-q) / b$ for binary outcomes; $f^* = \mu / \sigma^2$ for continuous returns. For the AV position with 15% estimated excess return and 50% annualized volatility, full Kelly = 60%—clearly too aggressive. Quarter-Kelly (0.25×) reduces expected return by only ~20% while reducing variance by ~80%. For AV: quarter-Kelly yields ~15% maximum thematic allocation.

Geopolitical overlay for China AV: (1) Political risk premium: +200–500bp discount rate, reducing position proportionally. If US AV warrants 15% and China carries a +300 bp premium, China's yield drops to ~12.5%. (2) Scenario sizing: base gradual decoupling 50%, escalation 25%, détente 15%, crisis 10%. (3) VaR adjustment: 1.5–3× stress multiplier, capping incremental VaR at 5% of portfolio risk budget. (4) Drawdown throttling: max 3% of total portfolio loss from China; if drawdown >10%, reduce 25–50%; beyond 15%, halt new purchases.

Integrated framework: Estimate scenario-weighted parameters → calculate full Kelly → apply 0.25× fraction → split US/Europe AV (10%) and China AV (5%) → apply 0.7× geopolitical discount to China (yielding ~3.5% allocation) → rebalance at ±20–25% drift with event triggers.

Bridgewater: China Total Return +34% in 2025. AUM ~$7.5B in China. Core principle: position sizing > directional accuracy. Max drawdown rule: never accept more than 1/3. Pure Alpha: 30–40 simultaneous positions.

BlackRock BGRI: Geopolitical Risk Dashboard tracks attention scores, market-driven scenarios, and likelihood assessments. China: neutral stance on EM—"valuations good, but trade risks loom."

Ed Thorp: Used Kelly at Princeton-Newport Partners for 28 years, generating 20% annualized returns. Maintained 100+ simultaneous positions.

D.2 Rebalancing Triggers and KPI Framework

Waymo weekly rides: Benchmark 450,000+. Bull: 500,000+ by 2027. Bear: flat or declining.

Baidu Apollo Go cumulative rides: Benchmark 17M+. Bull: 30M+ by 2027. Bear: regulatory restrictions.

Cities with large-scale robotaxi fleets: Benchmark 13+. Bull: 40–80 by 2035. Bear: stalling below 20 by 2028.

Cost per robotaxi mile: Benchmark >$2. Bull: <$1.50 by 2028. Bear: persistent >$2.

Remote operator ratio: Benchmark 1:3. Bull: 1:10 by 2028. Bear: stuck at 1:3–5.

US rideshare AV market share: Benchmark <1%. Bull: ~8% by 2030. Bear: <2% by 2028.

China L3 vehicle production: Benchmark ~46 vehicles. Bull: 1M units by 2027. Bear: regulatory delays.

Event triggers: Major regulatory approval → consider adding. Significant safety incident → reduce 10–25%. Key competitor exit (GM/Cruise model) → re-evaluate. Geopolitical escalation → reduce China by 25–50%—

technology breakthrough or cost milestone → re-run scenarios. Portfolio drawdown >10% → reduce per Bridgewater protocol.

Review cadence: Weekly: news signposts + BGRI. Monthly: VaR check + scenario probability. Quarterly: full rebalance + Kelly refresh. Annual: complete scenario overhaul + market sizing.

D.3 EU Regulatory Details

No equivalent to BIS connected vehicles rule as of February 2026. The approach combines UN R155/R156, the NIS2 Directive, and the Cyber Resilience Act. Risk assessment could designate Chinese suppliers as "high-risk" (as in the Huawei telecoms precedent), but has not. Anti-subsidy duties (October 2024): BYD 17%, Geely 18.8%, Tesla Shanghai 7.8%, SAIC 35.3% (on top of 10% import duty). Transitioning to the minimum import price mechanism (January 2026 guidance; February 2026 first exemption: VW Cupra Tavascan). DGAP (November 2025) called for an EU "binding rule similar to BIS." EC Automotive Industrial Action Plan (March 2025): committed to NIS2 risk assessment.

Commercial entanglement: WeRide (France driverless permit), Pony.ai (Stellantis MoU for European robotaxis), Baidu (Swiss Post), XPeng (Magna Steyr Graz). VDA survey: ~70% plan to increase China investment; 75%+ prioritize R&D. UK Automated Vehicles Act 2024: comprehensive but technology-neutral; MoD banned Chinese-component EVs within 2 miles of intelligence sites.

GLOSSARY

of

Terms, Frameworks, Characters & Metaphors

✦ ✦ ✦

Dragon vs. Eagle

The Trillion-Dollar Autonomous Demolition Derby

A Note on Usage

This glossary defines the analytical frameworks, cultural metaphors, technical terminology, and allegorical characters that operate throughout *Dragon vs. Eagle*. It is organized by category rather than by alphabet, because in this book's architecture—as in a Theyyam performance—the mask must be understood before the dance can be read.

Where possible, definitions reflect the book's diagnostic lens: the Kuttanad boatman's epistemology, where two currents flow through the same channel and the halocline between them is visible only to those who navigate both. Terms drawn from Sanskrit, Malayalam, and Kerala's ritual traditions carry their original pronunciations in parentheses. Financial and technical terms are defined as the manuscript uses them, which may differ from their broader academic or industry usage, just as the word "permanent" carries a different meaning in corporate finance than it does in geology.

Section references indicate where a term is introduced or most fully developed. Cross-references (in *italic*) point to related glossary entries. Numbers and data are current as of February 2026.

✦ ✦ ✦

I. THE BOOK'S ORIGINAL FRAMEWORKS

Proprietary analytical instruments developed across the manuscript to diagnose fragility, map interdependence, price illusion, and size risk. The investor's toolkit—forged at the burning ghat, calibrated in the backwaters.

Dinosaur Meter — Seven-factor fragility scoring framework for legacy automotive companies (Section 11.12.1). Scores range from 0 (Adapting) to 100 (Critical) across: ICE Profit Dependence (20%), Dealer/Service Dependence (10%), Fixed-Cost Rigidity (15%), Supplier Fragility (10%), EV Margin Gap (25%), Autonomy Stack Deficit (10%), and Policy Exposure (10%). Composite scores: Ford 83.4, Volkswagen 79.1, Toyota 70.6—all in the Critical band. "Its utility lies not in predicting bankruptcy. It predicts the moment when the capital markets stop pretending." Chapter 11. *See also: Fragility Bands, Refinancing Wall.*

Interdependency Web — Five-node platform map of embodied intelligence: (1) Autonomous Mobility, (2) Autonomous Logistics, (3) Robotics, (4) Distributed Energy, and (5) Financial & Data Rails. The Web's central insight is that these five sectors share software stacks (70 percent common code), supply chains (40 percent-plus BOM overlap), and data feedback loops, making them a single, interconnected platform rather than five separate industries. An investor who prices any node in isolation misses the loop. Chapter 11. *See also: Interdependency Web Score, Convergence Multiplier.*

Interdependency Web Score — Five-node, four-nation scoring matrix (Section 11.12.2) rating each country's capability across the Web on a 1–5 scale. Composite scores: China 24/25 (Platform Leader), United States 18/25 (Competitive Position), Japan/Korea 15/25 (Structural Deficit), European Union 11/25 (Structural Deficit). The strategic revelation: America scores 5/5 on Financial & Data Rails—the brain—while China scores 19/20 on the four physical nodes—the body. Chapter 11. *See also: Platform Leader, Structural Deficit.*

Quarter-Kelly Sizing — Position-sizing framework (Section 11.12.3) derived from the Kelly Criterion, applying a 0.25 fraction to cap thematic exposure at 15 percent of portfolio value. Reduces expected return by approximately 20 percent while reducing variance by approximately 80 percent. For the AV/embodied-intelligence thesis: 10 percent US/Europe, 3.5 percent China (after 0.7× geopolitical overlay), 2–3 percent short legacy automakers. The Kuttanad farmer's mathematics applied to portfolio construction: enough to profit from the monsoon, not so much that a flood destroys you. Chapters 11, 14. *See also: Kelly Criterion, Geopolitical Overlay.*

Māyā Meter — Valuation diagnostic measuring the per-vehicle implied gap between American and Chinese autonomous vehicle companies. Waymo: ~$50 million per vehicle. Pony.ai: ~$5 million. WeRide: ~$3 million. Ratios range from 14:1 (Waymo/WeRide) to over 1,000:1 (Tesla/WeRide by independent fleet tracker). Named after the Sanskrit concept of Māyā—not a lie, but something more dangerous: a partial truth elevated to the status of the whole. Each table includes a Steelman Column presenting the best case for the higher valuation. Prologue; fully developed Chapter 13. *See also: Māyā, Narrative Immunity.*

Extinction Pattern — Six-phase industrial displacement pattern derived from the British motorcycle industry's destruction by Japanese manufacturers (1955–1975): (1) Market-Entry Dismissal, (2) Quality-Gap Closure, (3) Supply-Chain Collapse, (4) Financial-Engineering Retreat, (5) Political Intervention, and (6) Ecosystem Colonization—this last phase is unique to China's embodied-intelligence platform. Western Automotive is assessed as having completed Phases 1–2, with Phase 3 underway and Phases 4–5 active. Chapter 11, Section 11.10. *See also: BSA Path, Norton Path, Triumph Path.*

Four Temples Framework — Archetype taxonomy for mapping autonomous-vehicle ecosystems across civilizations: (1) The National Champion (Baidu Apollo Go, Waymo), (2) The Pure-Play Scaler (Pony.ai, WeRide), (3) The Industrialiser (BYD, XPeng), and (4) The Stack Integrator (Huawei, Momenta). America's temple has one occupied altar and two empty stalls—no Industrialiser, no Stack Integrator. Chapter 2; applied in Chapters 7 and 14. *See also: Empty Stall.*

Three Monsoons — Scenario-planning framework for 2030–2035: (A) Two Galaxies—separate US and Chinese AV ecosystems with gradual convergence (base case, 50% probability); (B) The Monsoon—Chinese AV technology sweeps global markets via Belt and Road infrastructure (bull China, 25%); (C) The Dam—geopolitical forces constrain Chinese expansion to domestic markets (bear China, 25%). Named after Kerala's monsoon seasons: Edavapathi (southwest), Thulavarsham (northeast), and the dry season between them. The investor's task is not to predict which monsoon arrives but to size positions that survive all three. Chapter 15. *See also: Two Galaxies, One River.*

Fragility Bands — Three scoring ranges in the Dinosaur Meter. Critical (70–100): refinancing wall within 3–5 years; bond spreads widen to distressed levels when ICE utilization falls below 65–70 percent. Stressed (40–69): viable if self-cannibalization begins within 18 months. Adapting (0–39): structural adaptation underway or not required. All three scored legacy OEMs fall in the Critical band. Chapter 11. *See also: Dinosaur Meter, Self-Cannibalization.*

Euphemism Catalogue — Satirical taxonomy in Section 11.0 cataloguing the language Western automotive executives use to disguise strategic retreat as strategic choice. Sample entries: "disciplined capital allocation" (we stopped investing in the future), "focused EV strategy" (we cancelled most of our EV programs), "leveraging our ICE strengths" (we are riding the dinosaur until it collapses), and "partnership-led approach to autonomy" (we have no autonomy stack and are hoping someone will sell us one). Chapter 11.

Self-Cannibalization Imperative — The central strategic dilemma facing Western automakers: destroy your own profitable ICE business to fund an EV/AV transition where Chinese competitors have a five-year head start and a structural cost advantage—or protect the ICE margins and watch the platform economy pass you by. The Stressed fragility band is viable only if self-cannibalization begins within 18 months. Chapter 11, Section 11.1. *See also: Dinosaur Meter, Fragility Bands.*

II. ALLEGORICAL CHARACTERS & NARRATIVE DEVICES

The voices that carry the analysis. In a Theyyam performance, multiple deities may be embodied within a single ritual. Here, multiple analytical lenses are brought to bear in a single chapter.

The Boatman — The book's implied reader and navigational persona. Unlike the gambler who bets on the weather, the Boatman reads the current beneath the surface. Drawn from the Kuttanad tradition of navigating brackish waters where two currents coexist, separated by a halocline invisible to outsiders. The Boatman does not weep at the ghat; he reads the weight of the vessel and the tilt of the current. Prologue; present throughout. *See also: Kuttanad, Halocline.*

Marcus — Composite fund manager whose cognitive errors form the book's narrative spine. First appears in Chapter 4, pricing "40,000 tombs" as friction alpha; sells Pony.ai on a headline in Chapter 6; misses the global procession in Chapter 10; receives the Māyā Meter diagnosis in Chapter 13; runs the three frameworks in Chapter 11; and chooses his Boatman's profile in Chapter 14. Marcus is not a specific person—he is the reader. Marcus arrives at the ghat carrying the assumptions of Western capital markets. The chapter's frameworks are the tools that help him see what his Bloomberg terminal cannot.

Gekko — The ruthlessly pragmatic investor archetype, named after Gordon Gekko from Wall Street (1987) but repurposed: this Gekko does not worship greed—he worships data. He carries three instruments (the Dinosaur Meter, the Interdependency Web Score, and the Quarter-Kelly Sizing) and uses them to strip sentiment from allocation decisions. Gekko sees what Marcus cannot yet see. Chapter 11. *See also: Marcus, Integrator.*

McKinsey the Priest — The management-consulting industry's role in providing intellectual legitimacy to strategic delay. McKinsey the Priest performs the rites of "transformation" for legacy automakers—the slide decks, the frameworks, the "strategic pivots"—that create the appearance of adaptation without requiring the substance of self-cannibalization. The Priest who blesses the dying does not cure the disease. Chapter 11.

Milton the Trickster Economist — Free-market orthodoxy's role in rationalizing shareholder-return maximization over long-term industrial investment. Milton whispers that buybacks are efficient capital allocation, that the market will self-correct, that government industrial policy is always inferior to private enterprise, while $912 billion in Chinese guidance funds builds the infrastructure that private enterprise alone cannot coordinate. Chapter 11. *See also: Hunter vs. Farmer, Civilizational Capital.*

Integrator — Recurring structural element in Chapter 11, appearing as a boxed passage at the end of major sections. The Integrator synthesizes the preceding analysis into a single investment-relevant insight, connecting the section's evidence to the chapter's overarching thesis. Written in Gekko's voice—compressed, direct, unsentimental. A priest offers consolation; the Integrator offers allocation percentages. *See also: Gekko.*

Worked Dollar — Pedagogical device in Section 11.5 tracing a single $150 Hesai AT128 LiDAR sensor through all five nodes of the Interdependency Web: manufactured in Shanghai (Robotics), mounted on a Pony.ai robotaxi (Autonomous Mobility), its perception data trains JD.com routing algorithms (Logistics), charging patterns feed CATL grid optimization (Distributed Energy), transactions flow through Alipay M2M rails (Financial & Data Rails), and aggregate data informs the next-generation sensor at $120 (back to Robotics). "The investor who prices Hesai as a 'LiDAR company' sees the sensor. The investor who prices the Web sees the loop." Chapter 11. *See also: Interdependency Web.*

Steelman Column — Methodological discipline inside the Māyā Meter tables: the best arguments supporting a valuation the author considers inflated, presented with genuine rigor to avoid strawman comparisons. The Boatman who reads only one current drowns in the other. Chapter 13. *See also: Māyā Meter.*

III. THE KERALA EPISTEMOLOGY

Concepts drawn from Kerala's geography, ritual art, and navigational traditions serve as diagnostic instruments. The halocline is not a metaphor. It is a method.

Māyā (माया) — Sanskrit. In the Advaita Vedanta tradition, Māyā is not a lie but something more dangerous: a partial truth elevated to the status of the whole. The book uses Māyā as a diagnostic term for the cognitive architecture that sustains the 3,000-to-1 valuation gap—not deception, but the grand illusion of perception built on an elegant, unquestioned premise. Pronounced: MAH-yah. *See also: Māyā Meter, Advaita Vedanta.*

Theyyam (തെയ്യം) — Ancient ritual art form of North Malabar, Kerala, in which a performer, through elaborate costume, face-painting, and physical transformation, becomes a living deity. The transformation is not metaphorical—the performer embodies the divine. More than 500 distinct forms exist. The author has personally funded documentation of over 200 performances. In the book's architecture, Theyyam represents embodied tradition—intelligence carried in the body, not merely computed in the mind—prefiguring the concept of embodied intelligence at an industrial scale. The three lenses of the book—the Boatman (hydraulic knowledge), the Theyyam performer (inner Vision), and Gekko (capital pricing)—correspond to three modes of seeing. Pronounced: TAY-yum. *See also: Ullil Kaanal.*

Ullil Kaanal (ഉള്ളിൽ കാണൽ) — Malayalam. Literally "inner vision" or "seeing-beyond-seeing." The epistemological tradition underlying Theyyam, in which the performer perceives structural forces invisible to surface observation. The book's diagnostic lens: ullil kaanal reads the undercurrents beneath the ICE empire's apparent health, the structural forces sustaining the Māyā Meter gap, and the convergence dynamics invisible to single-sector analysis. Pronounced: OOL-il KAH-nal. *See also: Theyyam.*

Kuttanad — Low-lying farming region in Kerala where rice is cultivated below sea level in reclaimed backwater land. The backwaters feature two currents flowing simultaneously through the same channel—freshwater from the Western Ghats and brackish tide from the Arabian Sea—separated by a halocline visible only to the boatmen who navigate both. The Kuttanad farmer's wisdom—plant enough to profit from the monsoon, not so much that a flood destroys you—is the metaphorical foundation of the Quarter-Kelly position-sizing framework. Prologue. *See also: Quarter-Kelly, Halocline.*

Burning Ghat — A cremation platform on the banks of a sacred river in Hindu tradition, where the dead are committed to fire and their ashes to the current. Chapter 11's central metaphor: the legacy automotive industry is arriving at its burning ghat, where century-old business models built on internal combustion are being cremated by the convergence of electrification, autonomy, and Chinese industrial scale. Structured in three movements—Descends, Ascends, Counts—modelled on the progression of a Kerala cremation ritual. Chapter 11. *See also: Ghat, Funeral Procession.*

Ghat — A series of steps leading down to a river in South Asian architecture, used for bathing, ritual, and cremation. The burning ghats of Varanasi are where Hindus cremate their dead and release ashes into the Ganges. In the book's metaphorical architecture, the ghat is where the old industrial order meets the river of transformation—the place where capital must choose between clinging to the bank and entering the current. *See also: Burning Ghat.*

Halocline — The boundary layer in a body of water where salinity changes sharply, creating a distinct separation between water masses. In the Kerala backwaters, the halocline separates the brackish Arabian Sea tide from the freshwater Ghats current—invisible to observers on the bank, legible only to the Boatman. The book's metaphor for the boundary between American and Chinese AV market perceptions: both are real, both flow through the same channel, and the analyst who sees only one current drowns in the other. Prologue.

Advaita Vedanta — The non-dualist school of Hindu philosophy in which the apparent multiplicity of the world is Māyā—illusion—and the underlying reality is unified (Brahman). The book draws on Advaita's specific definition: Māyā is not a lie but a partial truth elevated to the status of the whole. The Kuttanad boatman inhabits this philosophy naturally: two currents are one river. *See also: Māyā.*

Arthashastra — Ancient Indian treatise on statecraft, economic policy, and military strategy, attributed to Kautilya (Chanakya), c. 300 BCE. The book's epigraph—"He who controls the granaries controls the kingdom; he who controls the trade routes controls the granaries"—frames China's supply-chain strategy: LiDAR (89 percent global share), batteries (55.6 percent), and automotive AI chips (49 percent of China's ADAS market). Prologue.

Kshetram (ക്ഷേത്രം) — Malayalam/Sanskrit. A temple complex serving a dual purpose—the sacred and the commercial, inhabiting the same geography but operating in separate realities. The book's metaphor for the AV industry's investment archetypes and for Wall Street itself as a temple economy. Pronounced: KSHAY-trum. *See also: Four Temples Framework.*

Edavapathi — The southwest monsoon in Kerala, arriving in June with the fury of abundance, floods paddy fields and fills backwaters. In the Three Monsoons framework, Edavapathi represents the Monsoon scenario: Chinese technology sweeps global markets. Chapter 15. *See also: Three Monsoons, Thulavarsham.*

Thulavarsham — The northeast retreating monsoon in Kerala, arriving in October with quieter menace, unpredictable in timing and force. In the Three Monsoons framework, Thulavarsham represents the Dam scenario: Chinese expansion constrained by geopolitical forces. Chapter 15. *See also: Three Monsoons, Edavapathi.*

Teettu — Elaborate caste protocols in traditional Kerala society dictate who could approach whom, at what distance. In Chapter 5, used as a metaphor for America's fifty-state regulatory patchwork, where each jurisdiction demands its own rituals of propitiation before an autonomous vehicle may enter.

Pokkali Rice — Salt-tolerant, flood-resistant rice variety grown in Kerala's brackish backwaters, where freshwater meets seawater. Metaphor for investments that thrive in contradiction—the investor who can read both currents and plant where others see only contamination. *See also: Kuttanad.*

Kolam — Geometric patterns drawn on thresholds using rice flour in South Indian tradition—decorative but also functional, feeding ants and marking boundaries between sacred and profane space. The book uses kolam as a metaphor for the threshold between the ICE civilization and the embodied-intelligence platform: the pattern drawn at the doorway that the old order has not yet crossed.

IV. STRATEGIC & GEOPOLITICAL CONCEPTS

The civilizational frameworks, investment theses, and scenario architectures that structure the book's argument. Where the Hunter stalks and the Farmer plants.

Hunter vs. Farmer — The book's foundational civilizational thesis. The Hunter (American capitalism) optimizes for quarterly kills—share buybacks, dividend increases, cost cuts that satisfy this quarter's earnings call. The Farmer (Chinese state-directed capitalism) plants for harvests that may take decades to mature—subsidizing losses, building supply chains, training workforces across generational time horizons. The $93 billion that Western automakers returned to shareholders via buybacks and dividends (2019–2024) while Chinese manufacturers were building the embodied-intelligence platform, is the thesis in a single number. Prologue. *See also: Civilizational Capital, Patient Capital.*

Civilizational Capital — The book's term for China's $912 billion in government guidance funds deployed across the five nodes of embodied intelligence. Distinguished from venture capital by its time horizon (generational rather than fund-cycle), its risk tolerance (willing to absorb decades of losses), and its coordination across sectors. The Kuttanad farmer plants for the harvest his grandchildren will reap. Chapter 11. *See also: Guidance Fund, Patient Capital.*

Patient Capital — Investment capital deployed with a time horizon measured in decades or generations rather than quarters or fund cycles. Willing to fund BYD's losses for fifteen years, CATL's capacity expansion ahead of demand, and autonomous-vehicle testing for a decade before commercial deployment. The opposite of the quarterly-capitalism critique embodied by Milton the Trickster. *See also: Civilizational Capital, Hunter vs. Farmer.*

Two Galaxies — Base-case geopolitical scenario (50 percent probability). US-China technological decoupling deepens, creating two separate, autonomous mobility ecosystems: a Chinese galaxy (China plus Belt and Road nations) and an American galaxy (US plus allied nations). Both rivers are investable, but neither dominates globally. The picks-and-shovels layer benefits from supplying both galaxies. Chapter 15. *See also: One River, Three Monsoons.*

One River — Alternative geopolitical scenario. US-China technological decoupling fails or reverses, and a single global autonomous-mobility ecosystem emerges. Chinese manufacturers compete directly in Western markets. This scenario maximizes China's platform advantage and delivers the highest returns for investors positioned at the Web's dominant nodes. Chapter 15. *See also: Two Galaxies.*

Triumph Path — Most probable (50 percent) of three probability-weighted scenarios. Named after Triumph Motorcycles, which survived the British motorcycle extinction by retreating to a premium niche. Western OEMs abandon the mass market, retreat to premium and luxury segments, maintain approximately 20 percent global market share, and undergo $50–100 billion in aggregate write-downs. Painful but survivable for the strongest brands. Chapter 11. *See also: BSA Path, Norton Path, Managed Retreat.*

BSA Path — Second scenario (30 percent probability). Named after the Birmingham Small Arms Company, destroyed by Japanese competition in the 1960s–70s. Complete industrial displacement: Western OEMs lose not just the mass market but also premium segments as Chinese manufacturers move upmarket. Total Western automotive equity value destroyed. Chapter 11. *See also: Triumph Path, Norton Path.*

Norton Path — Third scenario (20 percent probability). Named after Norton Motorcycles, which survived as a niche luxury brand but never recovered industrial relevance. A handful of Western brands (Porsche, Ferrari, perhaps BMW) survive as boutique manufacturers while the mass market is entirely colonized. Chapter 11. *See also: Triumph Path, BSA Path.*

Narrative Immunity — A phenomenon in which a company's stock price becomes decoupled from operational performance and attached to a story so compelling that no empirical evidence can displace it. Tesla's $1.5 trillion market capitalization, with $450–700 billion attributed to robotaxi potential despite a fleet of 30–60 supervised vehicles, exemplifies narrative immunity. The Māyā is not a bug; it is the architecture. Chapters 3, 13. *See also: Māyā Meter.*

Tariff Mirage — The illusion that tariffs protect the domestic industry from Chinese competition. Evidence: Chinese vehicle registrations in Europe surged 91 percent in H1 2025 despite EU countervailing duties of 17–35.3 percent. The tariff does not stop the river; it reroutes it—through tariff-exempt PHEVs, local manufacturing, and joint ventures—and delays the adaptation required to survive when the wall eventually cracks. Chapter 11, Section 11.11.

Galapagos Effect — The evolution of Chinese AV technology within a connected, enclosed data ecosystem (120 million cumulative test kilometers, 35,000 kilometers of instrumented roads, data-localisation requirements). Species evolved within this habitat are optimized for Chinese conditions but may prove maladapted for export—unless the habitat itself is exported via the Digital Silk Road. Chapter 6. *See also: Digital Silk Road.*

Digital Silk Road — The infrastructure layer of China's Belt and Road Initiative: 5G networks, BeiDou positioning, smart-city platforms, and $17 billion in digital investment across approximately 80 countries. It creates the roadbed upon which Chinese AV technology travels globally, bypassing US tariffs. Chapter 10. *See also: Belt and Road Initiative.*

DeepSeek Moment — The point at which an established player realizes its cost advantage was never an advantage at all, but merely a reflection of its own inefficiency. Named after DeepSeek's R1 reasoning model, which achieved frontier AI performance at a fraction of OpenAI's training cost. In autonomous driving, XPeng's FastDriveVLA paper at AAAI 2026 represents a DeepSeek Moment—architectural innovation beating brute-force capital expenditure.

Geopolitical Overlay — A discount factor (0.7×) applied to position sizing for assets exposed to US-China geopolitical risk, reducing the Quarter-Kelly allocation from approximately 5 percent to approximately 3.5 percent of the portfolio. The overlay acknowledges that the thesis may be correct, and the timing may still destroy the position. Chapter 14. *See also: Quarter-Kelly.*

Picks-and-Shovels — Investment strategy of buying the suppliers to an industry rather than the industry's direct participants—named after the merchants who sold equipment to Gold Rush miners. In the Interdependency Web: Hesai (LiDAR supplying both Chinese and Western fleets), Horizon Robotics (AI chips), and CATL (batteries). These companies benefit from the Web's growth regardless of which nation's OEMs win. Chapter 14.

Managed Retreat — The Triumph Path scenario expressed as corporate strategy: deliberate, phased withdrawal from mass-market segments to concentrate resources in premium/luxury niches where brand equity provides pricing power. Financially painful—$50–100 billion in aggregate write-downs—but survivable. The company survives by becoming something much smaller, much more focused, and much more profitable per unit. Chapter 11. *See also: Triumph Path.*

V. INDUSTRY & TECHNOLOGY TERMS

The hardware, the software, and the infrastructure through which the embodied-intelligence platform operates. Defined as the manuscript uses them.

Embodied Intelligence — The book's unifying concept: artificial intelligence instantiated in physical systems that move through, manipulate, and generate data from the real world. Encompasses autonomous vehicles, logistics robots, humanoid robots, drone systems, and the energy and financial infrastructure that connects them. Distinguished from "disembodied" AI (chatbots, software agents) by requiring mastery of atoms, not just bits. The country that builds the body at scale trains the brain for the world. Chapter 11.

Autonomy Stack — The integrated technology layers required for autonomous driving: perception (LiDAR, cameras, radar), prediction (AI models), planning (route and maneuver decision-making), and actuation (steering, braking, acceleration). The depth and maturity of a company's autonomy stack are among the seven factors in the Dinosaur Meter. *See also: Dinosaur Meter.*

ADAS (Advanced Driver-Assistance Systems) — Electronic systems (typically SAE Level 1–2) assisting drivers with lane-keeping, collision avoidance, and adaptive cruise control. In China, ADAS is becoming standard equipment at near-zero marginal cost (BYD's God's Eye at approximately $385 per vehicle across 2.3 million units). In the US, these are often premium subscription features. The distinction matters: mass deployment generates the data monsoon; premium deployment generates revenue. Chapter 1. *See also: God's Eye, Data Monsoon.*

ADS (Automated Driving System) — The complete software-hardware stack enabling a vehicle to perform the full dynamic driving task without human intervention. Distinguished from ADAS by the absence of a human fallback driver. Under the BIS connected-vehicle rule, ADS components from countries of concern face prohibition beginning with Model Year 2027.

L4 / Level 4 Autonomy — SAE International's classification for vehicles capable of full self-driving within a defined operational design domain (specific geographic areas, weather conditions, speed limits) without human intervention. Waymo, Pony.ai, Baidu Apollo, and WeRide operate L4 robotaxi fleets. Distinguished from L5 (full autonomy in all conditions), which no manufacturer has achieved. L4 is a commercial platform; L3 is a regulatory quagmire; L2 is a feature. Chapter 1.

Robotaxi — A driverless ride-hailing vehicle operating commercially without a human safety driver. Waymo delivers approximately 450,000 paid rides per week across six US cities. Pony.ai has achieved city-wide unit economics breakeven in Guangzhou. Baidu Apollo Go operates 250,000 fully driverless rides per week in Wuhan. The robotaxi is Node One of the Interdependency Web—the data-generating tip of the spear of embodied intelligence. Chapter 1.

God's Eye (天神之眼) — BYD's advanced driver-assistance system, deployed across the company's entire lineup (21 models from $9,550 to $233,000) at an incremental hardware cost of approximately $385 per vehicle. As of February 2026, 2.3+ million vehicles are equipped, generating 150 million kilometers of daily training data—roughly three times Waymo's total accumulated autonomous miles since inception. Chapters 7, 11. *See also: Data Monsoon, ADAS.*

LiDAR (Light Detection and Ranging) — Remote-sensing technology using pulsed laser light to generate precise 3D maps of the surrounding environment. Cost declined from approximately

$150,000 per unit (2012) to approximately $150 (Hesai AT128, 2025)—a 99.9 percent reduction driven by Chinese manufacturers who now control 89 percent of the global automotive LiDAR market. The Worked Dollar example traces a single AT128 through all five nodes. Chapter 1: Worked Dollar in Chapter 11. *See also: Worked Dollar, Hesai.*

LFP (Lithium Iron Phosphate) — Battery chemistry favored by Chinese manufacturers (CATL, BYD) for its lower cost ($50–70/kWh at cell level), longer cycle life, superior thermal stability, and freedom from cobalt and nickel supply-chain constraints. LFP's cost advantage over NMC (nickel-manganese-cobalt) chemistries used by most Western manufacturers is a structural enabler of China's EV price competitiveness. *See also: CATL, BYD.*

VLA (Vision-Language-Action Models) — AI architecture fusing large language models with visual perception and motor control, enabling autonomous systems to reason about complex traffic scenarios the way humans read sentences—understanding that a police officer's hand signal overrides a stop sign. XPeng's FastDriveVLA, accepted at AAAI 2026, achieves a 7.5× reduction in computational overhead. The post-sensor-debate frontier. Chapter 1.

Sensor Fusion vs. Pure Vision — The philosophical schism in AV development. Sensor Fusion (Waymo's approach) uses LiDAR, cameras, and radar for redundancy—"truth is compound." Pure Vision (Tesla's approach) relies on cameras and neural networks alone—sola scriptura. The book argues Fusion has superior safety proof, but Vision has superior scaling economics. The debate may be rendered moot by VLA models. Chapter 1. *See also: VLA.*

V2X (Vehicle-to-Everything) — Communication technology enabling vehicles to exchange data with infrastructure (V2I), other vehicles (V2V), pedestrians (V2P), and networks (V2N). China's C-V2X standard, using 5G cellular networks, underpins 35,000 kilometers of instrumented roads and 11,000+ roadside units. The US has not adopted a unified V2X standard—the neuron vs. nervous system divide. Chapter 8. *See also: Vehicle-Road-Cloud Integration.*

Vehicle-Road-Cloud Integration — China's six-element national infrastructure framework: vehicle (C-V2X onboard units), road (intelligent roadside infrastructure), cloud (data fusion platforms), network (5G/LTE-V2X), map (HD mapping and BeiDou positioning), and safety (cybersecurity protocols). Funded with over ¥600 billion across 20 pilot cities. The infrastructure-level complement to vehicle-level autonomy. Chapter 8. *See also: V2X.*

BeiDou — China's satellite navigation system with 55 satellites, 1.1 billion users, and adoption across 30+ Belt and Road nations. The Chinese equivalent of GPS, providing positioning data for C-V2X and autonomous navigation. Part of the Digital Silk Road's infrastructure export. *See also: Digital Silk Road.*

ICE (Internal Combustion Engine) — The reciprocating-piston engine burning fossil fuels that has powered automobiles since the 1880s. In this book, ICE represents not merely an engine but an entire civilization: forty million jobs, three-quarters of a trillion dollars in annual profit, and a capillary economy of refineries, gas stations, and service networks. ICE profit dependence is the most heavily weighted factor in the Dinosaur Meter. Ford scores 92/100: virtually all operating profit comes from the F-150, Bronco, and Expedition. *See also: Capillary Economy.*

BEV (Battery Electric Vehicle) — A vehicle powered exclusively by an electric battery. Distinguished from PHEVs (which retain a combustion engine) and hybrids. The EU's countervailing tariffs of 17–35.3 percent apply specifically to BEVs imported from China—a design Chinese manufacturers exploited by pivoting aggressively to tariff-exempt PHEVs and hybrids, driving the 91 percent registration surge.

NEV (New Energy Vehicle) — China's regulatory classification encompasses BEVs, PHEVs, and fuel-cell vehicles. China reached approximately 60 percent NEV penetration as of early 2026—the highest of any major market and the reference point from which the IEA's "approximately 80 percent by 2030" projection extends.

EV Penetration — The percentage of new vehicle sales that are electric (BEV + PHEV). China: approximately 60 percent. Europe: approximately 25 percent. United States: approximately 11 percent. These rates drive the non-linear cliffs in legacy automaker profitability: ICE utilization becomes unsustainable not at 100 percent EV penetration, but at 35–50 percent, when fixed-cost absorption collapses. *See also: Non-Linear Cliff, S-Curve.*

Non-Linear Cliff — The point at which a gradual trend produces sudden, discontinuous effects. In automotive, the cliff occurs when EV penetration crosses approximately 35–50 percent: ICE factory utilization rates fall below the threshold required to absorb fixed costs, transforming profitable plants into cash-burning liabilities overnight. Invisible at 25 percent penetration. Catastrophic at 40 percent. Chapter 11.

S-Curve — The characteristic adoption pattern of new technologies: slow initial uptake, rapid acceleration through a steep middle phase, and gradual saturation. China's EV adoption has passed the inflection point and is in the steep middle phase. The danger: the difference between 25 percent and 45 percent penetration may take only two to three years. *See also: Non-Linear Cliff.*

Data Monsoon — The daily torrent of real-world driving data generated by China's massive fleet of ADAS-equipped vehicles. BYD's God's Eye system alone generates 150 million kilometers of training data per day—roughly three times Waymo's total accumulated autonomous miles since inception. The monsoon does not wait for the slow farmer. Chapters 7, 11. *See also: God's Eye.*

ODD (Operational Design Domain) — The specific conditions—geographic, weather, speed, road type—under which an autonomous system is designed to operate. Waymo's ODD includes specific metro areas; Pony.ai's includes four Tier-1 Chinese cities. Expansion of ODD is the primary scaling metric for L4 operators.

BOM (Bill of Materials) — The complete cost breakdown of raw materials, components, and assemblies required to manufacture a product. The 40 percent-plus BOM overlap between autonomous vehicles, logistics robots, and humanoid robots is the mechanical reason the Interdependency Web functions: shared components drive learning curves across all five nodes simultaneously. A sacred text of the Farmer logic. *See also: Interdependency Web.*

VI. FINANCIAL & INVESTMENT TERMS

The language of capital allocation, credit markets, and corporate finance as deployed in the manuscript's investment frameworks. Some of the meanings in this book would be uncomfortable for Milton the Trickster.

EBIT (Earnings Before Interest and Taxes) — A measure of operating profitability excluding financing costs and tax effects. Ford's Model e division reported $16.7 billion in cumulative EBIT losses from 2022 through fiscal year 2025 (Ford Q4 2025 earnings, February 10, 2026)—the metric used to quantify the financial hemorrhage of legacy automakers' EV transitions without the distortion of one-time write-downs.

Refinancing Wall — The aggregate maturity schedule of corporate debt. Between 2027 and 2030, the Western automotive industry faces approximately $180 billion in maturing bonds, credit facilities, and supplier financing instruments that were issued when ICE cash flows were assumed to be permanent—a word that in corporate finance means "until the quarter someone notices they aren't." Each refinancing event forces the borrower to prove sustainable cash flows to credit committees. Chapter 11. *See also: Credit Spread.*

Credit Spread — The yield premium a corporate bond pays over a risk-free government bond of equivalent maturity. Widening spreads signal the bond market is pricing higher default risk. The Dinosaur Meter's near-term trigger: supplier credit spreads exceeding 400 basis points—the point at which refinancing becomes prohibitively expensive. *See also: Refinancing Wall.*

Kelly Criterion — Mathematical formula developed by John L. Kelly Jr. at Bell Labs in 1956 for optimal bet sizing. The full Kelly fraction maximizes long-term geometric growth rate but produces extreme volatility. Deployed by Ed Thorp to generate 20 percent annualized returns over 28 years at Princeton-Newport Partners. The Quarter-Kelly variant bets 25 percent of the optimal amount. *See also: Quarter-Kelly.*

Cash-Secured Put — Options strategy in which the investor sells a put option while holding sufficient cash to purchase the underlying stock if assigned. The Quarter-Kelly framework employs cash-secured puts on Chinese ADRs (e.g., BIDU) to generate income while establishing positions at lower prices—the mathematical equivalent of getting paid to wait for the monsoon. Chapter 14. *See also: LEAPS.*

LEAPS (Long-Term Equity Anticipation Securities) — Options contracts with expiration dates exceeding one year. The Quarter-Kelly framework uses LEAPS on Chinese equities as a leveraged way to express a long-term thesis while limiting downside to the premium paid—time-bounded bets that align the option's expiry with the thesis's expected materialization window. Chapter 14. *See also: Cash-Secured Put.*

ADR (American Depositary Receipt) — A negotiable certificate representing shares in a foreign company, traded on US exchanges. Chinese ADRs (Baidu, NIO, Xpeng, Pony.ai, WeRide) allow US investors to access Chinese equities without trading directly on the Shanghai, Shenzhen, or Hong Kong exchanges. Subject to VIE structure risk and potential delisting under the HFCAA. *See also: VIE, H-Share.*

VIE (Variable Interest Entity) — Legal structure used by Chinese companies to list on US stock exchanges while complying with Chinese restrictions on foreign ownership. The foreign-listed entity (e.g., Alibaba's Cayman Islands holding company) does not directly own the Chinese operating company but controls it through contractual arrangements. VIE structures underpin approximately $1.5 trillion in financing. Chinese authorities have never formally endorsed them. Chapter 14. *See also: ADR.*

H-Share — Shares of Chinese mainland companies listed on the Hong Kong Stock Exchange (HKEX). Provides international investors access under Hong Kong's regulatory framework without the VIE structure risk of US-listed ADRs. Dual listings (Nasdaq/NYSE + HKEX) provide delisting insurance. *See also: ADR, VIE.*

Goodwill Impairment — An accounting write-down of the intangible value recorded when one company acquires another. Stellantis's $26 billion restructuring charges—the largest single write-down in automotive history—signal the market's reassessment of what legacy automotive franchises are actually worth in an era of Chinese platform competition. Chapter 11, Section 11.0.

Wasting Asset — An asset that declines in value over time. In options trading, all options are wasting assets because their time value erodes daily. The book applies the concept to ICE-dependent business models: the apparent safety of Western auto stocks—shielded by tariff walls—is a wasting asset whose expiry date is printed in the cost curves the tariffs cannot reach. *See also: Tariff Mirage.*

Runoff Book — Financial term for a business expected to generate declining cash flows as its underlying assets depreciate. ICE manufacturers are not being disrupted in the conventional sense—they are being repriced as runoff books, valued on terminal cash flows rather than growth multiples. The funeral procession is an accounting event, not merely a metaphorical one. *See also: Funeral Procession.*

Stranded Assets — Assets that have suffered unanticipated or premature write-downs, devaluations, or conversion to liabilities. Applied to ICE-dependent manufacturing plants, dealer franchises, petroleum infrastructure, and pension obligations underwritten by ICE cash-flow assumptions. The capillary economy represents $180–220 billion in stranded real-estate value. *See also: Capillary Economy.*

Capillary Economy — The downstream economic ecosystem built around the internal combustion engine: refineries, gas stations, auto-parts stores, quick-lube outlets, and service networks. Estimated at approximately 2.5 million American jobs and $180–220 billion in stranded real-estate value. The forest burns not only at the crown; the root system dies too. *See also: Stranded Assets.*

China Discount — Structural undervaluation of Chinese technology companies relative to Western counterparts, driven by geopolitical risk, VIE concerns, index exclusion, and regulatory pessimism. The MSCI China Index typically trades at a 50–60 percent discount to the S&P 500. The Dragon 7 Chinese tech companies carry an average PEG ratio of 0.7×. The Māyā Meter measures whether this discount reflects risk or illusion. Chapters 13–14. *See also: Māyā Meter.*

Floorplan Financing Crisis — The impending credit event facing Western auto dealerships. As residual values of ICE vehicles collapse and EVs demand vastly less maintenance, dealerships are left hoarding unsellable, depreciating ICE inventory worth less than the revolving credit lines used to purchase it. The fire does not start at the factory. It starts at the lot. Chapter 11.

VII. REGULATORY & POLICY ARCHITECTURE

The legal and institutional structures defining the bifurcation of the global market. Where the Iron Curtain runs through the dashboard.

BIS Connected Vehicle Rule — Final rule published by the US Bureau of Industry and Security (90 Fed. Reg. 5360, January 16, 2025; effective March 17, 2025). Prohibits connected-vehicle software from countries of concern (China, Russia) beginning Model Year 2027, and hardware beginning Model Year 2030 or January 1, 2029, for components without model years. LiDAR, radar, and cameras are explicitly excluded from the hardware prohibition. The book's "technological Iron Curtain drawn through the dashboard." Chapters 5, 11. *See also: ICTS, VCS.*

ICTS (Information and Communications Technology and Services) — The legal category under which the BIS connected-vehicle rule operates. The ICTS supply-chain framework gives the US Commerce Department the authority to prohibit transactions involving technology from countries of concern that pose national security risks. *See also: BIS Connected Vehicle Rule.*

VCS (Vehicle Connectivity System) — Hardware and software enabling a connected vehicle to communicate externally—telematics control units, cellular modems, Bluetooth/Wi-Fi modules, satellite communications, and associated firmware. The BIS rule's hardware prohibition targets VCS components, with compliance deadlines of Model Year 2030 (model-year-associated hardware) or January 1, 2029 (standalone components). Two triggers for the same prohibition applied to different product categories. *See also: BIS Connected Vehicle Rule.*

HFCAA (Holding Foreign Companies Accountable Act) — US law (2020) requiring foreign companies listed on American exchanges to comply with PCAOB audit inspections or face delisting. The immediate threat was resolved in December 2022 when PCAOB gained full access to Chinese audit firms, but Treasury Secretary Bessent has stated, "everything is on the table." Part of the structural risk is priced into the geopolitical overlay. Chapter 14. *See also: VIE, ADR.*

MIIT (Ministry of Industry and Information Technology) — China's central regulatory body for industrial and technology policy. Unlike US agencies that "permit" technology, MIIT "orchestrates" it via Five-Year Plans, national standards, and municipal competition. Granted China's first L3 market-access permits in December 2025. The architect of the permission temple. Chapters 6, 8.

Belt and Road Initiative (BRI) — China's multi-trillion-dollar infrastructure and investment program spanning more than 140 countries. In the context of embodied intelligence, Belt and Road provides the physical corridors—ports, rail, digital infrastructure—through which China's autonomous logistics, energy, and financial rails extend globally. The Digital Silk Road is its technology-specific component. Chapters 9–10. *See also: Digital Silk Road.*

SAFE LiDAR Act — Proposed US legislation (H.R. 6576) to extend BIS restrictions to sensors. Zero co-sponsors as of February 2026—highlighting the tension between security hawks and an automotive supply chain that cannot source domestic LiDAR at Chinese prices. Chapter 15.

VIII. THE FIVE NODES OF THE INTERDEPENDENCY WEB

Each node of the embodied-intelligence platform is defined by the manuscript scores it. The Web is not five industries. It is one flywheel with five contact points.

Node One: Autonomous Mobility — Robotaxis, autonomous ride-hailing, and ADAS-equipped consumer vehicles that generate the Web's highest-value perception data. China scores 5/5: Pony.ai, Baidu Apollo, WeRide operate commercial driverless fleets; BYD's God's Eye generates 150 million km/day of training data. The United States scores 4/5: Waymo leads on safety proof and consumer trust, but operates at a higher cost with a smaller fleet. Chapter 11.

Node Two: Autonomous Logistics — Autonomous trucks, delivery drones, warehouse robots, and last-mile vehicles. China scores 5/5: JD.com and SF Express operate autonomous delivery at commercial scale; autonomous trucking corridors connect major ports. The United States scores 3/5: Aurora and Kodiak operate limited autonomous trucking routes; the Transfer Hub Model simplifies deployment but lacks infrastructure integration. Chapter 11.

Node Three: Robotics — Industrial robots, humanoid robots, and the manufacturing ecosystem that produces sensors, actuators, and compute hardware. China scores 5/5: KUKA (Chinese-owned), BYD's vertically integrated manufacturing, Hesai's LiDAR production at scale. The 40 percent BOM overlap with autonomous vehicles creates cross-platform cost deflation. Chapter 11. *See also: BOM.*

Node Four: Distributed Energy — Solar generation, battery storage, vehicle-to-grid (V2G) technology, and grid optimization. CATL and BYD's combined 55.6 percent of global battery cell production anchors this node. Autonomous vehicles become rolling energy-storage devices; their charging patterns feed grid-optimization algorithms; the grid's efficiency reduces the operating cost of autonomous fleets. The loop feeds itself. Chapter 11. *See also: V2G, CATL.*

Node Five: Financial & Data Rails — Payments infrastructure, AI compute platforms, and data ecosystems connecting the other four nodes. China's Alipay and WeChat Pay process approximately $35 trillion in annual transactions and are closest to enabling M2M payments for autonomous fleets. America's strength in this node (Google, NVIDIA, OpenAI, Palantir) represents its highest Web score—the brain. But the brain without the body is a thought experiment, not a product. Chapter 11. *See also: M2M.*

V2G (Vehicle-to-Grid) — Technology enabling electric vehicles to discharge stored energy back into the grid during peak demand, turning parked EVs into distributed energy-storage assets. Connects Node One (Autonomous Mobility) to Node Four (Distributed Energy): autonomous vehicles optimize their own charging and discharging patterns, generating revenue while balancing the grid.

M2M (Machine-to-Machine) — Direct communication and transactions between devices without human intervention. In the Interdependency Web, M2M payments—an autonomous vehicle paying a charging station, a logistics drone settling a landing-pad fee—represent the frontier of Node Five. China's Alipay and WeChat Pay infrastructure is closest to enabling M2M transactions at scale.

Convergence Multiplier — The amplification effect when five technology platforms share supply chains, data, and learning curves. ARK Invest's Convergence Network Strength metric increased

35 percent year-over-year in 2026. The compound growth rate of the Web exceeds any individual node's growth rate by approximately this factor—the mathematical proof that the investor who prices nodes in isolation underprices the system. Chapter 11. *See also: Interdependency Web.*

Platform Leader — Highest composite band (22–25) in the Interdependency Web Scoring Matrix. Possesses dominant or strong capability in four or more nodes, with self-sustaining feedback loops between them. Only China qualifies at 24/25. The defining characteristic: the platform generates more data, greater cost reductions, and greater capability as it grows—a flywheel that competitors cannot replicate node by node. *See also: Structural Deficit.*

Structural Deficit — Second-lowest composite band (10–15) in the Web Scoring Matrix. A nation with nascent capability in some nodes but critical gaps and external dependencies in others. Both Japan/Korea (15/25) and the EU (11/25) fall into this category. Characterized by the absence of a domestic platform integrator and dependence on Chinese supply chains for critical components. *See also: Platform Leader.*

IX. KEY ACRONYMS — QUICK REFERENCE

Acronym	Full Term
ADAS	Advanced Driver-Assistance Systems
ADS	Automated Driving System
ADR	American Depositary Receipt
BEV	Battery Electric Vehicle
BIS	Bureau of Industry and Security
BOM	Bill of Materials
BRI	Belt and Road Initiative
CAGR	Compound Annual Growth Rate
CATL	Contemporary Amperex Technology Co., Limited
C-V2X	Cellular Vehicle-to-Everything
EBIT	Earnings Before Interest and Taxes
EV	Electric Vehicle
FSD	Full Self-Driving (Tesla's branded L2 system)
HFCAA	Holding Foreign Companies Accountable Act
HKEX	Hong Kong Stock Exchange
ICE	Internal Combustion Engine
ICTS	Information and Communications Technology and Services
IEA	International Energy Agency
L2/L3/L4/L5	SAE Levels of Driving Automation
LEAPS	Long-Term Equity Anticipation Securities
LFP	Lithium Iron Phosphate (battery chemistry)
LiDAR	Light Detection and Ranging
MIIT	Ministry of Industry and Information Technology (China)
M2M	Machine-to-Machine (communications/payments)
NEV	New Energy Vehicle (Chinese regulatory classification)
ODD	Operational Design Domain
OEM	Original Equipment Manufacturer
PHEV	Plug-in Hybrid Electric Vehicle
TAM	Total Addressable Market
V2G	Vehicle-to-Grid
V2X	Vehicle-to-Everything
VCS	Vehicle Connectivity System

Acronym	Full Term
VIE	Variable Interest Entity
VLA	Vision-Language-Action (AI architecture)

This glossary is intended as a reference companion. Terms are defined in the context of this book's usage; some carry specialized meanings that differ from their broader academic or industry definitions. Numbers and data are current as of February 2026. Cross-references indicated by See also point to related entries within this glossary. Section references point to the chapter and section where the term is introduced or most fully developed.

The Boatman does not define the river. He reads it.

HUMBLE REQUEST TO REVIEW MY BOOK

I trust that you enjoyed reading this book. I'd like to hear from you and humbly request that you take a few minutes to post a review on Amazon. Your feedback and support will significantly improve my writing craft for future books and make this book even more commendable. This is a living manuscript and will continuously evolve based on your constructive feedback (contact @ https://www.theyyam.us/about or www.Tiger-Rider.com or https://www.linkedin.com/in/goodtogreat/)

FROM PARIAH TO PEAK
THE DIVINE'S DESCENT
KATHIVANOOR VEERAN
THE CRUCIFIED GOD
OF GOD'S OWN COUNTRY
SAJI MADAPAT

THE NIGHT WHEN THE GODS DANCED
CHIRAKKAL PERUMKALIYATTAM
The Cradle of The Gods of The Gods' Own Country
THEYYAM
SAJI MADAPAT

Cradle of Communism to Catacomb of Capitalism
THE GODS MUST BE CRAZY
A Proposal to Bring Back the House of Roosevelt's **TIGER RIDER**

THE DANCING GODS
GODFATHERS OF **GOD'S OWN COUNTRY**
SAJI MADAPAT

DANCE OF THE DIVINE
GODMOTHERS OF **GOD'S OWN COUNTRY**
SAJI MADAPAT

GODS OF GOD'S OWN COUNTRY
STORIES THEYYAM
TIGER RIDER **SANTHOSH VENGARA**

THE GODMOTHER OF **God's Own Country**
KARIM CHAMUNDI
SAJI MADAPAT

TEARS OF THE DIVINE
PILGRIMAGE IN GOD'S OWN COUNTRY
MAKKAM
SAJI MADAPAT

Proceeds from this book will be donated to Mother Teresa Mission
MAKE ENTERPRISE GREAT AGAIN
THE GODS MUST BE CRAZY!
From the Cradle of Communism to Catacomb of Capitalism: A Proposal to bring back the House of Roosevelt's
EPM MAVERICKS

Proceeds from this book will be donated to the Mother Teresa Mission

(Missionaries of Charity) or similar missions.

www.ingramcontent.com/pod-product-compliance
Lightning Source LLC
Chambersburg PA
CBHW082007230526
45468CB00023B/2677